# From The Projects to the Palace

# From The Projects to the Palace

*A Diplomat's Unlikely Journey from the Bottom to the Top*

*Interview conducted by Charles Stuart Kennedy*
*Initial Session: October 21, 2005*

*Diplomatic Oral History Series*
*Association for Diplomatic Studies and Training*

## Johnny Young

Copyright © 2013 by Johnny Young

ISBN:      Softcover         978-1-4797-6042-8
           Ebook             978-1-4797-6043-5

All rights reserved. No part of this book may be reproduced or transmitted in any form or by any means, electronic or mechanical, including photocopying, recording, or by any information storage and retrieval system, without permission in writing from the copyright owner.

The opinions and characterizations in this book are those of the author and do not necessarily represent official positions of the United States Government or the Association for Diplomatic Studies and Training.

This book was printed in the United States of America.

**To order additional copies of this book, contact:**
Xlibris Corporation
1-888-795-4274
www.Xlibris.com
Orders@Xlibris.com
104726

# CONTENTS

Foreword ...................................................................................................9

Beginnings ...............................................................................................11

Going International: Off to Madagascar ..............................................32

On to Guinea ..........................................................................................43

Dream Job in Kenya ...............................................................................54

Getting to Know the Qataris .................................................................62

Life is a Beach: Barbados ........................................................................79

Managing Personnel in Washington .....................................................85

Office of the Inspector General .............................................................92

Back to the Middle East: Jordan ............................................................98

Europe: The Hague ...............................................................................110

Senior Seminarian ................................................................................122

First Ambassadorship: Sierra Leone ....................................................136

Washington: Career Development and Assignments ........................163

Africa Again: Ambassador to Togo .....................................................174

Ambassador to Bahrain .......................................................................192

Fourth Ambassadorship: Slovenia ......................................................220

Selection as Career Ambassador and Life after the Foreign Service ...... 250

Dedicated to Lucille Pressey, the only mother I have ever known; my wife Angie, whom I have always loved and imagined loving; my children, David and Michelle, who have made me proud; Sol Berenholz, friend and role model; the late Assistant Secretary Mary A. Ryan, a courageous champion in supporting careers of officers like me; and finally, my grandson Phoenix, who awaits the future and all it offers.

# FOREWORD

## The ADST Diplomatic Oral History Series

For over 235 years extraordinary diplomats have served the United States at home and abroad with courage and dedication. Yet their accomplishments in promoting and protecting American interests usually remain little known to their compatriots. The Association for Diplomatic Studies and Training (ADST) created the Diplomatic Oral History Series to help fill this void by publishing in book form selected transcripts of interviews from its Foreign Affairs Oral History Collection.

The text herein acquaints readers with the life and career of Foreign Service officer Johnny Young, who rose from humble beginnings to become a four-time ambassador and attain the personal rank of Career Ambassador. We are proud to make his interview available through the Diplomatic Oral History Series.

ADST (www.adst.org) is an independent nonprofit organization founded in 1986 and committed to supporting training of foreign affairs personnel at the State Department's Foreign Service Institute and advancing knowledge of American diplomacy. It sponsors books on diplomacy through its Memoirs and Occasional Papers Series and, jointly with DACOR (an organization of foreign affairs professionals), the Diplomats and Diplomacy Series. Information about ADST's programs is available at www.adst.org.

*Kenneth L. Brown*
*President, ADST*

# BEGINNINGS

*Q: Let's start at the beginning. Could you tell me when and where you were born?*

YOUNG: I was born in Savannah, Georgia on February 6, 1940.

*Q: Let's talk about your parents first. Can you tell me about your father's side first?*

YOUNG: Well, on my father's side, he was one of eleven children. There were two sisters and nine boys. One sister figures quite significantly in my life and I'll explain that in a minute or two. On my mother's side, she was one of three. There was a sister and a brother in addition to my mother. Both of my parents were poor folks. They had nothing. We lived in an extended family relationship with my grandmother and my mother and father and some other uncles and their children. We lived in one big house, cramped in a couple or several rooms. Now, I had mentioned an aunt who figured significantly in my life. Shortly after my birth my mother became ill and realized later on that she was terminally ill. She had heart problems, and being a black woman in the South, twenty-seven years old at that time, she didn't have access to good medical care and good doctors, so that was a factor. I mean we realize it now in retrospect. In any case, she turned to her sister-in-law, my father's oldest sister, and asked her if she would take me upon her death and raise me and that's exactly what happened when I was eleven months old. My mother died and this aunt took me, her name was Lucille Pressey.

She took me and my sister, Loretta, and raised the two of us. Another sister by the name of Lottie was taken by my mother's sister and she had already moved to New York. This aunt raised me and she was the only mother that I knew. My father was with us, but he was a sometimes-father. He was here, he was there. He had his friends and his life and what have you, so I didn't have the kind of fatherly support that I would have liked.

*Q: Did you grow up in Savannah?*

YOUNG: We stayed in Savannah until I was seven years old. My sister and I were baptized as Catholics in Savannah. There's a story to that as well. This aunt, the one who raised me, found herself at a low point in her life in the 1930s when things were pretty bad economically. She was hired as a domestic by the Cathedral of Saint John the Baptist in Savannah, Georgia, and she began cleaning the cathedral and the rectory for the priests there. They took a liking to her and asked her if she could cook and she said yes, so she became their cook and in the process they converted her to Catholicism and she in turn converted a number of her brothers to Catholicism. By the time I came along it was just natural that I would be baptized a Catholic, so that's how I became Catholic.

*Q: Yes, because when one thinks of the deep South—certainly in the African American community—you think of Baptists.*

YOUNG: Baptists, absolutely. There was no question about that so I became a Catholic. I started Catholic school there as a matter of fact. It turned out to be the same school that Clarence

Thomas went to, but I don't want to get into that at all, since we are at opposite ends of the spectrum philosophically.

*Q: He's very conservative.*

YOUNG: And I'm a knee-jerk liberal. So, that's all I'll say to that.

*Q: Had your family been a long-time Savannah family?*

YOUNG: No, they originally came from one of the Sea Islands and that will be significant later on. They were from an island called Lady's Island, from where the family then migrated. This was all on my father's side and they then migrated to Beaufort, South Carolina and from Beaufort to

Savannah, Georgia. My sister and I started school there. We continued school there and then one day in July of 1947 my mother, my Aunt Lucille, came to us and said we're going north. I learned later that the nuns at the cathedral and at Saint Benedict's Church had given her money. It was a nun, the Mother Superior, and her name was Mother Blondena. She gave my mother the money and said, take these children north because there's no opportunity for them in the South. That was in June, early July of 1947. On July 3, 1947, we took a train called the Silver Meteor, which still runs to this day. We boarded it in Savannah, carrying with us our little shoe boxes of fried chicken and biscuits and I don't know what else. I thought this was the most exciting thing that I had ever done in my life. I had never been on a train and to think that I was going to go for such a long, long ride. I was just mesmerized by the whole thing, seeing the passing images of buildings and factories and things like that. This was really quite something for a boy who had come out of nothing. We had nothing. We were as poor as can be.

Then we were on our way to a new life in the North. I would like to go back for a moment to say that those early years in the South, as poor as we were, were happy years for me. I knew we didn't have any money and there were times when we had absolutely nothing to eat, I mean nothing except a piece of bread, and we had water which we would put sugar in. We called it tea so we had bread and tea and that was all that we had, but we were still very happy. We had times during that period when we had difficulty with the Ku Klux Klan and they would come to our street and absolutely terrorize us. I remember my mother would hold us close to her with her hand over our mouths so that we wouldn't make a sound and they couldn't hear that there was anyone in a particular house for them to target for more mischief-making.

So, I still remember those things. My overall memory is one of happiness and contentment during that time in the South.

*Q: As a small child up to seven, was it a completely black experience? I mean, did you see whites in your neighborhood or not?*

YOUNG: We were in a totally black neighborhood except for our grocer and his family. There was a grocer there by the name of Mr. O'Brien who had a son my age. I remember him to this day. It's like I can still see him.

He had red, red hair and we became just the best of friends and never for a moment can I think of anytime when he referred to my color or I referred to his color. We played together with the other kids in the neighborhood and that was life. We never gave it a thought. The only time we were aware of our race and being targeted because of our race was when we had these sessions with the Ku Klux Klan, when they would burn a cross in the middle of our street.

*Q: I'm surprised because I speak for somebody who lived in the North. I always thought the Klan was out in the countryside.*

YOUNG: No, this was in Savannah. We lived in a place in Savannah that was not in the heart of the city. It was not country, but it was an old, broken down area with ramshackle houses with corrugated tin roofs in a little area on the edge of the city. We lived on a street called Hall Street and the Klan used to come to an area called Bilbo Canal. I remember it to this day.

*Q: Was it named for Theodore Bilbo, the racist senator from Mississippi?*

YOUNG: I don't know, but that was the name of it. Bilbo Canal. To give you some idea of where it was, it was right on the edge where the carnival would come every year. They didn't use it for farmland or anything like that, but we were on the edge of the city at that time.

We went from Savannah directly to Philadelphia. We arrived in Philadelphia on the Fourth of July, 1947 and we were met by my Aunt Bertha who was my father's other sister. She took us into her home. We lived in a project in Philadelphia called the Shipyard Naval Homes. She had five children, who slept in one room, and she and her husband slept in another room. They took us in, so that made seven children in one little room and then my aunt, my mother, got a room across the street in the home of another woman in the project. That's where we lived for a very short period and then we moved to Wilmington, Delaware. We moved in with an aunt in Wilmington, with my father's brother and his wife. They didn't have any children, no children the age of my sister and I. My grandmother was there as well and later on, we were joined by my father. We continued going to Catholic school.

*Q: This was in Wilmington.*

YOUNG: Yes. We went to Saint Joseph's Catholic School on French Street, in Wilmington. The school is no longer there, but the church is still there. Some very prosperous banks took over the land that the school was on and there are great big buildings there at the moment. We stayed there for about four years. I was very active in the church, very active in the school as well. I was a good student, but I horsed around quite a bit and I remember the nuns liked me a lot. There was one nun in particular, Sister Mary Joseph who used to say, "I don't know what's going to happen to him. He's smart as can be, but he's constantly fooling around." Sometimes she'd get so frustrated with me. I can see her now. She was a large lady and she had sort of a W.C. Fields face and nose and she wore a brown habit and a big rope around the middle with the big cross dangling on the side. When she laughed, she looked like Santa Claus, but she would get so angry with me sometimes she would get her yardstick and shake it at me and say, "Boy, I'll make powder out of you." I'm glad she didn't. I think if she saw me today she would be quite pleased.

After about four years in Wilmington, my father and the aunt that we lived with had a falling out. We then moved back to the projects in Philadelphia with this aunt. This time my sister went with my aunt and her five children. My aunt, the one I called my mother, and I took a room in another lady's house, but it was all in the projects.

Q: *I'd like to go back to Delaware. You spent some time there. What was Wilmington like? You were a kid, but by this time we're talking about seven to . . . ?*

YOUNG: Eleven.

Q: *Eleven, so you were an observant kid. How did you find Wilmington?*

YOUNG: Poor, rundown. We were poor, but we had a little house and I had lots of fun. I didn't think of race. Everyone was black except the people who owned the stores and shops and that sort of thing. I just didn't think in any racial terms. One thing I think is significant was that while we were there, my sister and I did two things. We were very active in the Catholic Church, but we were simultaneously very active in the Baptist Church because the aunt and uncle we lived with in Wilmington were Baptists. So, on Sundays my sister and I would go to mass dutifully at 9:00, and then at 11:00 we would go to the Baptist service and at night we would return for the evening service as well. For that reason, and I'm not unusual in this regard in terms of blacks who have had the kind of experience that I have, having come out of the South and having been converted to Catholicism and what have you. They have a foothold in both religions. For that reason, to this day I go to a mass that features the black gospel tradition, which I like, and I'm very comfortable in that kind of setting. That did happen in Wilmington and it did have an impact on me.

*Q: What about school? You're saying you were a bright kid . . .*

YOUNG: That's what they told me.

*Q: Looking at this in our profession, the Foreign Service, mostly bright people end up doing well in the Foreign Service, it's just a given. Do you think part of the problem about being an active kid was that you were a little bit bored in class and all that?*

YOUNG: No, I wasn't bored with the classes. I can't say that was a factor at all. I honestly can't. I never thought of boredom. I didn't even know what the word meant. I was just full of beans and full of energy and it has been that energy that has kept me going and has seen me through to this day.

*Q: In school, which subjects did you particularly like, and which didn't you care for as much?*

YOUNG: I liked math a lot, although later on I learned to detest it. But at that time I liked it a lot. I was very good in math and I was very good in geography and English. Maybe the liking for geography was some indicator of something in the future, I really don't know. At that point I didn't give it a thought frankly, but I liked school a lot. It was fun.

*Q: How did you find the nuns? One has all sorts of stories about nuns and their discipline.*

YOUNG: They were strict. They were really as rigid as you could expect. They exacted a certain toll on you in what they wanted, and they wanted discipline, they wanted excellence, and they wanted things done in a proper and correct way. They just were not very flexible. They were unyielding in their demands that you perform at least in those areas.

*Q: Were you by this time much of a reader?*

YOUNG: Only to the extent that reading was required for school. My interest in reading came later on, and I'll get into that later on, but it didn't happen during those years. No, not at all.

*Q: In the Catholic Church at that time, were there black priests?*

YOUNG: I never saw a black priest or a black nun from the time I was small until I was a teenager.

*Q: Did this send you a message?*

YOUNG: No, I didn't think about it. I lived within my world of black people in Wilmington, and that was it. I didn't think beyond that world. I didn't ask myself, well, why don't I see some here and why don't I see some on TV, and why don't I see some in the newspaper, and on and on. It didn't occur to me. As a young boy, eleven years old, that just was not in my mind.

*Q: Well, given what has happened in so many of our cities these days, was there crime around you? Was it a different world in a way?*

YOUNG: It was a very different world, as poor as we were. And I'll get into some of this later on when I tell you about what happened when we went to Philadelphia. I think what I saw in Philadelphia was also indicative of what was happening in Wilmington, Delaware at that time.

*Q: Delaware in a way is poor, but comfortable; did you feel you had enough to eat?*

YOUNG: We did, those days were behind me in terms of hunger, but it's something that sticks with you, that has stuck with me forever. To this day, if you were to go to my home and open up my pantry, you would say, "My God, he's prepared for World War III." My wife is constantly after me because I love to shop for food. I just get such a thrill out of it and I think it's from those early years when I didn't have any, and now that I am secure and can buy, I love buying food. I love sharing food with other people. I love cooking and I think that some of that is from those early days.

*Q: I'm a child of the Depression and I adhere to the idea that when you get a job you hang onto it, you don't mess around. Well, then we'll go to Philadelphia. You were in Philadelphia from . . . ?*

YOUNG: From about 1951 until, well, until forever.

*Q: Philadelphia became your base.*

YOUNG: Right. We went to the projects, the three of us; we went back to Philadelphia and moved back into the Naval Shipyard Homes with my aunt and her five children. My sister stayed with my aunt, and the aunt that I called my mother and I took a room in another house in that project.

*Q: When you say project, what was it?*

YOUNG: Subsidized government housing, a housing project. Like the one project you might know about, the Cabrini-Green in Chicago, except these were not high rises. High rises had not come to that part of Philadelphia at that point. These homes were originally built to house naval families during World War II. They were literally built out of wood and tarpaper.

They were temporary quarters and they had a wooden stove in the kitchen that served not only to heat the house in the wintertime but was used for cooking also. They had a coal bin to hold a supply of coal for the winter months and there was a small kitchen, living room, two bedrooms. That was it. There were one thousand units, located right next to the U.S. Naval Shipyard in Philadelphia. Now, when you extrapolate how many were crammed into one unit, we were one thousand families, and we were totally surrounded by the white community, totally.

*Q: The projects were almost all black?*

YOUNG: They were. I think we had maybe three or four white families in the projects, but the rest were all black. So, we moved there. My aunt attempted to enroll us in the Catholic school. We wanted to continue our

Catholic education, but we were totally rejected by the Catholic school that was right next to our project but on the white side of the line at Saint Richard's Roman Catholic Church. It was one of the most devastating things that I can remember. It was the moment in my life that race entered my mind and I was touched by it, hurt by it, and deeply troubled by what happened. I'll never forget the moment when we went to the rectory, asked the priest, and he said, "No, we don't want them here." That's the way he put it. There were no blacks in that school and the time had not come for us to be a part of it. I became very discouraged with the church.

*Q: You were at the right age to understand what was going on.*

YOUNG: Oh, yes; that was the defining moment for me and without question for my sister, for both of us, but I think I was more dedicated to the church than she was. At that point I stopped going to church and just became very dissatisfied. We couldn't get into the public school system because we didn't have any ties in Philadelphia. We had just come from Wilmington from a Catholic school there. For a year we did not attend school. My aunt, the one we stayed with who had the five children, was a domestic for a schoolteacher in Philadelphia, by the name of Mrs. Grossman. She told Mrs. Grossman our story and Mrs. Grossman said, "Don't worry. I'll get them in." Mrs. Grossman was a librarian at Vare Junior High School in Philadelphia, on Twenty-fourth and Snyder Avenue. She did. She got us in.

My sister and I entered Vare Junior High School, where I did two years and my sister did a year and then she went on to the high school. Mrs. Grossman was later called up by the Congress's Un-American Activities Committee. She was judged to be unworthy, a Communist, and was drummed out of the Philadelphia school system, both she and her husband. They were never able to work again. It was a dreadful thing. Again, this was a defining moment for me in terms of the realization of what could happen in our country. It was a terrible time. I didn't fully appreciate it until later on, but Mrs. Grossman unfortunately got caught up in that, and yet this good soul had gone out of her way and helped us in our hour of need. I did well at Vare Junior High School. I remember I was getting ready to graduate and to go to high school, I went to the school counselor and asked her, "What should I do?" because I had no guidance from home. None of my folks were educated. The woman I called my mother was a domestic. Her sister was a domestic. I mean that's what they did.

*Q: There weren't that many men around were there?*

YOUNG: No. My father was there, but he was on and off. The counselor at the junior high school said, "Well, I think you ought to go to a vocational high school and take up carpentry or something like that." No encouragement whatsoever about anything academic, just take a trade, carpentry. She said, "You know, one of your cousins is studying carpentry, you take up carpentry." I said okay; what did I know?

I finished junior high school in 1954. That was an important point because my mother, my sister and I moved to a small efficiency apartment on Lombard Street in Philadelphia. That was a major move. For me, quite significant, because it was the first time that I ever slept in a bed by myself. Prior to that I always slept in the same bed with a cousin or with my mother but never had a bed of my own.

*Q: This apartment was still in the project?*

YOUNG: No, this was the break from the projects. This was private. We paid for it ourselves. I didn't have a job then, but I'll get to that in a moment. Lombard Street at that time was part of one of the biggest slums in Philadelphia. It was run-down, old broken shacks and dilapidated houses and what have you. We were in a relatively decent place. It was okay. There was a plan at the time by the mayor of the city and by a man who was probably one of the greatest city planners in the United States, Edmund Bacon. He died just recently. The plan was to redevelop that portion of Philadelphia, because it was the historic section of Philadelphia, and to rehabilitate it to the glories of the eighteenth century. One or two people had begun to do this and one of them was the mayor himself, who bought an old house. He completely refurbished it to the colonial style and it was very nice. When we moved there it was still a major slum.

One day in March of 1954, I was walking down the street around the corner from Lombard Street. There was another street called South Street. It ran parallel to Lombard Street. Lombard was residential; South Street was a commercial street with all kinds of shops and stores and what have you. We were one block away. I was walking along Fourth Street one Saturday morning and I was just getting ready to cross South Street when this gentleman came out of the store on the corner of Fourth and Lombard, the store was at 347 South Street, right on the corner, and was called My Lady's Specialty Shop. He came out and he said, "Hey boy, would you like a job?" I said, "Sure." I followed him into the store and went down in the basement. Now if you think about that in today's context, these would be alarming things for someone to say, but at that time there was certainly nothing wrong. I went downstairs with him and he said, "I want you to take these boxes out." He had cartons and so I took the boxes out of the carton. I don't know what made me do it, but I looked for patterns on them as I took them out of the boxes and I arranged them according to these numbers that I saw on the boxes. I went up and told him I had finished. He came down and he said, "Why did you do this this way?" I said, "Well, I saw a pattern on them, so I thought I'd just arrange them in that way." He said, "Pretty good." He seemed pleased. He asked, "Would you like to work here?" I responded, "Sure." He said, "Well, you can help out in the shop, you can sweep the floor, do different things like that." I said, "Okay." He said, "You come after school and we'll teach you." I said, "Okay."

I began working in My Lady's Specialty Shop when I was fourteen years of age. I would work there on Monday, Wednesday, and Friday from 4:00 to 9:00 p.m., Thursday from 4:00 to 6:00, and all day Saturday and Sunday. I just worked all the time and then went to school. Then in high school, I went to Edward Bach Vocational Technical High School and I majored in carpentry and in academic subjects as well so that I would graduate with a high school diploma and some technical skill.

Anyway, over the years I learned quite a bit about the retail trade. I continued to do well in that store and moved up to basically the position of assistant manager of the shop. That was my de facto responsibility, but the most important thing was this man that I met, the man who offered me the job originally. His name is Thal Berenholtz. His family had come over from France. They were Holocaust survivors. They had brought their money to the States and had opened up the shop. They had seen what was occurring in Europe before they left. What they did was arrive in the States, and buy up every single pair of nylon stockings that they could get their hands on when they arrived and they stockpiled them. During the war, ladies would line up almost for a block to get into that shop to buy a pair of stockings, and that's how they made their money and were able to open up a bigger shop and on and on. I liked him so much. I thought he was such a wonderful person. To me he was the kind of father that I had hoped for, and I thought at that point, "Now that's what a father is supposed to be like." I watched him with his kids and his wife. I thought he was a wonderful husband, a wonderful father, just a good person. I'd listen to him talk about music and books and about the theater and art and things like that and that's what opened up my interests to these areas as well. He was the one who was responsible for opening my mind in these areas. I held him as a very dear friend and he was a very compassionate and understanding man as well.

The other members of his family were different in their personalities. He was more like his father. His father was a very gentle, compassionate soul. His brother was a cutthroat like his mother, I mean literally. But I thought that I could identify with his qualities more. Whenever I have been sworn in as ambassador, I've had him at my side and that's the least I could do in showing him how much I appreciated his influence in my life.

*Q: I just wanted to go back. While you were at the junior high, the church had turned you down. Did you return to the church?*

YOUNG: That happened after we moved, when we were on Lombard Street, that I began to return.

*Q: A different church?*

YOUNG: A different church, a different community. We were in a mixed neighborhood. I mean everybody on Lombard Street was poor, but it was mixed. We had Polish, Italian, Turkish, black, I mean it was a wonderful polyglot neighborhood, but everybody was poor. At the end of our street there was St. Peter Claver Church. It was basically a black Catholic church and it was the mother church of the black Catholic churches in Philadelphia. We met some people in the neighborhood who were Catholic and they said, "Why don't you try Saint Peter Claver's?" We started going to Saint Peter Claver and that's when I began to go back to the church and reconciled with the church.

*Q: You lived in what you described as run-down, almost a slum; this was on Lombard Street?*

YOUNG: Yes.

Q: *Compare it to today, the problem of gangs and all this. Would you talk about the ambiance?*

YOUNG: Sure. I wanted to say earlier that even when we were in the projects, we never saw a gun. We never heard of anyone with a knife or anyone being injured with a knife. There were no problems of drugs and that was true for the high school as well, although I mean Bach High School was not the greatest school in Philadelphia and it was known primarily as the school for underprivileged children. We never had those kinds of problems, it was just a completely different world and it was the same on Lombard Street. As integrated as the neighborhood was in terms of different groups and what have you, we didn't have those problems. In the projects, we did have racial problems. We used to have race riots because we had to go through the white neighborhood to get to their junior high school and from time to time we would have clashes between the whites and the blacks, but you'd be fighting with the same kids you'd see in high school.

Q: *What about while you were going through these early experiences, what about men around you? Was there much drinking? Were they working, were there any male models?*

YOUNG: There were male models at that time. As I said, I didn't have them in my family because we were in Philadelphia. My father continued to live in Wilmington, Delaware. He stayed on in Wilmington. There were some, but they were not particularly strong models, the ones that I saw. It was the women who kept us going.

Q: *Well, this of course is one of the great traditions in life. What about drinking? In your family were the men going around on Saturday night?*

YOUNG: I can only speak for my own experience. I mean my father had a weakness for drinks and the ladies, but not a lot of ladies. He would devote his attention to one and would put his earnings into that particular person and he did like to drink. We didn't think about well, we don't have any men in our lives. We didn't think about that. We needed to survive and we survived the best way we could. We got all kinds of odd jobs and we did everything imaginable to make ends meet. I did farm work when I was in Philadelphia. I was a day laborer. They'd pick us up in a truck from the projects, take us out to New Jersey. We would pick tomatoes, strawberries, blueberries, peaches, things like that during the summer months, washed floors, washed dishes, you name it I've done it all.

*Q: In high school, how did you find the academic side?*

YOUNG: The academic side of it was good. I mean we had to meet the requirements in order to graduate and we had to do our technical side also. Some fell asleep in his class, but I certainly wasn't one of them. I remember once this one fellow did fall asleep and I recall the teacher tiptoed over to the fellow and he screamed in his ears, "The British are coming, the British are coming." The fellow woke up and didn't know where he was. Of course the class just roared with laughter, but the teacher was just wonderful.

*Q: Philadelphia was in the North, but were you aware of Brown versus the Board of Education, of integration?*

YOUNG: Heard of it. It didn't affect us, because we were already in an integrated school. There junior high was a fully integrated school. So at least from what I saw in '54, Philadelphia was already integrated and Bach was already an integrated school. That pattern had happened decades before my time. It wasn't the same as the kind of impact it would have in places that were totally segregated.

*Q: How about given your future career, did the outside world intrude much by the time you graduated from high school?*

YOUNG: Absolutely not. Had no clue of it, none whatsoever, except I remember one thing. In Mr. McMaster's class, he said, "You know, there's a country in Africa that's going to become independent very shortly. Can anyone tell me what country that is?" I remember putting up my hand and saying, "Ghana." He said, "Absolutely right Mr. Young." I felt so proud that I had become aware of that, but part of that was my working in that shop with Mr. Berenholtz and his interest in world affairs and world events, and overhearing him speak about these issues and things like that. That's where I learned a lot.

*Q: You graduated from high school when, what year?*

YOUNG: 1957.

*Q: 1957. Where were they pointing you, telling you to go out and get a carpenter job?*

YOUNG: Oh, very interesting. Before I graduated I went to the high school counselor, Mrs. Muir, and asked her about what I should do next and she said, "Get a job as a carpenter." I said, "What about going to college?" She said, "Are you kidding? No college in its right mind will take a look at you." That's what she told almost all of the black kids in the school. I remember her to this day as well and not with great fondness. Then I graduated and I did attempt to get a job as a carpenter, but the unions were segregated and you couldn't get into the union. It was a useless exercise. I mean I could have, I guess, sort of been a day laborer or something like that, but I didn't want that. I continued working at the store. I then began to work full-time at My Lady's Specialty Shop.

I then took the college entrance examination, the SAT and didn't do well at all on it, didn't get a good score at all, didn't have good preparation to tell you the truth. In any case, I got from Mr. Berenholtz and his family and what have you a sense of the value of education. I heard them talking to their friends and relatives about this one going to university and that one going to university and how important it was and on and on and they suggested that it was something I should keep in mind. I didn't have money to go to college, didn't have any money at all. I went to Temple University and got a catalog and asked about going to school at night and I found out that I could go to school at night. It wasn't too expensive; I could afford it. It was eighteen dollars a credit, can you imagine? I didn't know what to take. I knew I was going to take something in business because I liked working in that shop. I had aspirations of maybe owning a shop of my own, managing a shop for the Berenholtzes because they had spoken to me about that prospect.

I began to go to school at night and took accounting and found out to my surprise that I had an aptitude for accounting. I had never done anything in accounting in my life, but I just had ability for it, and I think I started in 1958. At the time Temple University had a certificate in accounting program. You had to get, I think, forty-eight credits. You took a lot of accounting courses and you could get a certificate of proficiency in accounting. So, I began taking a lot of accounting courses. I mean I took other things as well, Spanish and anthropology and a lot of other things, but I was really gunning for those forty-eight credits in accounting, because I wanted that certificate. In 1960 I was laid off from the shop because business was so bad I couldn't continue on there. I was at loose ends, didn't know what to do, and tried all kinds of different possibilities, but none of them worked out. That's again a time when race came into play. I began to realize that I'd be called in for jobs, and the minute I walked in the door I knew that it was because of my color that I wasn't going to get the job.

I then went to the city of Philadelphia and looked at their announcement of openings and saw there was a position for junior accountant. The requirements were a bachelor's degree or a certificate in proficiency in accounting and you could take the exam. I was very close to getting my certificate and I worked and worked and got my certificate in 1960. I sat for the junior accountant exam for the city of Philadelphia and I passed it at the top and was offered a position in 1960. I started working for the city of Philadelphia as a census enumerator, which was interesting. That took me into parts of Philadelphia that I wouldn't think of going into today. When I look back on where I went and those doors I knocked on and the people I encountered and what have you, there's no way in the world that I would do that today. I was fearless. I just didn't think about it. I mean it was literally the worst crime-ridden area of Philadelphia at that time. Anyway, I think it was September of 1960 I began working as a junior accountant for the city of Philadelphia and that was a major step in my life because it was the beginning of my entrée to the middle class.

Q: *Did the election of 1960 cross your path at all?*

YOUNG: Oh, I couldn't vote at that point, because I wasn't twenty-one, but oh, everybody was excited by Kennedy, everyone. The hope was palpable. You could just feel it. I mean it was unbelievable.

Q: *Was it in your community?*

YOUNG: Oh, within the black community I mean he was like God.

Q: *We're talking about Kennedy?*

YOUNG: Kennedy, yes, absolutely, absolutely. I mean he was adored, loved, and everybody I can think of supported him. I worked for the city of Philadelphia and I began to save a little bit of money and I continued to go to school at night.

*Q: Temple University?*

YOUNG: Temple. I got the certificate. Then I decided I wanted a degree, so I continued to go to school at night but I wasn't a matriculated student. So after I got the certificate I went to the dean and I said, "I'd like to be admitted as a degree student." He said, "Well, you know, according to your SAT scores, you wouldn't get in, but my God, I look at the courses you've taken and you have done so well. There's no question in my mind that you can do the work. You're admitted." That's how I got in. I didn't get in on the basis of the test scores; I got in on the basis of demonstrated work. They let me in and I continued to do well in my studies.

*Q: Could you talk a little bit about Temple at the time, what kind of a school it was?*

YOUNG: Temple was primarily a working person's school. It was an urban university. It was a school where most of the students were first generation college students in many cases. At the time not many black students, just a few you could spot around the campus. The majority of the blacks who were in university were either in historically black universities or they were in Cheney State Teacher's College, which was one of the historically black schools, or Lincoln University or someplace like that. There were not too many in Temple and even fewer in Penn, because I took a couple of courses at Penn as well, or Saint Joseph's or La Salle. I mean integration was not bringing minorities into those schools, not just in terms of blacks, but in terms of other minorities as well. The schools had not evolved at that point.

*Q: What sort of course were you moving towards?*

YOUNG: I majored in business with a minor in Spanish. I found out again that I had a talent for Spanish. I took a lot of Spanish courses, did very well in Spanish, very well in anthropology. The only subject I didn't do well in was statistics. Statistics was a killer for me and I didn't do too well in one of the economic courses that had a lot of numbers involved. General economics I did fairly well. Those were the two drawbacks, but I did well in all my studies, very well. I continued going to school at night and continued to take exams to get promotions.

Q: *Within the Philadelphia system?*

YOUNG: Right, and then I went from junior accountant to accountant I and then eventually I became Accountant II and was doing quite well. The next major event that occurred in my life was in 1961, a year after I had begun my work with the city of Philadelphia.

I had been working for the city for a year and the Catholic employees of the city were getting ready to host something called the communion breakfast. I bought two tickets for this event that was to take place a couple of months later, not having any idea of who would go with me to this event. Anyhow, the week before the event I went to a dance at International House in Philadelphia. During the course of the dance I looked across the room and just like in the play *South Pacific*, "one enchanted evening, you will find a stranger." There she was. I saw this lovely, young lady and I invited her to dance. We started talking. I found out that she was Catholic. She gave me her phone number, her address, name, the works, and this is key because there's a dispute between the two of us to this day as to how events transpired, but anyhow she did give me those key bits of data.

The next week, the event was supposed to take place on Sunday. That Saturday I had to go to New York. I came back and when I entered the house, my mother said, "Some girl called here about some dance tomorrow or some breakfast or something." I said, "Well, did you get the message straight?" She said, "Well, I'm not sure." I said, "Did she say she was going or wasn't going?" "I don't know." "Oh my God, the thing is tomorrow. I've got to have a better answer that that." It was dark, I mean it was late at night. I didn't have a car, so I got on the bus. I got on the elevated train and I took another bus and I went to her home. The house was black, dark, no lights at all in the house. I knocked and knocked on the door and finally a light came on at the top of the steps. I think they might have been peeping out of the door or something to see who was down there because she came to the door and I said, "Are you going to go tomorrow or not?" This is the second point where we have a dispute as to what was said. I say she said yes and she tells me that she said maybe.

Anyhow, the next morning I got dressed and went to her home and I knocked on the door and her mother greeted me and she said, "Step inside young man. I want to talk to you." I thought, oh my God what have I done. I couldn't believe it, and her mother was quite a formidable large lady and she said, "Please have a seat." So I sat on the sofa. Angie was not to be seen anywhere. Her mother said, "Sit down. I want to talk to you." I said, "Yes, ma'am?" She said, "I want you to know that I'm a single parent and I'm raising my two daughters to be good decent girls" and they don't do this and they don't do this and I don't allow them to do that and on and on, "and I don't allow her to date; after all she's only fifteen years old." At that point if there had been a trap door in the floor I would have gone through, because I had no idea that she was fifteen years old. She looked so mature. She never gave a hint about her age and then her mother said, "But I'm going to let her go with you this time because your intentions seem good." I said, "Thank you very much, Mrs. Clark." Her name was Virginia Clark and the girl that I had asked out was Angelina Clark. We went out the door and as soon as we got outside I said to her, "Why did you lie to me?" She said, "I never lied to you. You never asked me my age." We went out on that date and we subsequently went on other dates and six years later we were married, so that's how I met my wife in 1961 and that was a key point in my life.

*Q: Well, how did you find working for Philadelphia? One thinks of the civil service in Philadelphia as being at the center of city politics and all that. How did you feel?*

YOUNG: None of the politics bothered me at all and we had an excellent mayor. We had Mayor Richardson Dilworth at the time. He was a man of integrity, honesty, imagination, a lot of drive and energy, and a good manager. He was a superb mayor. None of that bothered me and his administration had a good reputation. The office I worked in was the procurement department. I was the accountant for the procurement department and it was not at all affected by any of the politics.

*Q: I would think that the procurement department would be ideal.*

YOUNG: Ideal?

*Q: Ideal, the ideal place for people with connections, and you were buying things.*

YOUNG: It didn't happen. The head of the procurement department was a political appointee. The one when I was there was a fellow by the name of Otto Winter. Dilworth demanded integrity and honesty, and I don't recall any scandals during his administration. That turned out very well. In the early to mid-60s I also became very active in the YMCA (Young Men's Christian Association) and in what they call their Young Leadership Development Program. So I banded with a lot of other young people my age and we would go to conferences and seminars, and the goal was to sort of develop us as potential leaders for the future in the community and business, et cetera. A combination of social and some career formation as well. It turned out quite nicely. I mention that because that's another significant point in my life story.

*Q: By this time where were you living? What sort of life were you living?*

YOUNG: Oh, I was still on Lombard Street, but we had moved into a three-room apartment at that point and my sister had moved to Wilmington, Delaware, and my aunt and I continued in our three-room apartment in Philadelphia. We got that apartment after I had begun to work for the city of Philadelphia. As I say, that was my entrée to the middle class. The first thing I did was get this larger apartment, where I had a room truly to myself for the first time. We continued to live in that apartment until 1964. I had saved a little bit of money. I continued to save my money and then in 1964 the transformation of the neighborhood had clearly begun. I. M. Pei, the famous American architect, designed three apartment towers not too far from where we were and also a complex of townhouses. I remember looking at those townhouses and saying, now this is what I want one day. This was 1964. I looked at one of those townhouses and they were $48,000. I think my salary at that time was something like $6,500, which was a decent middle class salary at that point. I thought these houses were the most beautiful things I had ever seen, but they were clearly out of my reach and the condo apartments were also out of reach, so I thought well, maybe I can buy a shell of a house and have it rehabilitated. I called up the redevelopment authority and asked about one of these shells and they said, "Well, you can have one of these shells for $400, $500, $600" and I said, "Oh, that's great. What about how much to rehabilitate it?" They said, "The cheapest we've done has been about $60,000." This is in 1964. I said, "You're kidding." They said, "No, because it's basically building a new house." So I said, "No thank you." I forgot about staying in that neighborhood, but I loved that neighborhood. I really loved that neighborhood.

*Q: Did it continue to be a mixed neighborhood?*

YOUNG: No, it didn't. It was transforming to a solidly white middle and upper-middle class neighborhood. Who else could buy a $48,000 townhouse or put $60,000 into rehabilitating a home? I can tell you very few blacks could at that point. I began to look into other sections of the city and found a very nice duplex home in what is called West Oak Lane in Philadelphia. The home was on the market for $18,500. It was a two bedroom apartment downstairs, a two bedroom apartment upstairs, and I figured we could rent out the one upstairs and that would help pay the mortgage, plus my contribution, and I bought it. My aunt and I moved. We had a garage. I didn't have a car, but we had a garage and it was a very nice place. When we moved into that neighborhood we were the second black family in a neighborhood that had been predominantly Jewish and Polish and Italian. As this neighborhood was transitioning eventually to become all black, the neighborhood we moved out of on Lombard Street was transitioning to become all white. In 1964, I bought that house and my aunt and I moved into it and I kept it until after her death.

# GOING INTERNATIONAL: OFF TO MADAGASCAR

In 1965 I was asked by the YMCA to be a U.S. delegate to an international conference to be held jointly by the YMCA and the YWCA (Young Women's Christian Association) at the American University in Beirut (AUB) in Lebanon. I was terribly excited by this prospect. I had not been overseas at all except for a trip to Puerto Rico for about a month or so and for a trip to Canada. I'd never been really very far so I was very excited by this trip. It would take us to Switzerland, Lebanon, Greece, Jordan, and then back to the States. I agreed. I paid my portion and was signed up for the trip, and in August of 1965 we went to the American University in Beirut. We were there for a couple of weeks for the conference and then we made these other trips as I mentioned to Switzerland and Greece, and while we were in Lebanon we went to Jordan as well.

That trip was a transforming experience for me. I had never met so many people from so many different cultures, and to hear their stories about their countries and their cultures and their traditions and what have you was fascinating to me. I say to this day that that was my conversion on the road to Damascus, except mine occurred in Beirut at AUB. It was at that moment that I said I have got to do something in the international sphere. I was going to graduate the next year in 1966 and I said I've got to find something that will put me in that kind of arena. I began to apply to a number of American companies. I wanted to work in the international division of an American company abroad and I thought in 1965, 1966 the United States had changed enough to make that possible. I learned later on that it was not possible, that it wasn't going to happen. I was called for a number of interviews. I remember going to New York and going into Citibank and going into insurance companies in different companies for interviews and they were very charming and very nice and they'd say, "Oh, Mr. Young, you have a really impressive resume and you have a superb academic record." But the minute they said let's go to the executive dining room and the minute those doors opened and I looked inside and saw what was there and realized that mine was the only black face in the place and I wasn't going to be the one to change things, I knew that it wasn't going to happen. They gave all kinds of excuses and what have you, but the fact is the U.S. had not changed enough for that to happen.

Then I began to look to the federal government and I began taking every exam that I could think of and finally succeeded in 1967 in getting into the Foreign Service.

*Q: While you were discovering that the American business world had not changed, there were black power movements going on. I mean, you've got the qualifications but you realize, this is not for me. You got your nose pressed against the glass looking inside. How did this affect you in regard to the movements that were going on?*

YOUNG: Oh, when we had demonstrations in Philadelphia, I'd be part of them. I'd do the marches and things like that. I didn't travel to the South to participate in any of those. I didn't travel to Washington in '63 to participate in the March on Washington, but I was active in the NAACP (National Association for the Advancement of Colored People) in the branch office in Philadelphia. So that was my involvement in an effort to try to improve things with whatever kind of contribution I could make.

*Q: Was there any movement within your circle of friends in Philadelphia, I mean getting together and talking and saying, "What are we going to do about this?" Was this a subject of conversation?*

YOUNG: Oh, yes, the majority of my friends in Philadelphia because of my initial connection with the YMCA were white. They were very concerned and very active. We would all demonstrate together and do these various kinds of marches and what have you together. We were very active in an organization called Fellowship House in Philadelphia, which was a great meeting point in bringing us all together and bringing this integrated community together. I remember we had planned an outing to Wildwood, New Jersey for a weekend, this group of friends that I belonged to. We drove to Wildwood on a Friday evening. We arrived at the hotel and I was the only black in the group. The minute the owner of the hotel saw me, he said, "You all can stay here, but he can't stay here." They said, "Why not?" He just said, "He can't stay here." They knew, of course; he wouldn't come out and say it, but they knew why. They said, "If he can't stay here, then we're not going to stay here either." We tried a couple of other places and we ran into the same thing in each place, so we ended up staying in a couple of black hotels on the black side of town in Wildwood, New Jersey. I subsequently filed a complaint with the New Jersey Civil Rights Commission against this particular hotel. There weren't any claims of monetary benefit or anything like that, but I did win a complaint against them. They got their wrists slapped, and that sort of thing.

*Q: You say you took the Foreign Service exam among others. Did you know what you were taking?*

YOUNG: No, because I looked at the FBI (Federal Bureau of Investigation), I looked at the Navy, I looked at anything that would sort of get me overseas. I also applied to an organization called Opportunities Industrialization Center that was run by Dr. Leon Sullivan, because they were opening offices overseas as well.

*Q: Sullivan later became very renowned.*

YOUNG: In South Africa, that's right, exactly. We're back in 1966-67. As I said, I succeeded in getting into the Foreign Service and was offered an initial assignment to Madagascar, and I had no idea where it was. It was called the Malagasy Republic at that time and I thought it was somewhere in the Philippines. I just didn't know where it was.

This created a dilemma in my relationship with the woman I had fallen in love with, Angelina. I was going to go away in the fall and I had asked her to marry me, but the question was when and how and I first talked about getting married by proxy. I talked about coming back and marrying her. I talked about her coming out and marrying me. I mean we just discussed all kinds of things. It was on the 16th of September 1967 that I really asked her to marry me quickly and she said okay. Then I got home at about 2:00 in the morning, and my aunt would always wait up for me. She couldn't sleep until she heard the door close. I went in and I could tell that she was awake and I said to her, "Lucille, I'd like to talk to you." Her answer was,

"If you want to get married go ahead, that's your business." She knew. She could see it coming. One week later, on the 23rd of September, we had a full-fledged wedding at Sacred Heart Catholic Church on Sixteenth Street, with all of the usual things and that was the beginning of our married life together as a Foreign Service couple.

*Q: How did Mrs. Clark take this idea of one of her two daughters running off with a guy who was going to be all over the place?*

YOUNG: Well, that's a good question. She initially was not very pleased because it meant that her daughter had not fully realized the dreams that she had for her in terms of finishing her studies and things like that. Initially she wasn't pleased, but it didn't take many years for her to realize the kind of husband I was and the kind of person I was. She became one of the best supporters I could have had in life. Really, she just became a wonderful mother-in-law.

*Q: Let's talk about your entry into the Foreign Service. Could you talk about the oral exam? I'm always curious to get the feel for it.*

YOUNG: Yes, and I remember that to this day. At that time it was just three people. They sat behind the desk and asked me all kinds of questions and I tried to answer them to the best of my ability and then they said, well, you can take a break. They wanted to deliberate, to decide what the agreement was, and I'll never forget one person who was on the board. It was a woman by the name of Georgiana Prince. I don't know if you ever ran into her in the Service and we're friends to this day although I don't see her. She is still living and she must be in her eighties now. She sends us a card every Christmas and what have you. She said, "Oh, I was looking for you." I said, "Oh, really? What for? What did I do, did I fail?" She said, "No, you passed. We're very pleased." To this day I've been trying to find out who the other members of the board were, but I can't remember them. But I do remember Georgiana.

*Q: Do you recall any of the questions that were asked?*

YOUNG: I can't. I just really can't. That's out of my mind.

*Q: When you came in, it varies, were they looking for a particular field or "cone" for you to go into?*

YOUNG: At that time I was asked to go in as an administrative officer and went on an initial assignment as a budget officer to Madagascar.

*Q: Did you have an A-100 course?*

YOUNG: We did have a course.

*Q: How did you find the group of people?*

YOUNG: They were quite good. Some of them became such good friends that we remained friends throughout their time in the Foreign Service. I think they've all moved on now. I'm the last one to go.

*Q: Did you have any feel for what the Foreign Service did?*

YOUNG: Well, you have to keep in mind that when I came in, in 1967, you could count on one hand, not even two, the number of black officers in the Foreign Service. I mean very few. I went to Madagascar. I was the only one and then later on another African American officer came and the ambassador could not distinguish between the two of us. This second officer's name was Irving Williamson and the ambassador used to call Irving Johnny and he used to call me Irving. Irving was the economic officer and was just there for a short time before he moved to Mauritius, where he went to work. I just was quite surprised that there weren't more of us in the Service, but it was very few. Of the few who made ambassador at that time, as I recall back in the late sixties, they almost all came from USIA (United States Information Agency) and not from the State Department. The only one that I can recall at that time might have been Terry Todman, and there might have been one other or so, but almost all were from USIA.

*Q: You were in Madagascar from when to when?*

YOUNG: I was in Madagascar from 1967 to 1969, but I was also accredited to Mauritius. I have to tell you about one of the first things that happened to me on that first assignment. It was in 1968, when the students in Paris were rioting.

*Q: This was May or June of '68?*

YOUNG: That's right. They were rioting and they had a major impact on airline service and the students in Madagascar identified with the students in France and they, too, were rioting and sort of stirring up things. Well, one of the problems was that we couldn't have usual pouch service between Mauritius and the rest of the world. I had gone to Mauritius to help on the administrative arrangements to get the post set up for its independence in 1968. I went to buy furniture and help set up offices and check the books and all kinds of things like that. My wife went with me and when our work was done, which was I guess after about a week or two, we prepared to return to Madagascar and I was asked to serve as a non-pro courier. I think this occurred in about April or May, something like that. I was to be the non-pro courier taking these pouches back to Madagascar and then from Madagascar, I think, they would be put on Air Madagascar and sent to France. That's how we would get things from Mauritius to the rest of the world. I had five pouches and when I got to the airport I was told to check them in. I checked them in, these were classified pouches. I got the courier letter, the works.

When we arrived in Madagascar we went to claim the pouches and there was one, two, three, four, but there was no five and panic struck. My wife and I looked in every corner of the whole airplane. We couldn't find that fifth pouch. I was getting frantic. Before we had set out on our first assignment I had been ill and I'd been in the hospital in Washington for internal bleeding. They didn't know what the reason was. I never reported it to the State Department. I just took off on my assignment and my wife was worried that I was going to get sick again. We looked and looked and we said, well, we have no choice but to call the embassy. I called the embassy and explained what happened. They said to come in right away. I went in with the four pouches. They took the four and contacted Mauritius right away to explain what happened. Mauritius found the fifth pouch and said there was no evidence that it had been compromised in any way.

Telegrams flew back and forth. The country team was assembled. I thought oh my God, this is the end of my career. It hadn't even gotten off the ground yet. We had arrived in late October, so we had only been at post about five months. I thought that's it, my career hasn't even gotten started, finished. The communicator who took me to the airport said that he accepted responsibility because he never briefed me on how I should handle a pouch as a non-professional courier. Everyone said to me, oh, they certainly took care of that in orientation class. They surely told me. No one ever mentioned anything about how you behave as a non-professional courier. I didn't have a clue. He accepted responsibility for that and I thought that was a very big thing on his part. It really was. It's amazing what goes around, comes around.

Now, we had become friendly with this communicator and he was a very bright fellow and we remained in touch with him. He was not a high school graduate. He was very clever, though—his name was Theodore Boyd, Ted Boyd—and we told him, "Ted, you know, you're a very bright man. Why don't you finish your GED (General Educational Development diploma) and take the Foreign Service exam?" He took the Foreign Service exam and passed it with one of the highest scores recorded at that time, and succeeded in passing the oral as well. He was brought into the Service and he became a U.S. Information Agency officer. USIA put him through school. He did his bachelor's degree, did his master's degree, and worked toward his Ph.D. Some decades later he ended up as my public affairs officer when I was in Togo. That's jumping ahead a little bit, but that's what happened on my first assignment. Losing a classified pouch was quite something.

*Q: Let's talk a bit about when you arrived in Madagascar. What was Madagascar like? What was happening there and what sort of government did it have?*

YOUNG: It had a very stable government, one that was basically directed from behind the scenes by the French. It was a forgotten little paradise. When I describe the kind of Madagascar we had then, compared to the Madagascar that people talk about today, they can't believe it's the same place at all. At the time we were there it was the second most popular place among French colonials. They loved it. They adored it. We all had a great life there. We lived in wonderful houses, ate the best food, and had the best clothes. It was a good life. We were kind of like a little forgotten place.

I'll tell another story that I think is a great little story. The embassy was next to these very long steps that led up to a market. I think there were like eight hundred steps up to this market that was up on a plateau. Back in 1968 when the students were rioting in Paris, the students in Madagascar were following in a similar vein and one day the students came descending down these steps screaming and what have you. We had a young political officer who was, I think, on his third assignment at that point, one of the brightest guys we've ever met, full of beans as well. His name was Fred Rondon and Fred said, "Oh, my God the revolution is here." We said, "Oh, Fred, keep quiet. No revolution is here. We're a forgotten island. Nobody knows we're here. They've forgotten about us," and on and on. He says, "I tell you the revolution is coming. This country is out of step with what's happening in the rest of Africa and its going to come here." We said, "No revolution is going to come here. This is an island of stability and peace and calm and the good life." He insisted, "I tell you it is coming here." So Fred would write these very thoughtful think pieces for what we called at the time airgrams, and he'd keep sending these things in about the changes he saw coming to Madagascar. Now, when we were there, only Western countries were represented.. There were no Russians, no Chinese, no Eastern Bloc countries, strictly the West, and the place was stable, solid, with the French pulling the strings behind the scenes. Fred left and moved on and we all went to different assignments after that.

A few years later it happened just as Fred had predicted and there was a revolution and a very extreme turn to the left. As a matter of fact we got into trouble with them and in a fit of anger the Government of Madagascar PNG'd (declared persona non-grata) the ambassador, the DCM (Deputy Chief of Mission), the administrative officer, the political officer, and, I think, one other officer, about five of them in all. They were gone in no time. Our relations hit rock bottom and remained that way for many, many years until we came to the understanding that times had changed enough for us to reestablish relations at the full diplomatic level. We decided that we would name an ambassador once again to put things back on track, and as it turned out that ambassador was Fred Rondon. It was a wonderful way for Fred to have a first ambassadorship.

*Q: Who was your ambassador when you got there?*

YOUNG: That's an interesting story. Our ambassador when we got there was a fellow by the name of David Space King, and I remember him because I was a bit concerned as to how we would get along. He was a Mormon. He had been a member of Congress, did not succeed in his reelection bid and was given this ambassadorship to Madagascar. Well, I thought, my God, I'm going to work for a Mormon ambassador and the Mormons don't believe that we should belong to their church and believe that we are the descendants of Ham and are cursed, and on and on. Not only am

I black, but they're sending this man to a black country also. I wondered how this was going to work out. As it turned out, he was wonderful. He was also in the forefront of trying to push for change in the church, which he eventually succeeded in doing. He was a very good ambassador, very effective. He learned how to speak the local language. He wrote a book on the country. He was very good. I liked him a lot. Spoke superb French.

*Q: How did you find being the B&F (Budget and Fiscal) officer?*

YOUNG: Not very much to my liking at all, because I found it too confining. I wanted to be with the people more and I wanted more contact with the outside as well. I didn't want to just sit in an office and do numbers and work with just the FSNs (Foreign Service National employees). I did two things. Number one, I began teaching English as a foreign language at USIS. The other thing I did was to begin giving international folk dance lessons. During the period when I was active in the YMCA, I did international folk dancing. You know, dances from Romania, Bulgaria, Israel, and Hungary and different places like that. I started teaching a class in that and that got me out and made it possible to do what I was expected to do inside and then have friends on the outside, getting to really meet Malagasy.

*Q: How did you find them?*

YOUNG: Loved them. Wonderful people, absolutely wonderful. Beautiful, gentle, kind. They invited us into their homes. My wife and I had an enormous number of Malagasy friends, unlike a lot of other people in the mission. We just reached more and as a result it paid off in friendships on the outside.

*Q: Was there a difference between the highlanders and lowlanders?*

YOUNG: A big difference. Most of the people in the capital city, Antananarivo, where we were, were highlanders. Most of the people around the coastal area were a mixture of African and Indonesian stock. They had a certain look to them and it wasn't the same look that you would see in the highlands. The people in the highlands you could put on the streets of Jakarta and you'd never find them again. Some of the ones from the coast, you put them on 125th Street in New York and you'd never find them again.

*Q: You were there during a time of turmoil in the United States, particularly with the Vietnam War, but also on racial things, too. Were the Malagasy tuned in? Were they interested?*

YOUNG: Very interested, oh yes. They didn't have riots and demonstrations and that sort of thing. They were attuned and very keen on things American and particularly things black American; music and culture and plays and, you know, we'd get groups out from the U.S. We'd get dance troupes and musical groups, almost always black groups that were enormously successful in their presentations in Madagascar.

*Q: Did you feel at the time, "I'm a budget and fiscal officer, but I'm sure not going to do this again"? Did you feel like you were locked into this?*

YOUNG: In fact I wasn't sure I was going to stay in the Foreign Service, because my wife and I began to discuss what we should do. At one point we decided we would call it quits because she wanted to return to school and I was prepared to go back and do that. Then we discussed it some more and we decided, well, maybe we ought to give it one more shot. By that time it was too late, because all of the jobs had gone, so there was nothing left for me. I had a wonderful DCM, a man we became friends with and remained friends with until the time of his death, and he was just a great mentor and friend and a real big helper. His name was Peter C. Walker, a great guy. We are friends with the family to this day. Anyhow, I went to him and I said, "Peter, this is our story. We weren't sure we were going to leave. We waited and we made up our minds, and now we're going to give it one more shot. Do you think you can help me with a job?" He says, "Well, this is late in the cycle and I don't know what we can do. The executive director of the Bureau of African Affairs is a friend. Maybe he can help you with something." I think it was Ed Dobbins. Peter said, "Maybe he can help you. I'll write to him." He wrote to him and told him about me. Then Peter came to me one day and said, "There's one job that he can offer you." I asked, "What's that?" He said, "It's as general services officer (GSO) in Conakry, Guinea, but it would be following some training." Now, in the meantime, I had become very ill on three separate occasions in Madagascar and on the third occasion, which was toward the end of my assignment, it was decided that I would go back to the States for treatment. Peter had factored all of this into his letter to Dobbins.

Then I returned to the States and I got a tentative assignment as GSO in Conakry, preceded by a huge chunk of training. This was 1970. I finished the Madagascar assignment in 1969, came to the States, got medical treatment that entailed a major operation, moved into this training program in January of '70, and was in the training program until June. This training program was intended to create the next generation of administrative officers for the next century. I've forgotten the name of it, but it had some fancy title and we were all highly honored that we were selected for this thing, and I must say we did quite well when I recall some of the people who were in it. I entered that management training program and then I took a little bit of brush up French because I hadn't reached a 3/3 yet. I got the 3/3 and went on to Conakry, Guinea.

*Q: Tell me more about the management course.*

YOUNG: This was a course created by the Department in an effort to develop a cadre of the next generation of management officers. We weren't called management officers at that time, although it was called the management course. We were called administrative officers. This was a bold, new initiative. It was a very lengthy course. It went from February to June, which was quite extraordinary for that time. We're talking about 1970, and to put administrative officers, GSOs, personnel officers, into that kind of broad administrative training was quite a jump. We were quite a group. Our class included Brian Atwood, Irv Hicks, and Larry Grahl, and it included myself. I'm just mentioning a few people, all of whom went on to become chiefs of mission or even higher.

*Q: What were some of the emphases that you were getting?*

YOUNG: Well, the goal was to try and instill in us the importance of service, the importance of creativity, the importance of risk-taking, the importance of innovation, the importance of dealing with change, and things like that. That was the thrust of it. We had speakers—I can't remember all of them now—but we had them from the outside and from the Department and all kinds of universities and what have you. It was quite a course. It didn't last in the curriculum very long, mind you. I think it lasted a couple years and that was it.

# ON TO GUINEA

*Q: Then in 1970 you went to Conakry. Is that right?*

YOUNG: Went to Conakry, Guinea as general services officer. At that time it was probably one of the worst places in Africa.

*Q: When were you there?*

YOUNG: From '70 to '72.

*Q: Describe the situation in Guinea at the time.*

YOUNG: Well, I went ahead without my wife, who remained behind to have our first child. She was pregnant with our first child and we learned very quickly that Guinea had no facilities at all for her to give birth at post, so she stayed behind and I went ahead. I arrived I think in July. It was the height of the rainy season. I moved into a good size house. Things were kind of run down and shabby and it was raining like I had never seen rain before. I mean it just poured. I've never witnessed that kind of rain before. At our previous post in Madagascar, we would have rain occasionally, but never anything like this. I mean torrential rains. The houses had corrugated tin roofs so the rain would pound down on this roof. I mean something just unbelievably loud and frightening if you were not used to it. I was not used to it.

When I moved into this house I was very lonely. I missed my wife quite a bit and there was another single young man there and we became friends. He was new at the post as well, so we used to pal around together. We would go out at night after hours into the beer gardens and drink beer and watch the local folks dance and we'd chat and make friends and what have you. I figured well, this is not a nice place, but we'll make do. It was clear to me as I looked around that everything was shabby and broken down and I could see very readily what had happened when the French pulled out in the late fifties and literally ravaged that country. They were going to teach them a lesson, because Guinea was the only country of the then Francophone African countries that said it didn't want to be a part of the Francophone set-up, that it wanted to go it on its own, and France was furious. They pulled out all of their people. They ripped out the electrical wires for the street lighting, for the apartment buildings and offices, broke the generators of the local hospital, tore up the streets. I mean, everything you can think of, they did. It was horrible. They broke the elevator to the one skyscraper, which was just mean and vicious. It was ugly and the country had not been able to overcome that. It was readily apparent. I mean holes in the streets, broken down lights. You couldn't get electricity on any kind of continuous basis, so it was just a dreadful situation in terms of the infrastructure. They broke things and the cranes. You just name it, they broke it. They were determined to teach that country a lesson and they did.

Anyhow, there I was, lonely, in the rain, miserable, and I'll never forget my early introduction to Guinea. One morning I got up and I felt something crawling on my back and I took off my pajamas and sort of gave myself a good shake and out dropped this huge cockroach. It had been in the bed with me. On another occasion I remember going home after work and reading a *Herald Tribune* that was two weeks old at that point and being very happy to get it, an *International Herald Tribune*. I had a scotch in one hand and the newspaper in the other and suddenly I heard this thing fly in from the rain and right towards my head. Boom, it bounced off my head. It was a huge flying cockroach. I had never seen one of those in my life and so the newspaper went in one direction and the scotch in another direction, and I think I started to take off in another.

After several introductions to the bugs and insects and things like that, I got used to it and went on with life and got on with my job. My job was a tough one, because the infrastructure, as I mentioned earlier, was so broken down. Nothing worked in that country. To get goods from the port was worse than pulling hens' teeth. It was almost impossible, but we had a third country national, a Lebanese fellow who was the miracle-worker of the embassy, and he could do anything. He got all of our goods in and out of the country. I'll never forget, the ambassador told him once, "Don't ever tell me how you do these things, because if you do I'll have to fire you." We knew that a lot of it was done through little bribes and what have you to the port officials. It was the only way you could get anything done and he did it and we were grateful for it.

I remember on another occasion the ambassador saying to me, "Johnny, you're the most important person at this mission." I said, "Well, thank you very much Mr. Ambassador, but I find that hard to believe." He said, "No, really, you mean more to morale at this post than I do." Well, I never took him seriously for a minute. I thought he was just being very kind. He was an extraordinary ambassador. His name was Bud Sherer. I just loved him. I never ever thought that I would ever become an ambassador, but years and years later when I did, he was my model. He was an incredible man and I'll get to something else in a minute that will indicate what an extraordinary person he was, both he and his wife, Pam Sherer, just a fantastic couple.

Anyhow, we struggled to get our work done in Guinea. It was a struggle for the ambassador to meet with Guinean officials. Everything was so leftist at that time. It was unbelievable. You couldn't buy something as simple as an airline ticket and say, I want to leave tomorrow. You had to go through all kinds of government offices to get an airline ticket to leave and we worried particularly in the case of medical evacuation about delay and in several cases the ambassador had to intervene at the presidential level to get these authorizations to buy tickets to get people out on an emergency basis. It was tough for the ambassador, tough for the mission, tough all around to get things done. The government was inward-looking, it was leftist leaning and didn't have anything good to say about the United States and the West. If you called a government office, the first thing you would hear on the other end was not hello, but it was about the revolution. "Ready for the revolution" was the mantra all over town. That was how the phones were answered. It was an indication of the kind of indoctrination that the local population was going through.

*Q: The president was?*

YOUNG: Sekou Toure, an extraordinary leader. At the time we were there, he was still at his height in terms of power and influence on the continent. Sekou Toure was the kind of man who could stand up in a stadium and speak for seven hours straight without a single note and have the people enthralled. He also had his country divided in terms of having people express their loyalty to the government. That was the only way that they could get a little bit of food that was available and distributed by the government. Those who expressed the greatest loyalty to the government were the ones who got the little bit of meal, a little bit of rice, a little bit of tomato paste, whatever the case may be, because all of the food was handled through the government. There were no private grocery stores or markets or anything like that. I remember my wife couldn't find a single onion in its entirety. She could buy a half an onion and buy several halves because things were so scarce. You could not get anything. We had to bring everything into that country, everything. We hooked up, for example, with a company in Belgium called Belex Cargo and they brought in everything. Planeloads of goods would come in every Friday and I'd send out my GSO trucks and we'd get everything in and bring it to the embassy, divide it up and distribute it, and we all ate like kings and queens. As tough as it was, we did put in a great effort and we did eat quite well.

As I mentioned earlier, my wife was waiting to have our first child, who was due on October 25, but on October 25, no baby, and no baby a week later and a week later and a week later. Finally, it was several days after November 18 that I got a telegram from Washington. In fact, I used to call the communicator every morning to see if he had received a telegram. He would say, "No telegram, no telegram." One morning he called me.

*Q: So, you were calling the communicator.*

YOUNG: Right, the communicator, everyday. Any word yet from my wife? No. So, one day he called me and he said, "Hello Johnny?" I answered, "Yes?" He said, "I have a telegram you'd be interested in." I said, "What does it say?" He read, "Mother-in-law Virginia Clark advises son David John Young born Wednesday, November 18, 1980, weighing nine pounds, three ounces; mother and baby fine." He said, "That's the biggest goddamn baby I ever heard of." I had a good laugh, we all had a good laugh. I had stopped smoking at that point for several years and I said to someone, "Give me a cigarette" and I started smoking again and I continued smoking for another five years. I got the telegram several days late, so it was about November 20 or 21. Now, I mention this because I was home in bed on the evening of November 22, which is a fateful day in Guinean history. I was stirred out of my sleep by what sounded like cannon sounds. We had made a huge investment in food that we had shipped to the post and put in a storeroom at the end of one of the hallways in the house. I kept saying to myself, "Who's trying to get into my storeroom?" All I could think of was the value of all that food we had in the storeroom. I kept getting up and going to check the storeroom and everything was fine. I kept hearing boom, boom, rat a tat tat, boom. I couldn't figure it out.

The next morning I got up to go to mass. I was standing outside of the gate waiting for the person to pick me up to take me to church and it was the administrative officer who came by and said, "Johnny, you can't stay here." I lived in an area that was close to what they called the ministerial village, which was near where a lot of the ministers lived. He said, "Last night there was an attempted coup. There's still trouble in the air. We're all meeting over at the DCM's residence." The DCM at that time was a fellow named Don Norland. So we all gathered at Don Norland's house. We gathered all of the Peace Corps volunteers, as many as we could. We all went to Don Norland's house and that's where we stayed for literally several days until we could return to our respective homes. On the night of the 23rd, things were still uncertain so we stayed at Don's house. Suddenly, I guess as dark descended, the cannon fire started again and we could see the tracers through the trees, and I remember Don screaming to all of us to get down on the floor. We all got down on the floor and that's where we stayed for the rest of the night, down on the floor as these bullets and cannon shells and what have you sailed through the trees. The Guinean forces were challenging rebel forces that were attempting to come in from the sea, and Don's house was right on the coast. We could see what was going on. That went on all night long. On the 24th we didn't have that at night and by the 25th we could return to our houses.

Well, things were pretty bad after that. Sekou Toure turned on his own people that he suspected in being involved in the plot to overthrow him. He turned on a number of people in the foreign community he thought were involved in the plot as well, including a number of Lebanese. I'll never forget a couple of days after that, going to work one morning and going under an overpass and seeing the hanged bodies of people we knew, including the director of the electricity department, whom I had dealt with just a few days before in an effort to get electricity to several of our houses.

We saw people who were strung up in the public square for everyone to see. It was a very tense time. Now, this witch hunt that Toure had embarked on stretched out over a number of months and a number of people we knew were involved, including a number of Guinean officials. It was really pretty grim and many of them were never heard from again. They were killed and murdered or never heard from again. This was a time when we were concerned about human rights but frankly couldn't do very much about it. Diallo Telli was a famous Guinean, for example, who had been caught up in events of that time and was tortured terribly and eventually killed.

Some months later the Lebanese fellow who worked for us had gone on vacation with his family while this hunt for coup plotters was still on. He was planning to return to Conakry with his family. He was housed in an apartment along with our other diplomatic personnel. This was at a time when we treated third country nationals basically the same as we would an American diplomat. He lived in an apartment building that we had and we treated him the same as everyone else, as I mentioned earlier. But during this time we suspected that if he returned to the country he would be in great difficulty. We tried to get a message to him in Lebanon. We tried also through our embassy in Paris, because we thought he was traveling to and from Lebanon through Paris. We did succeed in getting the message to him, but he decided he would send his family back anyhow. He sent his wife and daughter and his brother back to Conakry and we didn't think that was particularly wise, but that's what he opted to do. He stayed out longer. I went together with my wife to the airport to meet his wife, daughter, and brother. We met them and took them to their apartment building. The apartment building we lived in at the time was under surveillance by the government and Guinea police. From time to time, they would have one of their policemen sit outside of this building in a chair. I arrived. My wife went home with our baby. I went with his family to the apartment building. We got them settled.

We were sitting in the apartment building having a Coke when there was a knock on the door. We opened the door and in marched I think about four Guinean policemen who wanted to know who let these people into the building. I said, "I let them in this building. Why are you here?" They said, "We are part of the Government of Guinea and we are the authority here and we have a right to be in this building." I said, "You have no right to be in this building. This is U.S. government territory and you should leave immediately." Well, they said, "No, you will leave immediately." I responded, "I will not." They said, "You have no right to have allowed these people in this building. This building is under surveillance and you have to get out." I said, "I'm not going out." They said, "Yes, you are." So, we got into a little back and forth. They then took a bayonet, they had a submachine gun with a bayonet, and they put that in my back and said, "You will go with us." I said okay and went with them.

They left the Lebanese family there and they marched me out of the building and the other Americans in the building all had their doors cracked at that point, because they knew there was some commotion and something was going on in the building. As I descended the steps, I passed the ambassador's secretary, a woman by the name of Marcella Wheeler. She had her door cracked and she was looking out the door. I said, "Marcella, be sure you tell the ambassador what has happened to me." She said, "I will." They marched me out. They put me in the back of a little Jeep and then they took me to jail. At the jail, they sat me in a cell and they gave me a piece of paper and a pen and they said, "You will now write your deposition which is your confession." I said, "I will not." They said, "Yes, you will." I said, "I will not write any deposition." They said, "You will or you will stay here." I said, "I'll just stay." I remained there in the cell and the policeman who was outside of the cell would occasionally answer the phone when it rang and each time the phone rang I would say, "Is that my ambassador?" He would say to me, "No" in very clear terms. He said, "Are you ready now to do your deposition?" I said no. So, we went back and forth on that for a while. Each time the phone would ring I would say, "Is that my ambassador?" "No." This went on for several hours.

At one point, we said to them, "You will not receive a single further shipment of food from the United States government." We said, "We have sent a message to Washington. It was received in the White House." I learned later from a friend of mine who was in the White House, Fred Rondon, and Fred said, "I was in the situation room and this cable came through that you had been arrested and you were in jail. I thought I couldn't believe Johnny Young had been arrested and was in jail." It was that leverage of no further shipment of food that persuaded President Sekou Toure to act to get me out of jail. I mention all of that to just illustrate what a difficult situation Guinea was in at that time.

After the attempted coup and difficulties in the ensuing months, I remember the ambassador called the staff together and said, "This has been a really rough time for us. Some of you may want to leave and if any of you want to go, I will do everything I can to see that you get good onward assignments, but you don't have to stay on here if you don't want to. Just let me know if you want to do it and I will take care of it for you." Not a single person at the mission took the ambassador up on that offer, because they had such great respect and admiration for him. They were prepared to undergo whatever the hardships were at that time in order to continue their work with him at that mission. I'll never forget him.

*Q: How about just day-to-day working? You need clearances and everything else. Was the government out just to be nasty to you or was this just the way it was, to you as Americans or were other countries having the same problem, including, say, the Soviets?*

YOUNG: Oh, no, any Western country; they were very difficult. The Soviets were in their glory days there. The Soviets and the Eastern Bloc countries were treated very nicely, and we did not hear of difficulties they had. The French have an embassy there, because Guinea had broken relations with the French when the French pulled out in the late 1950s. I think in '57 or '58.

*Q: What happened to the Lebanese man?*

YOUNG: He finally returned after things quieted down, packed up his bags and left. We got him a job at the embassy in Cameroon. He went to Cameroon and he was there for a little while and they finally caught him with his hands in the till and he was released and we didn't hear from him anymore after that.

*Q: Could you get out into the country or outside?*

YOUNG: Absolutely not. We were basically under city arrest. My wife and I made one of the few trips possible before they completely shut down any travel out of the country. On that trip we were able to go to Freetown, Sierra Leone. We went by road and returned by road. Again, it shows you how fate operates. Little did I know that many years into the future I would return to Sierra Leone as the American ambassador. We went there and we saw colleagues there that I had met. We met two young gentlemen who later came into the Foreign Service and have done very well. Steve Noland and his brother; they were teenagers at the time. That was one of the last trips anyone was able to make by road outside of Conakry. We were literally confined to the city.

*Q: Since you're a Catholic, what was the fate of the church?*

YOUNG: That's a good question, because the church was fine. No problem with the church. After the coup, the church was kind of implicated in being part of the coup and it was our embassy that managed to get a message to the Vatican on the whereabouts of Archbishop Kimball. We did play a role in that, since the church unfortunately had no way of communicating, at least to the Vatican. The Catholic Church was fine.

*Q: Did you feel the hand of the Soviets or the East Germans there?*

YOUNG: We had pretty good relations. I mean to the extent that you could have good relations with Soviets back in 1970. I'll never forget the Soviet ambassador would invite our ambassador over to his residence from time to time for them to sit down and have a tête-à-tête. The ambassador would always say, "Well, I'm going to the Soviet embassy for lunch. I won't be back for the afternoon because they're going to ply me with vodka," which they did, and of course he couldn't return to the office after that. The relations were good but limited. For example, the goods that we were able to obtain locally from any kind of store, we were able to get from a big Yugoslav store that was set up to cater to the diplomatic community in hard currency. That worked out very nicely. We were very happy for that. I mean, it wasn't the caliber of goods that you would get in a Western store, but the Yugoslav store was good and it peddled Yugoslav products and they got dollars for it and they were very happy and we were happy. So it worked out very nicely.

*Q: I realize your job wasn't political reporting, but I imagine there wasn't much going on there.*

YOUNG: Oh, there was a lot going on. The problem was you couldn't get it first-hand. You had to get it from bits and pieces that you would glean from different contacts. We had a very active political section and a superb political officer, a young man at the time who has subsequently done well in the Service, a fellow by the name of Al Thibault. Al has done quite well.

*Q: I've actually interviewed him.*

YOUNG: A terrific officer, a wonderful reporting officer, but you couldn't just go to the ministry and have a discussion with officials. It was what you could get off of radio, reading between the lines, what you could glean from the few contacts that you had. Very few people had real Guinean contacts except for our public affairs officer, Hank Ryan. He was exceptional in terms of how he was able to get into the Guinean community, and we got good bits and pieces of information from him as well. We were trying to read the country and get a sense of where it was going and how the political decisions were being made.

*Q: Did you get any feel for the Guineans' regretting that they'd broken off with France the way they did? Were other countries like Senegal seemingly doing much better?*

YOUNG: They knew that other countries were doing better. Senegal and Ivory Coast at that time were really models of success. Guineans were fiercely loyal, fiercely proud, but they were also terrorized by their own government. They were afraid to voice their opinion about what was going on in their country. They couldn't speak to each other. They didn't know who would turn them in. They lived in a state of terror. A huge community of Guineans lived outside in Togo, in Benin, or in the Ivory Coast. I mean they were just all over, a huge community of them. I think it was up to a quarter of the population. It was very large.

*Q: Did Guinea have a society segmented into important tribal units?*

YOUNG: Oh, it's tribal; I mean lots of tribes there. But the main tribe I think was the president's tribe. I think he was what they call Mandinka, if I'm not mistaken. All those tribes, I can't even remember them all. It was not a major issue at that time. People were held together through terror, through sheer force, and in that situation they suspended their tribal beliefs just to survive.

*Q: How did your wife with a new baby adjust to this?*

YOUNG: Well, my wife is an extraordinary person. She realized the limitations of the situation we were in and she managed to have a very good life there. She developed a group of friends and she would visit with those friends. They had all kinds of projects that they would work on, but they couldn't do the kinds of volunteer work that she would do in the future in other countries. I mean there were no local ladies' group or local charities or that sort of thing. None of that existed in Guinea. Her focus was on her baby and helping him to grow and develop. She did that very nicely and made a very lovely home for me.

*Q: Well, was it '72?*

YOUNG: 1972. While we were there she became pregnant with our second child and became so dehydrated that the regional medical doctor who was resident in Conakry, a Dr. Corey Marko, had to confine her to bed. Eventually we left and then she had to be treated in the States for her dehydration. We left somewhat in an emergency situation. I'll never forget I had to pack up the entire house myself and this was at a time when we couldn't call the GSO section, although I was the GSO, or call the contractor to do the packing. They gave us boxes and tape and paper and we had to do it ourselves. I packed up the entire house myself. Mind you we had only been married a couple of years, but it was amazing what we had accumulated in just a couple of years. That was my first time to pack up the entire house and I had to do it on one other occasion, but I'll tell you about that later.

# DREAM JOB IN KENYA

Following Conakry, I was looking for an onward assignment. We had had a temporary admin officer in Conakry, Marsha Martin, who liked my work. She liked me. She had received an onward assignment to be the admin officer in Nairobi, Kenya and she told me later on, "You know I like your work a lot. Would you mind coming to Kenya to be the GSO?" I said, "I would love it, but that's sort of like a triple stretch." At the time I was an FSO-6 and she said, "Well, I'll see what I can do, but I can't make any promises." She left and we, of course, put our bids in on a number of other things. I can't remember what they were, but in the back of my mind I had it in my head, "Well, maybe this will work out." One day we got a call and she said, "I think I have it worked out. I think they're going to allow you to go into this stretch assignment as the supervisory GSO in Nairobi." That's what happened. That was my reward and we were assigned to Nairobi. We went to Washington for a while to have some more training and then in the summer of 1972 we arrived in Nairobi. My wife was very pregnant at that time with our second child and she planned to give birth in Nairobi. Our relatives, her mother and my mother, thought that I was out of my mind to allow her to give birth in Kenya. They had in their mind an Africa of huts and things like that. They had no idea that we were going to a pretty sophisticated city, with good facilities and things like that.

We went there and that assignment turned out to be really quite a nice one for several reasons. The place is spectacularly beautiful. The job was a dream. As I said, it was sort of like a triple stretch. The people were nice; the country was stable. We had a good embassy and a good ambassador. Terrorism wasn't something that we dealt with at that time. Anybody could walk into the embassy and come up and see me, and that was it. It was a different time altogether. It had so many positives working in its favor, and of course my daughter was born there, which made it very special. On October 11 she was born in the Queen Elizabeth Hospital and was healthy, never had a problem, which was really quite special. Our son was born in Philadelphia at one of the best hospitals in Philadelphia and shortly after birth had an infection, or rather my wife developed an infection and was isolated from the baby for about ten days. But we didn't have any problem like that in Nairobi. She had a c-section, which was what she had in Philadelphia as well, but it all turned out very well.

We were very happy there, very pleased. I had an assistant GSO, a fellow who had been an army officer, had left the army, and had come into the Foreign Service. A guy by the name of John Nix, and he was quite good. He stayed for about a year and then I subsequently received another GSO to replace him. My wife and I went out to the airport to receive this replacement; this was in 1973, We stopped by Kentucky Fried Chicken, bought chicken, took it home, ate it and gave him some. We put him in the car and took him to his new house, got him settled, and my wife and I got in the car and we said we've got a winner. He was a winner. His name was James Walsh and he subsequently, many years later, became U.S. ambassador to Argentina.

Anyway, I'll tell you about some of the fun times in Kenya. Of course we enjoyed ourselves very much there. We were freed. I mean, we could travel all over the country, we could travel to neighboring countries and we took advantage of those countries. We went on safari and we did all kinds of things. One of the big events of our time there occurred in the fall of 1973. At that time, Kenya hosted the first meeting in Africa of the International Monetary Fund and the World Bank. It was a big event. The U.S. government decided it would send a huge delegation to this gathering. George Shultz was the secretary of the treasury, Arthur Burns was the head of the Federal Reserve, and Paul Volcker was the head of the Council of Economic Advisors. We had Andrew Young. We had Wright Patman, who was the chairman of the House Banking Committee. It was just an incredible group and they were going to be there for ten days.

We had them scheduled to be in two hotels with two control rooms set up for both. I worked the control room in the Hilton Hotel and I remember we were scrounging around for help in supporting this huge activity that was a first for the mission in Kenya. The executive director of the Bureau of African Affairs, Bill Bradford, offered to send some help. He said, "You know, I have this new young officer here who is bright and smart. I'm going to send him out there and he can lend you a hand and I think he'll help you out. His name is Pat Kennedy." We said, "Well, we're happy to take whoever you send." Pat came out and he worked with us on this. I'll never forget it. I went out to the airport to meet this group. We went out with the cars and we had a bus that we were going to put them on. Shultz and some of the other key VIPs were taken in cars, but I had the bus where I rode with the senators and the congressmen, and in the bus with me was Congresswoman Margaret Heckler.

*Q: Oh, yes, from Massachusetts.*

YOUNG: From Massachusetts. I'll never forget her as long as I live. There I am, in the bus with her and all these other senators. Andrew Young was in there and a whole mess of them. She said, "Oh, I'm so excited to be here. I'm happy to be here. This is great. This is wonderful. I've never been to Africa before. I'm so happy. I can't wait to get to the bush." Then she turned to me and she said, "Are you from the bush?" I said, "No, I'm not. I'm a Foreign Service officer. I'm from the United States, Philadelphia." It was really so funny. I then got them to their hotel and the majority of the senators and congressmen stayed in the Hilton Hotel, where I had the control room. Volcker and Burns and Shultz and company stayed at the Intercontinental Hotel, and that was another control room. We took care of them for ten solid days. They went on safari. They traveled around.

I'll never forget, I wish I could remember the name of the congressman, I think he was from New Jersey, but anyhow he went on safari one day and this is the way the story was recounted to us. He had been told not to take pictures unless he got approval from the person he wanted to take the picture of. They went on this safari and they were in this little minibus and he had his camera with the big lens and he was snapping pictures and he didn't see anybody around. They're way out on the way to their camp and suddenly the bus is totally surrounded by Masai tribesmen. He thought they were going to be harmed and the story goes that he said, "You want my camera? You want my watch? Please don't hurt me, whatever you want, don't harm me." They weren't there to harm them. That's the way it was. You could be out in the middle of nowhere and suddenly there would be Masai or somebody else and that's the way it was. They let them go and they had a good safari and came back and told us the story and everybody had a good laugh.

Wright Patman was a very distinguished-looking gentleman from Texas. He looked every bit the part of a distinguished ambassador or statesman, and a fine gentleman, there's no question about that. Well, I'd been working with all of them for ten days, day and night, in this control room, so I thought they knew who I was and what I was or wasn't. They all arrived at the airport and the plan was that everyone would get on the plane and the chairman would be the last one to get on and then that would be it and the plane would go. It worked that way. I escorted him to the steps of the plane. He turned to me. He said, "Thank you, son." He shook my hands and slipped me two dollars. I said, "Thank you very much Mr. Chairman, but I can't accept tips. I'm a Foreign Service officer." I returned the two dollars to him. He understood, I assume, and then he went on, but I thought that was rather amusing.

*Q: Oh boy. Who was the ambassador while you were there?*

YOUNG: We had two ambassadors. The first one was Robinson McIlvaine, who was a very fine ambassador, did an excellent job.

*Q: He was ambassador in a number of countries.*

YOUNG: Including Guinea. Yes, a good man, a good fellow; he did an excellent job. He was particularly keen on trying to limit growth at the embassy. He would face fights on that going and coming from his AID colleagues, because AID wanted to just grow and grow there. They were already bigger than any other component of the mission. They were giving about I guess seventy million dollars a year to the Kenyans and they were doing it with about fifty or sixty people. The Germans were giving the same amount of money with six people, but that's just the magnitude of how we had this huge AID apparatus to give this amount of money. The ambassador wanted to limit it. He said, "If trouble comes to this country one day, there will be a price to pay in having all of these people here. We don't need to be any larger. We want to keep it at a certain level, at least during my time here." He just refused to go along with it and it worked at least during that time. Subsequent ambassadors to Kenya did not succeed as well and some of them were very much in favor of growth.

*Q: Who succeeded him?*

YOUNG: Tony Marshall, a political appointee who had been PNG'd from Madagascar and came to Kenya. A very nice man, not the same as McIlvaine, but he was quite good. He wasn't just a run of the mill political appointee; he was someone who had considerable experience in Africa as a private businessman and private citizen. He had had interest in Africa and he had been appointed previously, as I mentioned, as ambassador to Madagascar, from which he had been declared persona non grata.

*Q: Do you know why he had been PNG'd?*

YOUNG: The Malagasy government thought the U.S. was involved in a plot to overthrow the government and they PNG'd the ambassador, the DCM, the political officer, the administrative officer, the economic officer, and on and on.

*Q: As the supervisory GSO could you talk a little bit about working in that environment. Were local employees getting things done?*

YOUNG: Getting things done was a dream compared to Conakry. You could actually do the job in a place like Nairobi at that time. The infrastructure was good. The government was stable. Systems were in place that had been put in by the British. They worked very nicely. The Kenyan civil servants were professional. We didn't hear of problems of corruption. We didn't have to bribe officials to get goods in and out of the country, so it was the way it should have been. It worked very nicely. The job was a pleasure. I had a super staff of Kenyan employees, and Asian Indians from Sri Lanka, Pakistan, India and Goa. The Goans in the embassy were an incredible group of extremely talented, very well educated people.

*Q: At that time Goans were still under Portuguese rule?*

YOUNG: It was part of India at that point. They were incredible employees. They all did very well. Now, they were there at a time when the situation for Asians in Uganda turned very bad. They became very frightened and they turned to us and asked if we could help them to leave, and we managed to get many of them jobs at our embassy in England. We got a number of them jobs throughout our missions in Canada, in Vancouver, Ottawa,

Toronto, and many of them moved on. As they moved on we replaced them with Kenyan employees, which was going to happen eventually in any case, and that worked out very well.

Q: *Did we have a subsidiary post in Mombasa?*

YOUNG: We had a consulate in Mombasa at the time, but it was very quiet and sleepy; not very much happened there.

Q: *Was this our port? I mean, did we have much in the way of port calls and that sort of thing?*

YOUNG: Yes, we did. In fact we were there when we received, I think it was for the first time, one of the U.S. aircraft carriers that came through.

Q: *A whole city coming through.*

YOUNG: They had not seen anything like it. Now, mind you, I have to put all of this in perspective. The aircraft carrier had come from the Arabian Gulf. You have on these aircraft carriers a lot of young men full of energy, shall we say, and coming from the Arabian Gulf they were looking for a bit of amusement. So Kenya and the Seychelles were places where the kind of amusement they sought could be found.

Q: *We're talking about females.*

YOUNG: Well, I didn't want to get to that. That's a fact.

Q: *There it is.*

YOUNG: That's it. It was like they had died and gone to heaven, and of course the economy in Mombasa welcomed them and did quite well during those visits. The aircraft carrier would not come into Mombasa, but it would anchor out and then bring 200 or 300 in at a time by boat, and it worked out very nicely.

Q: *When I was in Korea when we used to get aircraft carriers to come into Pusan, there would be buses loaded with young ladies. I assume there would be busloads in this case.*

YOUNG: Exactly. That's what happened. We were always on the lookout for trouble and what have you, but we had very little trouble.

Q: *I think the navy is used to this and it's something they have to deal with and it works.*

YOUNG: Yes. We loved that assignment in Kenya. It was good. It was interesting. We loved Jomo Kenyatta, a fantastic man.

Q: *Was he the president?*

YOUNG: He was the president and he had charisma. You felt that you were in the presence of a truly great and mysterious and wonderful man, which he was. He kept that country together. Everybody loved him. When we were there, the big question was what would happen when he was no longer be on the scene. There was all kinds of speculation as to who would replace him and how things would evolve as a result of that. When we left in 1974 he was still there and still doing quite well. In '74 we had completed our assignment. Our children had grown up a little. Our son was then four years old. Our daughter was going on two years of age and I was looking around for an onward assignment.

I got a cable one day asking me if I would be interested in setting up the American embassy in Papua New Guinea and I said yes. I was very excited by that prospect. This was at a time when Papua New Guinea was preparing for its independence. In preparation for their independence they had placed a number of junior government officials in British embassies around the world so that they would be part of a new Papua New Guinean diplomatic corps, and one of these fellows was at the British embassy in Kenya. We got a chance to meet him. There was also one at the Australian embassy in Kenya. We got a chance to meet him and we liked him very much. As it turned out, there was a delegation passing through Nairobi and this delegation included a fellow who was likely to be the new head of Papua New Guinea. So we got a chance to meet these people and we hit it off with them very nicely. We looked forward to it and we got ourselves very excited by this. People gave us farewell parties. We presumptuously told them we were going to Papua New Guinea. Mind you, we hadn't received any orders and then two things happened.

It was at the end of the fiscal year and at this time in 1974, the government had run out of money, so the State Department had no money for onward assignment travel. I got a cable saying we're very sorry, but someone else was selected for this opportunity. I was heartbroken. We basically had to stay in place until they found another assignment for us. So, our friends jokingly said, "We're not going to give another party for you. We've given all these parties for you. We're not having another one." We just cooled our heels and waited until something else came along.

# GETTING TO KNOW THE QATARIS

Then I got a cable asking if I would be interested in setting up the new American embassy in Doha, Qatar. I said yes I would be. They said, "We will be sending the first American ambassador there, and we need someone to set up the embassy." I said, "Sure I'd be glad to." Mind you, I had no clue where Qatar was, but it was just the opportunity that was so exciting. I discussed it with my wife and we agreed that we would do it. That's what we did in 1974.

Following the oil embargo of 1973, the U.S. government had decided that it needed fuller representation in the new countries of the Persian Gulf, these countries that had been part of a trucial state. We decided that we would move from basically a one-person operation, as I used to call it, the person who basically flew the flag and drank gin all day long, to a full-fledged embassy.

*Q: In the late 1950s I used to go from Dhahran to Qatar and to the trucial states in Bahrain to do my consular work there and pick up tidbits, and that was pretty much it. That covered Saudi Arabia.*

YOUNG: The flow of funds that came from oil and the importance these states assumed following the oil embargo just changed the world completely. I agreed to this assignment and in the summer of 1974, I left my wife and two children in the States. My wife was left with our son, who was four years old, and our daughter, who was two, and I took off for Doha. I couldn't take them with me, because there wasn't any housing and it was my job to find such things. I was to be the administrative officer. I ended up being the administrative officer/DCM, before that kind of nomenclature became as common as it is today, but I was really in the vanguard of persons who perform that dual function. I arrived there in the summer. We did have a building that we had leased for an office. It was my job to furnish it and to fit it out so that it could function as an embassy. I got busy with the one national employee we had working for us and with the person who was assigned as the ambassador's secretary. We were like the three musketeers in going through that town and visiting all of the shops and buying desks and typewriters and chairs and refrigerators and things like that. Then finding residences where we could put the people who were coming in. We were all staying in hotels. Of course the national employee was on the local economy. He was an Indian fellow who still works for the embassy to this day; he has worked for the mission for over 40 years now.

We began to buy and buy in order to get things set up. We found houses that were suitable and we began to lease and furnish them. The Department had arranged for sets of furniture to be shipped via Beirut to the mission, but we had to get all of the other things to go with it. The basic living room and dining room sets were provided by the Department, but we had to buy the refrigerators, the stoves, the washing machines, the dryers, and all of those kinds of things to give people some semblance of normal life. We did that and we had no communications whatsoever. All we had was a small telex machine. The Department really didn't want to go the full route in providing all of the equipment we needed to function as a mission. There we were trying to set up a full-fledged mission, but yet we had no communications.

*Q: Could you describe what Doha was like at that time? I'm surprised you were able to find houses.*

YOUNG: Well, it didn't have very much. I often describe it as just emerging out of the sand at that point. There weren't many things. There were some shops. Some nice houses were being built. There was the realization that good times were on the horizon. Entrepreneurs and merchants and real estate developers were all flooding the country to find opportunity and to make way for what was surely to be an influx of expatriates who were going to come in and help this country to develop and prosper.

*Q: Who was building? I can't imagine that you'd find at that point much building expertise among the Qataris.*

YOUNG: There was one Qatari engineer in the country, I mean a truly trained engineer. There were small contractors and what have you.

There weren't many trained engineers and contractors in the city at that time, but there were a few. Some people had come in from the outside to do construction, particularly a lot of Lebanese builders. They had arranged partnerships, with basically the Qataris providing the name and perhaps some of the capital and the Lebanese or Palestinian builder taking it from there. They built houses, they built office buildings. Then, also some American architects were invited in because the city had begun to work on a master plan for development. One of the big projects envisioned was development of a seafront area that had nothing but the sea then. The idea was to fill this in with dredging and to build on it. A big American architect named William Pereira, the architect of the famous the pyramid shaped building in San Francisco, came. We worked with him and with the Government of Qatar and he designed a famous hotel there, the Sheraton Hotel, which is built like a pyramid. That was realized years later, but the initial planning for that occurred during our time there. We located houses. As we furnished them people began to come in. A political officer came and an economic officer and a consular officer. The ambassador arrived.

*Q: Who was the ambassador?*

YOUNG: The ambassador was a fellow by the name of Robert Paganelli.

*Q: I know Bob; he was my DCM in Rome.*

YOUNG: He arrived and we got him settled in a very nice house. It was owned by one of the few trained engineers in the country, a Qatari fellow who had been trained in the United States. He had married an American woman and had returned to Qatar. That in itself was something exceptional at that time, to have a Qatari married to an American woman. The Government of Qatar had made very generous arrangements for people to be educated abroad. However, they did not particularly like the idea of their young men returning with foreign brides. That caused that fellow some problems later on in limiting his access to government contracts and in his appointment to positions for which he was well qualified. Anyhow, things began to move there.

We had this big problem, as I mentioned, with not being able to communicate with Washington and the rest of the world. We solved that problem initially by preparing reporting telegrams and operational messages on the regular telegram forms, those regular old green forms from years ago. We would do airgrams as well and we bundled them up and waited for someone going to Kuwait or to Lebanon or Syria, and then we'd send these along with them, and the mission on the other end would transmit them to Washington. Well, as you can imagine, this did not make for any kind of good current reporting because it wasn't timely by the time it got to Washington or by the time it got to whatever post it was going to. This was a great irritant and a great frustration. We would do messages, for example, and sometimes run down to the local hotel. If the message was unclassified then we would ask the hotel if they could send it by a telex to Washington or to Beirut or some place like that. That went on for a while. We kept badgering the Department to put in a communications system and sending us someone to operate it, but we didn't get anywhere.

Finally, there was the attack on the embassy in Lebanon and that attack had a major, major impact on the evolution of our mission in Qatar, not only in Qatar, but in the Gulf. The four embassies that were established at that time were Bahrain, Oman, the Emirates, and Qatar. It was a wakeup call for the Department when the embassy was bombed in Beirut in 1974. Ambassador Paganelli sent a really infuriated message to the Department. He said basically that if terrorists were after us, and we could not assume that we were not immune from this, we would be very easy targets and wouldn't even have the means to communicate with the Department to tell them that any of our people had been injured or killed. He also put a few expletives in the message that got attention. As a result, another office in the mission decided that it would provide everything we needed for a full-fledged communications operation and that office acted with alacrity and in no time at all a C-141 arrived and brought everything we needed, including the man who was assigned to the post to operate the equipment.

That is what saved us, and once they got there and they could provide our communications, then the State Department said, "We have to have some control over this as well." The ambassador said, "I don't give a damn. I want my messages in and out of here and I don't care who sees them. If you can do better, send somebody out here to take care of the State side of it."

State did then send someone out and sent the equipment to have basically a full-fledged operation that satisfied us.

*Q: Did you have any contact with my old post, Dhahran?*

YOUNG: Dhahran helped a little bit. When we needed to get these messages to the quickest post we could in order to get them further transmitted onward, we just took whatever options were open to us.

*Q: Did you drive there?*

YOUNG: Oh, no, there was no causeway at that point. Heavens no.

*Q: This would be going from Doha up to Dhahran without need for a causeway.*

YOUNG: That would have been a hell of a drive.

*Q: I remember we had somebody come from Doha in about the late '50s, but it was a sheik. He came with two burly guys who sat in the back of a Cadillac.*

YOUNG: No, we never drove. I mean, that came later on. My wife was on one of the first trips from Doha to Dhahran and I'll never forget, she went and then came back and told me what a spectacular experience it was.

We got equipment. We were then a full-fledged embassy. We could operate independently. We had everything we needed. We even had the emergency generator and everything else to be able to sustain operations in the event of an emergency. So business was going along very nicely. The Qataris were coming to us in droves to find out how they could build a factory here, build a plant there, and how they could get this American product in and get that American product in. And it was exciting trying to make connections between the Qataris and American merchants to make these deals.

Many of these deals worked. However, I must say we were very disappointed to find that with many of these proposals from the Qataris that were, let's say, in the neighborhood of twenty, thirty, or forty million dollars or something like that, many of the American companies that could do the kind of work that was needed told us at that time, "Thank you very much, but we're not interested." They said, "We have basically two areas of interest in this region. Those two areas are Iran and Saudi Arabia." They would let these projects go and as they did so, in came the French, the Japanese, the Koreans, the Germans, and everyone else, because we all opened up our missions in these places at the same time in the 1974-75 time frame. We watched these allies basically fill that vacuum that was left. I'm talking about American giants in communications and aviation and on and on that would pass up these opportunities. Other countries would come in and say, "Yes, we'll take two million here, five million, ten million dollars," and after some years they had a pretty solid footing in those countries.

*Q: Part of my job was commercial officer back in '58, '59, or so. It was the same damn thing, you know. It was absolutely ignored, although there was money to be made. It would take a little time and at that point it was selling Parker pens, other things of that nature, not the big things, but there was lack of initiative on the Americans' part.*

YOUNG: Yes, I agree wholeheartedly. Well, we kept trying and trying.

I would like to mention several things that were highlights of my time.

I was there from 1974 to 1977. We were there for three years and they were three wonderful years. A period that was very significant for me in my career. One thing that happened very shortly after I had sort of gotten settled was that we had hired a Foreign Service National employee, a Palestinian-American, but we engaged him locally as the commercial assistant. He was terrific. He was just wonderful. He had lots of personality and was a good talker, a real schmoozer. His father was the top advisor to the emir of Bahrain. His sister ran the Qatari TV service. They were a Palestinian family very firmly ensconced in Qatar. They had a lot of influence and we enjoyed their company very much. They were very bright and very well educated and good folks.

Well, this FSN was doing very nice work for the mission and he had some difficulty with one of our American residents a Lebanese-American. I don't remember the fellow's name now. He represented an American company there and he was a real difficult personality. Sometimes when you get two persons of the same ethnic group, there are difficulties instead of understanding. This was a case where there were difficulties and the two personalities just didn't mesh. He thought that this fellow was too demanding and that he was rude and arrogant and what have you, and he was. The fact is he was one of our citizens and we had an obligation to treat him with full respect and to provide him with full services offered by the mission. Anyhow, one day he came into the office and he spoke to the FSN and he and the FSN got into a confrontation. The FSN hauled off and socked him right in the nose. I mean cold-cocked him right there. The fellow was absolutely furious. "I'm going to write to my congressman. I'll have your head" and on and on. He was just furious. The key to this is that the ambassador had gone away and the ambassador had made me the chargé. We calmed the fellow down and then he left and then I called the FSN in and I said, "I'm sorry, but you're fired. I cannot have anyone who represents this mission slugging an American citizen. I cannot have that."

*Q: As much as it is often deserved.*

YOUNG: Believe me I think it was deserved in this particular case, but we couldn't have it. So, he said, "Well, you know, the guy asked for it" and on. I said, "He might have asked for it, but there is no justification for it and there's no way that I could accept this and there's no way that anyone would accept this." I told him, "Get your things and I'm sorry, but this is it." He left the embassy. I was scared because his father had such great influence and I knew the ambassador loved the FSN and loved the FSN's father as well, so I waited and waited and later on that evening a call came from the palace that the emir wanted to see me. I went out and I saw the emir and he asked me if I would reconsider and rehire the FSN. I told him that as much as I would like to and as much as we appreciated the great work that he had done for us, I could not in good conscience do that. It would not be acceptable; it's not acceptable to me personally. It wouldn't be acceptable to my colleagues and it wouldn't be acceptable to the folks back in Washington as well. He talked and he talked and I said, "I'm very sorry. I cannot rescind what I have decided." He thanked me and then I left. The next day I called the ambassador in the States and I told him what I had done and I thought he would be furious with me for having fired the son of his really good contact at the palace, but he said, if that was your decision, that was your decision and I'll stand by you and he did. That was my first big major problem as chargé.

Before the ambassador went away on this first trip, he had observed the different officers in the embassy and we were not a large embassy at all. We were very small. We had a political officer, an economic officer, a consular officer and a secretary, two communicators, and that was it, and I. He came to me one day, he said, "Johnny, I'm going away for" I don't know what the period was, a month or something like that and he said, "I want you to be chargé." I said, "Well, Mr. Ambassador, thank you very much, but there's no way that the Department will agree to an admin officer being chargé. That doesn't happen." He said, "I know, but I think you can do it." I said, "Well, you have a political officer, you have an econ officer, you have consular. They're going to say you should appoint one of them as chargé and not me." He says, "This is my embassy, goddamn it, and I'll do what I want to." If you worked for Bob Paganelli, you know the language.

Q: *There was a time around '74 or so when they decided to reach down into lower ranks.*

YOUNG: Yes, he was one of them.

Q: *He was an FSO-4 I think.*

YOUNG: It happened to all four of them. It happened to the one who went to Oman, to Bahrain, to Qatar and the Emirates. All of them were FSO-1s. Kissinger decided he would . . .

Q: *Reach down, and these were people for whom normally there would have been a ten-year wait.*

YOUNG: In fact when they were appointed, they were FSO-2s. Later on they were on the promotion list.

Q: *Yes, I think in the old days FSO-4s.*

YOUNG: Right. So, anyhow, Paganelli was insistent that I be chargé. I said, "Well, Mr. Ambassador I am not going to get into that battle with our staff and the Department. If you feel that strongly about it and you want to take that on, I'll leave that with you." He said, "No, I think you can do it and I like the way you do things. I like your judgment." and that's what he did. Now, the political officer was Ryan Crocker who hasn't done badly either. He was just brilliant, even in that early assignment. It was his second assignment in the Foreign Service and I was his boss at that time. That was Paganelli's decision and that's how I became chargé. As I said, for an admin officer that was extraordinary in that time. You know it might happen today, but that was really something in 1974. He allowed me to be chargé during the entire three-year period that we were there, every time he went away. This provided an opportunity for me to demonstrate that there was perhaps something a little bit more than the usual that would be expected of an admin officer. It brought me to the attention of some other people in the Department. That's what happened.

Now, in terms of the work, the work was fabulous. I did everything. Everything, economic work, and consular work. It was the easiest consular work I've ever done in the Foreign Service because the Government of Qatar provided full scholarships for anyone who wanted to study in the United States. The majority of their students who were going on to university either studied in the United States or they went to American University in Beirut (AUB), but not that many of them went to AUB. The majority of them went to the United States. A few went to a couple of other places, but it was mainly the United States and they had settled on two colleges in the Michigan area. One was a college called Hope College and the other one I think was called Holland something, but they had settled on these two schools. These students were not the greatest prospects, but they were bankrolled to the hilt. They were all from the ruling family, so they all got A1, A2 visas. They went to the States. We never had any problems with them. That's why I say it was the easiest consular work I have ever done and that was just really exciting.

I remember another exciting thing was trying to get the Qataris to buy an American airplane. At that time, it was a Lockheed 1011 and we succeeded in convincing them to buy some of those planes. Later on we realized that the Egyptian FSN who was helping us with that deal had had his hands deep in the kitty, and that surfaced later on. That surfaced many years later, but it was as a result of what was going on in the Gulf at the time that legislation was passed, which made it illegal to get kickbacks and that sort of thing. At least something good came out of that. The deals just kept flowing and small ones and more small ones and it was just an exciting time. I loved it. One of the best assignments I think I've had.

*Q: How did you and the rest of the embassy view the rule of the emir and the family? How did that work?*

YOUNG: At that time, during the time I was there from 1974 to '77, our goal was to keep these guys on our side and to keep the oil flowing. That was the bottom line. We didn't make any pitches about democracy. We didn't make pitches about human rights. I mean there weren't any overt human rights abuses because these guys really ruled with a fairly tight hand and we didn't concern ourselves with those kinds of issues. That wasn't the name of the game at that point. You have to keep in mind that we came as a result of a crisis in oil and we remained there to make sure that they stayed on our side and we didn't have a problem with Iran at that time, so that was not an issue. There was great concern in the Gulf at that time about Iraq. The fear was that Saddam, or Iraq anyhow, would move on the Gulf states and so the Gulf states had moved closer to Iran as a balancing power, and that was the way they saw things at that time.

*Q: Wasn't Qatar involved in a dispute over some islands?*

YOUNG: They were in a dispute with Bahrain over the Hawar Islands. That dispute had been going on at that point for thirty some years and it continued. It was resolved, as a matter of fact, when I was in Bahrain, but that was a dispute that had been going on for sixty some years.

*Q: How were relations with the United Emirates at that time?*

YOUNG: They were excellent. Qatar had good relations with all of its former Gulf colleagues, or Gulf states, excellent relations.

*Q: How about with Saudi Arabia?*

YOUNG: The Saudis are a force in the region, you cannot deny that, but Qatar was unlike Bahrain or unlike Oman. It had enough oil of its own. They had just begun to realize that they had this enormous reserve of gas. Gas had not taken on the importance that it has had since that time and they were looking for ways to develop that gas as well. They had good relations with the Saudis and no problems there. They had some border disputes, mind you, but they weren't that bad.

*Q: At that time you weren't looking towards Qatar and the trucial states as being military bases or something like that?*

YOUNG: Not at all, not at that time. No interest whatsoever at that time. Our base was in Bahrain.

*Q: COMIDEASTFOR (Commander, Mid-East forces).*

YOUNG: COMIDEASTFOR. That was the presence in the Gulf at that time and there was no talk of having anything anywhere else, certainly not in Qatar. I don't know what talks were going on elsewhere, but I don't recall anything else. We were content with how things were. We did attempt to influence them in terms of the Palestinian situation. We didn't have the issue of terrorism that came on the horizon later on. Those kinds of problems had not surfaced. Qatar was basically such a new state that it hadn't really gotten its footing yet in terms of its membership in a number of international organizations. So our multilateral relationship with them was rather limited as well. They were deeply involved in OPEC (Organization of the Petroleum Exporting Countries). I remember they had one of the OPEC meetings in Qatar while we were there and that was a big deal. A lot of attention on OPEC at that time and OPEC had more influence than it has today. Its influence has diminished quite a bit, but at that time it was quite a force to be reckoned with.

*Q: Were we acting as a mentor to the Qatar government on getting into the UN or establishing a diplomatic corps, or something like that?*

YOUNG: No, that was basically a British undertaking at that point. They were part of the British arrangement in the region. It was Britain that took on that role. We didn't do that at all.

*Q: Were they concerned about too many Iranians in the area?*

YOUNG: Not at all.

*Q: In Bahrain it was a great problem.*

YOUNG: It was a problem in Bahrain, but only after 1979. Prior to 1979, there wasn't the problem.

*Q: When I was there in the '50s there was concern that there were a lot of illegal Iranians working there.*

YOUNG: That's true.

*Q: That's when the shah was making noises about "it's not the Arabian Gulf, it's the Persian Gulf."*

YOUNG: But that wasn't the same as what occurred after '79, when the Ayatollah said, "Well, that's my island also." They made some attempts to extend their rule. Then the Bahrainis really turned on the Iranians in the country, including some of its own citizens who were in this category of stateless persons of Iranian ancestry but had never opted for Bahraini citizenship. Bahrain issued an ultimatum: either you accept Bahraini citizenship or you can accept Iranian citizenship and go to Iran. Many of them didn't opt for either and they stayed and became stateless persons. As far as Qatar is concerned, during '74 to '77 when I was there, we were excellent friends with the Iranians. The Qataris also had superb relations with them. As I mentioned earlier, they looked to Iran as a balancing power against the threat of an Iraq that might march down the Gulf. Things were good at that time.

*Q: Had they started at that point to have a lot of South Koreans, Pakistanis, and all coming in and doing the hard labor?*

YOUNG: Oh, at that point the Indians had already come. The Pakistanis had already come. The Bangladeshis had come. We were there when the first six Filipinos arrived in Qatar. I remember it so well because one of our officers in the embassy who is presently DCM in Tokyo, Joe Donovan, dated one of them for a while. It was the first six. When I left Bahrain in 2001, there were 35,000 Filipinos in Qatar.

*Q: We're talking about a little piece of land.*

YOUNG: That's it. I mean it's just incredible. So, the Koreans had not come yet, but they're there now. I mean they're all there. Filipinos, you name it; they're there and in thousands.

*Q: Well then is there anything else we should talk about while you were there?*

YOUNG: The emir was a fellow who was very quiet, somewhat aloof. We felt that he was basically directed by Mr. Fanoose and another Egyptian fellow who was one of his key advisors. There weren't many educated people in the country at all in terms of Qataris. There was one fellow who was a fantastic contact. He was the minister of information and a graduate of American University in Beirut. To this day, he remains an advisor to the former emir, who was deposed by his son in a coup. You could count the number of Qatari university graduates literally on one hand. They were so few. So, they used their money to buy expertise, to buy knowledge, and basically to buy the development that has made that country such a success.

Q: *What was the ruling family's name?*

YOUNG: The Al-Thani. The emir was Al-Khalifa, but the family name was Al-Thani.

Q: *What's the family name in Bahrain?*

YOUNG: Al-Khalifa.

Q: *I was going to say, was it the same?*

YOUNG: No, different families. The emir of Qatar when we were there was Sheik Khalifa bin Hamad al-Thani. In Bahrain you had Emir Isa ibn Salman al-Khalifa. In Bahrain, the majority of the population is Shi'a. It is the only place in the Gulf, other than Iran, with a Shi'a majority. The rest are all Sunni majorities.

Q: *Did religion cause any problems there?*

YOUNG: Not in Qatar.

Q: *You didn't have sort of the Wahabi type?*

YOUNG: No, none of that. Extremism and what have you in religion was not an issue there. In Qatar you couldn't openly drink alcohol. For example, when we were in the hotel, we couldn't get a drink with a meal, but we could go up to room 502 in the local hotel, knock on the door and say, hey, Bernie sent me or something and go inside and have a drink and then go down and have a meal. There were provisions for diplomats to buy drinks to have in their homes and what have you, so that was it. Women couldn't drive. It was a very restrictive society. It wasn't as strict as let's say Saudi Arabia, but it was still a restrictive society, not a lot of mixing, very little mixing and that sort of thing.

*Q: Women played no role?*

YOUNG: None.

*Q: Until later.*

YOUNG: That came later on. I can't think of a single woman who was in any responsible position in government. There were one or two out at the university. The woman that I mentioned who ran the television service was a Palestinian who was basically a foreign national, a resident alien, and there were a few other Palestinian women who were doctors. There were lots of Egyptian women teachers, but there weren't Qatari women in those positions.

*Q: Then you left there in '77. Whither?*

YOUNG: I want to tell about a little incident. In November of 1974 I found a house, got it furnished, and told my wife the time had arrived. We will meet in Beirut and then we will all travel back to Qatar together. We were very busy the day before my departure preparing the telegrams and messages that we wanted to get out to the rest of the world so I could take them as a non-pro courier and dump them in the embassy in Beirut and they would be sent out. We worked night and day a couple of days ahead of my visit to get these ready. The day before my departure, the ambassador was ill. We went over to his home, the secretary and I, and he was in his bathrobe and I was smoking at the time. I went in and I sat down, I was smoking my cigarette. He knew that I smoked. He said to me in the rudest way possible, "Put that cigarette out. It stinks and it's making me sick." I said, "Excuse me, I didn't know that was the case." I put it out and I can tell you it was like a sheet of ice that descended on me. I was so stunned. I had worked so hard all hours of the night and day in all of that hellish heat of the Gulf to make this guy look good as the ambassador, to set up that functioning mission for him. I was just deeply, deeply wounded to be treated like that in his residence.

He looked at all of the telegrams, made corrections. That meant we had to go back to the embassy, make the corrections and then return for a final review. We got outside and we went to the embassy and we made all the corrections and I told the ambassador's secretary, Libby Cooper, "Libby, I cannot believe what he just did to me. I can't tell you how hurt I am by this." She said, "Oh, don't worry about it, it's going to be okay." I said, "I can't forget it. My family is going to meet me in Lebanon tomorrow and I'm going to come back here and I'm going to have to work with this?" She did all of the corrections because she was doing all of the typing and we bundled up the whole package and went back to the residence. When we got to the residence I said to her, "You take them inside, I'm not going to set foot in that house again as long as I'm here." She says, "Oh, no, you're kidding." I said, "No, I'm not going in." She went inside and she must have told the ambassador that I wasn't coming in. I had said, "You can tell him that if I leave tomorrow I may never come back. I'm going to get my family and I may turn around and just go back to the United States. I just feel so badly about what has happened." She went inside and then later on he came outside in his bathrobe. He said, "Come inside." I said, "No, I'm not coming inside." He said, "Come on inside." I said, "No, I'm not." We went back and forth and back and forth. Finally I went inside and I sat there and I sulked the entire time and had absolutely nothing to say to him, nothing to say to his wife and he apologized. He said, I'm sorry and what have you. I heard his wife tell him, "Robert that was the rudest thing I've ever seen you do."

*Q: Donna.*

YOUNG: Donna, yes. Anyhow, I left and I said goodbye and that was it. When I left the next morning, I went on to Lebanon and I arrived at the hotel and went into the room and there awaiting me in the room was a big bouquet of flowers and a big bottle of champagne from Bob with a note that he was sorry and wishing me the best with my family. I returned and we got along fine. I thought it was amazing that despite our ups and downs, he believed in me and I'll always give him credit for that. He gave me full credit for the work that I did for him, because he could be a very difficult customer. We had a swimming pool, for example, at the residence that we couldn't get to work properly. We tried everything under the sun and he wanted that pool to work properly, and we did too, because it was going to be a community pool. He would call me on weekends and he'd say, "Didn't I tell you to do so and so?" I would say, "Yes." "Get over here right away." I'd go over to the residence or I'd go to the embassy, whatever. I remember one time he did this and it was sort of like Martin Luther with the so many theses nailed to the door. I got to the embassy, there was Paganelli's note nailed to the door: "I told you to do so and so." He would come through the embassy sometimes cussing like a mad man. Then he would calm down and he'd come back and say, "I'm sorry. I really didn't mean that," and on and on. I remember once he told me, "You know, you have a very restraining influence on my language," because he could really let loose with a few zingers.

*Q: Were there constraints on your wife?*

YOUNG: There were no constraints on what a foreign woman could do. Foreign women could drive, they could move around, no problem. And she drove all over the place in our 1972 Peugeot without air conditioning and she had no problems at all. She'd become very active in a number of groups there. Although she couldn't do the kind of volunteer and charity work that is customary in many foreign situations. Nevertheless, she had a good group of friends. She learned how to play bridge and how to do different kinds of arts and crafts. She taught women English at the university. We had a very good and full life, and then raising two small children was also a great challenge, along with managing a house.

We had an inspection headed by Maurice Dean and Ken Rogers. This story shows how astute inspectors can be. They've done this kind of work for a long time and they can see things that perhaps the rest of us can't or think we can cover up. I met them at the airport and brought them to the embassy. I had everything looking just perfect. They're looking around and they say, "Oh, very nice." Then the night of their arrival, we had I think it was a camel roast for them. One of our junior officers, a fellow by the name of Tom Wukitsch decided he would roast a camel for them. We said, "Oh, Tom, please don't roast a camel. You know, roast a cow or something." Tom said, "No, I'm going to do this camel," and he did the camel and it all worked out very well. That night they said to us, "Now, things are too perfect at this post. Tell us what the problems are." We said,

"Well, there are no problems, everything is wonderful." They said, "No, something is wrong here." Nothing was revealed that night. Then the night of the dinner at our home when we had all had I think a cognac or two too much, tongues loosened and they asked the wives as a matter of fact, what's wrong here? Then the wives said, "Well, you know, the ambassador picks on our husbands too much," and all that. Those kinds of things came out. That was to say that the inspectors smelled a rat despite all of our cosmetic arrangements to make things perfect. Not that there were grave issues that needed correction by the ambassador, but they needed that information in order to sit down with him to say, look, you're running a great mission here, lighten up a little bit. That was basically the bottom line.

My career counselor at that time was Mary Ryan. I remember we were going back and forth and she said to me, "I assure you before I leave this job, I'm going to get you a good onward assignment. You deserve it after being in that place for three years," because at that time Qatar had a reputation of being not a very nice place. There was nothing there. It was hot as hell and it was just considered a real hardship. It was and we were getting 25 percent hardship differential and we deserved it. She worked on various possibilities for me and she finally nailed down Bridgetown, Barbados as my reward, a three-year assignment there.

# LIFE IS A BEACH: BARBADOS

So we went to Bridgetown. The ambassador at that time was Frank Ortiz and the deputy chief of mission was John Eddy. We arrived in the summer.

We moved immediately into a hotel, the Southern Palms Hotel, located right on the beach, I mean a holiday setting if ever there was one. Our children were seven and five. They thought they had died and gone to heaven. When it was time for us to move into a regular house, they said, "What for? This is just heaven. What are we going to move into a regular house for?" They swam every day; they were on the beach every day. They just loved it and we also loved it, but it was no fun living in a hotel for over three months. We rented a house. It was the first posting we had been to where the government had not provided furniture, so we had to buy our own furniture. At that time we were able to buy furniture under the government contract. My wife and I scraped the money together and we bought a three bedroom set of Drexel furniture under the government contract and had it shipped to Barbados. We furnished our house with it and we had a very lovely home, up on the top of a hill overlooking the ocean. It was wonderful.

*Q: You were in Barbados from '77 to when?*

YOUNG: '77 to '79.

*Q: It's interesting that Frank Ortiz, a career Foreign Service officer, was ambassador there because that's the sort of place they usually toss to some political appointee.*

YOUNG: They had. In fact Frank was sent to clean up the mess.

*Q: Political ambassadors and then you send a professional to clean it up.*

YOUNG: We had an ambassador there who was a disgrace. He was a mess, an absolute mess. His reputation was that he was in every hole and alley and corner of Barbados and that can be a good thing depending on how it's done, but this was not in the most flattering way shall we say. He had gotten into fights with people in the embassy. Shortly before we arrived there he had locked the political officer out of the embassy. He had gotten rid of a couple of officers. He had made some changes to the residence that made parts of it look like it was rented out by the hour and things like that. He had painted every wall in the embassy sort of like sea blue. It was just unbelievable.

*Q: What was his background?*

YOUNG: Well, he had been an educator and a person involved in development work and what have you. He was a black Republican and that was his reward, Barbados. So, Frank was sent to clean up the mess because the mission was demoralized, unhappy, and the ambassador had earned a very bad reputation in the country. The Department wanted a major improvement in that situation so they sent Frank and he made a difference. He was a wonderful ambassador. He did a great job, established excellent rapport with the Bajans as they're called.

*Q: What are they called?*

YOUNG: Bajans, Barbadians are called Bajans. Excellent relationship. At that time Barbados was, and I think still is, a symbol of great stability in the Caribbean region. It is the oldest democracy, really a true practicing democracy in the region. It was a symbol that we wanted to use in expanding this kind of stability and success to other countries in the region as well, particularly in Trinidad. Jamaica was going to hell in a hand basket at that time and needed every example it could possibly get. I found it a very nice place, wonderful people, but given the breadth of work that I had carried out in Qatar, I found it dull. The work was not interesting.

*Q: You were the administrative officer.*

YOUNG: I was just the administrative officer there and I didn't find it very satisfying. After a short time I decided that three years of that would just not be my cup of tea, and I asked that my assignment be curtailed to two years, which it was. After the curtailment things began to become a little bit more exciting in the region. I was asked to travel to a number of the islands that were talking about independence to look over the situation to prepare for American delegations that would attend the independence celebrations of these different countries. I traveled to Saint Lucia, Dominica, and Antigua to find out what they had in the way of hotels and restaurants and this and that and talked to the leaders of the countries to get a sense of where things were going, and that was exciting. Things were beginning to happen. It made the assignment more interesting. Then we had a couple of other things that happened there that were fascinating.

There was a coup on the island of Grenada. There was a U.S. medical school there. Our concerns, of course, were for all American citizens on that island in the face of a coup, but we were particularly concerned about the students who were attending the medical school there. The ambassador wanted to know how we could get some information on what was going on. I had met a young man and his wife earlier when they were visiting Barbados. The woman had been a secretary in the embassy in Barbados and the fellow she subsequently married had entered the Foreign Service. They were passing through when I met them on the way to his first assignment, which was to Caracas. I knew that he was from Grenada. I said to Ambassador Ortiz, "You know we have a fellow in our embassy in Caracas named Roland Bullen. You should contact the ambassador there and see if he would release Roland and allow him to travel to Grenada and then he could get information and send it to us." He did that and it was a great success. Not only was Roland able to get into Grenada and get the information, it turned out his brother was appointed a minister in the New Jewel Movement government.

Q: *Was that New Jewel?*

YOUNG: The New Jewel Movement government. So, that's what happened. That was really a great thing and worked out very well. Roland has subsequently gone on to bigger and better things. He's now our ambassador in Guyana.

One other remarkable event was a volcanic eruption on the island of Saint Vincent. One night my wife and I were coming back from a function and we said, my God, we can't believe it is snowing on the island of Barbados, because it looked just like snow. I mean we saw all this white stuff coming down and thought, my God, this is very unusual. Then the report came out that this volcano had erupted on the island of Saint Vincent. Again, we had concerns about the U.S. citizens there and an evacuation.

The first of the countries to become independent was Dominica. I'll never forget, because I remember Pat Kennedy came out to help with the U.S. delegation. He accompanied the U.S. delegation on that trip. That was interesting because it was the first time I had ever attended an independence celebration. It was quite moving. At midnight when the British flag was lowered and the new flag of Dominica was raised, they played "God Save the Queen." A member of the American delegation gave me a little nudge and said, "Why are they playing My Country This of Thee?" I had to explain to him what that was all about.

We left Barbados in the summer of 1979. Before going, I attended the independence celebration of Saint Lucia and again received the American delegation and supported them throughout that exercise. That was memorable because Princess Margaret was the representative from the British government. These little children had rehearsed all day long for days for the presentation they were going to make when Princess Margaret made her appearance. We waited and waited and waited and those kids were in the sun and they waited and waited and she never showed up. I thought it was just absolutely awful. I thought it was just terrible. She never showed up for that. Then they continued on with the ceremony. That was it. That was indicative of the kind of person that she was. On various events, even when she came to Dominica, you saw the same thing.

*Q: She was very much the indulgent, aloof person. She didn't see any sense of duty.*

YOUNG: Not at all. I saw her actually in Dominica where she was supposed to officiate. In Saint Lucia, it was Princess Alexandra who came out and it was like night and day. I remember we made the comparison and we said, my God, this is a pro in Princess Alexandra.

*Q: While you were in Barbados and other places, I guess in Jamaica it was more pronounced, was there a racial element taking over, was there a sort of a white colonialist group that was being displaced?*

YOUNG: No, not in Barbados. In Barbados there was a long-standing community of white Barbadians. They were not all well off by any means. In fact they were called red legs and some of them were very poor. They were beginning to find their way off the island through immigration to England, to the United States, and to other places. There was a community of them there. They were well-entrenched. Some of them had good businesses. Some of them were also professionals, doctors. They were not the overwhelming element in terms of their influence in the country. They were important, they were there, they had a history there, but no, we didn't run into great racial problems there. The other thing I might add, we didn't run into some of the problems that you find today in Barbados. AIDS (Acquired Immune Deficiency Syndrome) didn't exist.

*Q: The disease.*

YOUNG: The disease, yes, it didn't exist at that time. Or crime. We had minor break-ins now and then, but no kind of assaults, no murders, that sort of thing. It wasn't a high crime wave. It was, however, beginning to be a transshipment point for narcotics. We were running into an increasing number of cases involving shipments from further down in Latin America or through other points in the Caribbean using Barbados as a transshipment point. I remember we had one case involving a very well-known family who had come through and someone had sent a box of dolls to this family. I don't know if it was in Canada or the United States. This package was addressed to the maid at one of their estates somewhere and the police knew what was in it and when the maid went to get it they nabbed her. Then revealed that inside the dolls there was marijuana or whatever the drug was. They were able to establish really that the maid had absolutely nothing to do with it. It was somebody else's. But I mean that kind of thing was beginning to happen. Now it's a major concern to us. As a matter of fact, I think we even have DEA people assigned to the mission in Barbados.

*Q: Also in places that had the cruise ship industry. Was there much of that at the time?*

YOUNG: The cruise ships were coming. You know Barbados has some incredible hotels, I mean unbelievable hotels and golf courses and a wonderful stretch of residences for the very well to do: Frank Sinatra and Claudette Colbert and so on. They'd have their beach homes there. Princess Margaret, Oliver Messel, the famous set designer, had his spectacular house there. So, many very well-known Americans had just gorgeous places there. They were lovely and they still have them and even more have been built. Sandy Lane Hotel, one of the top hotels of the world, is still there. It's gotten bigger and better, way beyond my means.

One thing we liked was that on Sundays we could go to mass and then after mass we'd select a hotel and go to the beach. Each Sunday it was a different hotel and it was a lot of fun. But only so much of that and you get tired of it.

# MANAGING PERSONNEL IN WASHINGTON

*Q: After this time in paradise, whither?*

YOUNG: Well, I had cut back the tour, and I was in Washington for a conference and I went to see my career counselor, Mary Ryan. As I was leaving the office she said to me, "What are you going to do when you leave Barbados?" I replied, "I don't know, I don't have anything in mind." She said, "You know what I would really like? I'd like you to replace me as a career counselor for administrative personnel in the Bureau of Personnel." I said, "Gee, that would be terrific." She said, "We may have a problem though with timing. I'll keep in touch with you and I'll let you know." I got a call from her one day and she said, "Things are looking a lot better. My supervisor, Bill Jones, is going to retire. He's decided that he would retire and he's asked me to replace him, and I'd like you to replace me. We still have some finessing to do to see if it will work because of the timing. I would be moving in right away behind him and we're not sure we can wait that long for you to come in." I said okay, "I'll have to leave it in your goods hands." Sometime later she called and said, "Johnny, it's a done deal. You're going to replace me and I replace Bill." She was the chief of assignments for administrative personnel and I was her deputy. That occurred in the summer of 1979 and that was the beginning of a very difficult year for us from a personal perspective.

*Q: This was '78. You were there for how long?*

YOUNG: I was in Washington for a total of four years, but '79 was when I made the transfer from Barbados to Washington, D.C.

*Q: What was the difficulty?*

YOUNG: What was the difficulty? There were many. We had purchased a house in 1974 before we went to Qatar and we had rented it out. When we returned to Washington the house was in dreadful shape. Not that it was a great house to begin with, but it was a small house in a great neighborhood. We had this three-bedroom, one-and-a-half bath, non-air conditioned, tiny kitchen home in Chevy Chase, Maryland on Leland Street. A great street, a great neighborhood.

It was a house that when we bought it, frankly, I couldn't really afford it, because we bought it in 1974. My salary was $17,500 a year and yet we bought a house for $69,000. That was outrageous, but it was possible because the realtors liked us very much and said you're a nice young couple and we want to help you out. So we got all kinds of balloons and all kinds of things like that. We went back to this house. The tenants had been a group of lawyers at one point and a group of nurses at another point. They didn't do justice to the house. We were in a state of shock when my wife and I walked in and saw it. That was one problem.

The other problem was our kids had never attended school in the United States. We arrived in the summer. We thought that that would be a good opportunity for them to make friends and what have you. Little did we know, everybody in Chevy Chase sends their kids away to camp in the summer. There we were and our children had nobody to play with because there was nobody around. We did meet one family down the street and we became very friendly with them. We didn't have any money. My wife didn't want to work. She said, "I'm not going to work until I get my family settled." I thought that money was more important than getting the family settled. I didn't know anything about the job that I was going into. I didn't know what it meant to be a career counselor. It was all of these factors.

I began to do the job and I didn't know that the job really had such a heavy toll on you. When you think about having to offer advice and counsel to people on their careers and what this means to them and to their families, it's an enormous responsibility. Maybe I took it too seriously, but it began to weigh on me. I began to worry about all kinds of things. As I said, we had this house we wanted to fix up and make it look nice and we didn't have any money. My wife didn't want to work and the kids were finally getting settled in a new school. I said to myself, "My God, what if I drop dead, what would happen to them?" I called the insurance company and said I needed to take out some additional insurance. They said okay, fine, we'll be glad to sell you some insurance. So, they sent a representative out and we filled out the application and then he said to me, "Oh your blood pressure is a little bit high. I'll wait a few minutes and I'll take it again." During the course of that evening he took it about five or six times and each time it was high. He thought that after a few minutes I'd calm down and it would go down, but it never did. He said, "I'll come back next week and take it again." He came the next week and took it and the same thing again, high. He said, "Well, I'll come back next week." He came back again and it was high. That's when I found out that I had high blood pressure. Mind you, I had had my physical exam before I left Barbados and I was in perfectly good health, no problem at all, which proved to me that stress can indeed bring on these problems and once they're there, once they're manifest in you, you have to deal with them. Then I began taking medication to control the high blood pressure.

After a year, my wife did begin to work and we were settled in our house. We had painted, we had fixed it up and it was a cute little house. I remember my wife used to say, "My God, I'm going to have to lose weight to get into this kitchen," because the kitchen was so tiny. We never got air conditioning. We were happy, very happy. The kids were doing well in school and I completed two years as a career development and assignments officer. I had gotten promoted out of Barbados and so things were really looking up very nicely.

In 1981, I was looking for a good assignment and I bid for different ones and had a couple of interviews. One was with the Office of the Inspector General for the job of executive director. At that time, the inspector general was a fellow named Brewer. They liked me and I got the job. I became the executive director of the Office of the Inspector General for two years from 1981 to 1983.

*Q: I'd like to go back to when you were here as a management officer. How did this system work? I mean, in the first place, you had essentially a stable of administrative officers?*

YOUNG: Oh, my stable consisted of not just administrative officers, but general service officers. We had a separate office for security officers and communicators and secretaries. My office was primarily building and maintenance people, general services officers, admin officers, those types. I forgot how many hundreds I had, and Mary Ryan had the other hundreds. She took them from FS, she had FS-1s and 2s and I had the 3s and 4s.

*Q: Could you work on projecting and working with your group to have both good development and moving up? I mean, was there a promotion and professional ladder to work with?*

YOUNG: Oh, there was. Our job was to say to them, "If you want to achieve this level in the Service, or what have you, these are some of the things you need to do and you need to do them well." They had to make those decisions for themselves if they wanted to go that route or not. We provided them with advice and counsel on how to get the assignments that would help them to advance in the system and help them to develop their careers.

*Q: When you came, were they really trying to develop professional administrative officers in a special program, or was it sort of a catch as catch can system as far as recruiting people was concerned? In other words, what did you think of the professional qualities in people?*

YOUNG: Well, the people coming in as administrative officers were very talented and well trained. They all had excellent credentials. The goal was to bring them in to do this kind of work and to bring them in trained. They came in either directly from university or from jobs in the private sector.

*Q: Was there a problem of social distinction or professional distinction between administrative and consular on the one hand and political and economic on the other, almost a class distinction?*

YOUNG: Oh, yes, it was a big thing for us. We could sometimes get an officer assigned as a DCM or as a political officer or as an economic officer. It didn't happen that often, but it was beginning to happen. That's why when I was serving in Qatar it was such an extraordinary thing for me to be able to serve as de facto DCM and then serve as chargé. So that was still there. There was no question that if you were a political officer or an economic officer there was a definite pecking order, and our job was to try and make opportunities for people to break through that and we did.

*Q: Did you find that on the administrative side there would be a tendency if somebody got into ARA or American Republics, or Asia, or Europe especially, if they knew people they would keep them there? Did you find that you had problems of getting somebody slogging away in Africa and giving them a chance to try something in Europe or elsewhere?*

YOUNG: It was difficult and I think it is still difficult, frankly, but we tried to encourage people to make that effort to break out so that they became known in more than one bureau. Sometimes it meant taking jobs that were not the most desirable, but it allowed you to establish a reputation in that bureau and you could then use that to move on. I was able to get into three different bureaus.

*Q: Did you have problems with the European Bureau?*

YOUNG: Oh, yes, definitely. It remains the most exclusive of the clubs in the Foreign Service other than, I would say, the Arabic club, which has at its core this language and culture that bind its members together. That's a tough one to get into because you need certain kinds of requirements to be a member.

In the case of Europe, it was the old boys' network and not just by specialty, but by gender as well, and certainly by race and ethnic group, no question about it. It's still the case.

*Q: On the administrative side, particularly in the time you're dealing with, would women either be on the personnel side or budget and fiscal?*

YOUNG: You had some of that, but at the same time you had women generalists as well, though not that many. Mary Ryan was a case in point. She was a generalist, but there weren't too many like her.

*Q: Do you want to add more about your family?*

YOUNG: Yes, I feel I've neglected my family in what I've said so far. They have been key to my survival and well-being and to my success—particularly my wife. She has forsaken her own interests and career aspirations in order to follow me around the world to these different posts. She set up house for us and served the U.S. government free of charge, representing and supporting our government in so many ways in her charitable work, humanitarian work, and her outreach to the community. She has been just absolutely extraordinary. I give great credit to my children as well for the moves back and forth to different countries, the breakup of their friendships and what have you, all to be with their mother and father who are off on this adventure. They quietly supported us and we're really very grateful for that. They too contributed to my successes, just no doubt about it.

Our kids have not shown any interest in following in my footsteps in joining the Foreign Service, but they love to travel. That is in their blood and I think it will always be there. They're particularly culturally sensitive people. If you throw them in a room of strangers, they'll seek out the foreigners in a minute and strike up rapport with them. I've seen it happen over and over again. They gained something special there and they acknowledge it. They have no regrets whatsoever for the experience that they had in accompanying us on these different assignments. They felt it was really an education in itself.

Q: *The spouse, usually the wife, is so important as you move from post to post, setting up a house, entertaining in a business-like sense, making contacts that can't be done by fax or telephone. I mean it's getting to know the people, making a home for the children and making acquaintances. So often it's the wife who can say, you know I heard that such-and-such is happening.*

YOUNG: Yes, oh yes, absolutely.

Q: *Sometimes it is something that the political, economic, and other officers haven't heard because the wives are usually more clued in than the men who were stuck in the office.*

YOUNG: Exactly, oh yes. That's why I say they contribute to your success in so many ways. For example, I have a wife who is an outward-looking person. She has that kind of personality. People just love her and they gravitate to her and they also provide her with information because they like her. She wins the confidence of people very easily and they share things with her, some of which has been very useful to me in my work on occasion. She has been like an officer in the embassy in terms of her outreach in the community, in her charitable work, and her work with the American community and in various organizations in the foreign community as well. In these positions, she is looked at as a U.S. government official, as someone who represents the United States. She has done it all for nothing and frankly with no thanks from the U.S. government. At the end of it all, you would think that someone would say, well done Mrs. So-and-So, here's a form of recognition for you for all that you have put in for the U.S. government free of charge. But that's not given at all, nothing. It's all for the love of the spouse and I must acknowledge that.

# OFFICE OF THE INSPECTOR GENERAL

*Q: Let's talk a bit about your time in the inspector general's office. You were there from when to when?*

YOUNG: I was there from 1981 to 1983. I had completed my work as the deputy to Mary Ryan in career assignments for administrative personnel and it was time to move on. I had looked around the Department for an appropriate level position, something that would give me some visibility and something that would really be good for me in terms of career development as well. So, I looked at post management jobs and various things and then I zeroed in on this position as executive director to the Office of the Inspector General. It wasn't a senior executive director position, but let's face it, title does mean something sometimes and "executive director" looks good on the old PAR as we used to call it. I applied and interviewed for the job. At the time the inspector general was moving on and a new one, Robert Brown, was coming on board. The deputies at that time were Frank Reddy and Dick Fox. I interviewed with them and some weeks later I got word that they were interested in me and eventually I was assigned there. Before going to that assignment, however, I went on a brief stint with the Board of Examiners; I did some initial training and then went out for several weeks to give the Foreign Service exam in New York, Boston, and Chicago. That was quite a wonderful experience.

*Q: What was your impression of the candidates?*

YOUNG: The candidates were excellent. We didn't pass very many, I must say. It was just as tough then as it is now, but I was impressed with the candidates. The one candidate that impressed us the most was a man in his mid-thirties who had been a postman. He didn't have a college degree, was working as a postman, and was absolutely superb and we passed him. I don't know if he ever came into the Service or not, but that stuck in my mind. I'll never forget it because it demonstrated that you can really accumulate quite a bit of knowledge and information and have a good understanding of the world if you apply yourself, and you don't necessarily have to go to school to get that in a formal way. This man had done it on his own and it was really remarkable, very impressive.

*Q: While you were doing this, did you go on inspections at all?*

YOUNG: I didn't go on any inspections at all. I would get sort of virtual inspections. The inspectors would come back and they would debrief us on their inspections. I thought that was just a fantastic experience because we would sit around and listen to these teams debrief the inspector general and his deputies on their work. We were able to get a sense of what was good and what was bad, and who was good and who was bad, and I found that very helpful. It was like a textbook exercise. It was quite helpful.

*Q: Did you see any areas where the inspectors were coming back and saying, we've really got a problem here. I'm talking about not necessarily the post but in general.*

YOUNG: Oh, yes. There were many times when they would come back and they would say, well, we have a broader systemic problem that we saw in this post and that post, and we need to look at it from a systemic point of view. They did that quite often, but more often than not it would be post-specific. Here are the problems we're having at this post, and I'll get to one in a moment that affected me personally.

*Q: Does that come up during the time you were with them?*

YOUNG: Yes, my job when I was there as the executive director was focused on basically three areas: finances, money, and getting money for the Office of the Inspector General. It was a time when the office was expanding and we needed more money. We needed more personnel. It was also a time when changes in legislation were being proposed to move from a career inspector general to a non-career inspector general. That was in the works as well. I had responsibility for personnel. I was responsible for bringing into the inspection corps all these senior officers, people who had been ambassador more than once, but on several occasions it would be people who had the title of career minister and what have you. I would establish contact with them, interview them, and I would then prepare a sheet that I had ginned up where I could provide the inspector general with a summary of basically how I saw that person, talking about their experience, education, where they had been, that sort of thing, and make a recommendation to him. I must say I had a pretty good record and the IG, if I made the recommendation, would go for it. I was responsible for bringing Mary Ryan into the inspection corps, which worked out very nicely. I'm just using that as one example. I brought in a number of ambassadors as well who were team leaders and that worked very nicely.

I remember one incident with an officer I had worked with in Kenya. We were junior officers together and he was really moving ahead very rapidly, leaving the rest of us in the dust and he was a very difficult personality. He called me one day from a Caribbean post where he was the counselor for economic affairs and he said, "Oh, I want to be an inspector." I told him, "Well, that's very nice, but you know we were junior officers together back in Kenya and things were not too good during that time." He said, "Well, that's true, I was difficult. I've grown up a lot and matured and I still don't suffer fools gladly, but I've learned a lot." I said, "Well, you know if I recommend you to the IG and he takes you, it's my reputation that's on the line." He responded, "I understand that, but I assure you, you won't regret this" and on and on. I accepted his word. I might as well be honest and give you his name. His name was Tom Forbord. I said, "Okay, Tom, I will recommend you to the IG." I did and the IG took him. He came on board several months later. Now, Tom was probably one of the smartest international economists in the Foreign Service at the time. He was absolutely brilliant, but as brilliant as he was, he was difficult and abrasive. Anyhow, he came in, started working with the other members of the office, and had been there just a couple of months when a delegation of secretaries came to me and asked, "Who brought this man into this office?" I said, "I did." They said, "Well, you better get him out of here because he's driving us crazy." I replied, "Well, I'm sorry about that, but there isn't anything I can do about that now." I just mention that to say that I did go out on a limb, I brought this guy in and he did good work for the office, there's no question about that, but he created difficulties in his interpersonal relations with the other members of the teams.

*Q: I think experience really shows people with interpersonal problems.*

YOUNG: They don't change. It's like a leopard changing its spots.

Later on, when I was a minister-counselor and the director of career development and assignments (CDA), I had the same problems in placing that officer. He, too, at that point had reached the rank of minister-counselor but was still a difficult person to place. Some things don't change, but I really did like that assignment in the inspector general's office. As I mentioned earlier, I was promoted to FS-1 out of that position. I had a good staff. I had a budget person and a personnel person and a couple other people in the office. They were all excellent people and we also did something there that was very interesting and had an impact on the Foreign Service. We were bringing in, and I sat on the examining team that brought these people in, what we called at the time "audit-qualified inspectors." These were inspectors who had training in finance and auditing and who could give an expert, close scrutiny of the financial operations at a post. That worked out very well. Some of these audit-qualified inspectors went on to much bigger and better things in the Department and in the Service. One of them is now the deputy assistant secretary for personnel, Linda Tagliatella, in the director general's office. She was one of them, I'm just using her as an example, and she has performed just absolutely beautifully. I could name a number of others who went on to become admin counselors and so on.

*Q: Were you sort of mentally making a list of what you were doing based on what you saw? You know, "If I ever run a mission I will do this, I won't do that." Seeing the problems, did that help?*

YOUNG: No, I never thought I was going to become an ambassador. I was making notes of what was good and what was bad based on the debriefs that we got from the inspectors, but I never made mental notes in terms of, "If I become an ambassador I'll do this and that." No, it never entered my mind. I made notes in terms of what a good admin counselor would do. I did that because my goal was to be the best admin counselor that I could be. That was how I made the notes in my mind. I learned a lot from that.

Anyhow, I was getting toward the end of that assignment and it was time once again to bid. That ugly monster of bidding had reared its head and it was time to deal with it once again. I began to look around for a position overseas. I had established very good relationships as a result of this executive director position. I got to know all of the other executive directors in the geographic bureaus and the functional bureaus and they were all very supportive. I narrowed down my list to two key jobs. One was admin counselor in Rabat in Morocco and the other was admin counselor in Amman, Jordan. I had spoken to Sheldon Krys, who was the executive director of Near Eastern affairs. He liked me. He was very supportive and arranged for me to interview with the political appointee ambassador in Morocco, Joseph Verner Reed. Ambassador Reed was here in the States at the time and I interviewed with him. He was a character. It all turned out very well. He offered me the job, but I didn't accept right away. I went back and conferred again with Sheldon Krys and Sheldon said to me, "Johnny, you can have either of these jobs. You can have Morocco or you can have Amman. If I were you" these were his words, he said, "both of those ambassadors are a pain in the ass, but I would go with the one in Jordan because he's a career man." I took Sheldon's advice and I opted for Amman. I was very happy. It was a very competitive job and in an exciting area. I thought it was just a perfect match. My wife and I were happy. Our kids weren't too happy, because they were settled in the States with their friends. My son was at the point of puberty and friendships are so important at that stage. He didn't want to leave them, so that required some work on our part.

Before I went to Amman an inspection team went out there in the spring of 1983 and they returned and provided a debrief that was a horror story, one of the worst horror stories I think I'd ever heard. I remember they looked at me and said, "You want to go to that post?" I said, "Yes." They said, "You're out of your mind." I asked, "Why?" They said, "It is the biggest mess we have ever run into." I said, "Well, what's going on?" They replied, "Well, it's been a raging battle between the ambassador and the administrative staff, particularly the admin officer and the budget and fiscal officer. The ambassador has already savaged both of them." The ambassador was Richard Viets, Dick Viets. So, I was terrified after hearing these stories. I didn't know what to think. I read the draft inspection report and it had something like 150 recommendations, almost all of them on the administrative side. I just couldn't believe it. I'd never seen anything like it. I was very worried and this troubled me for months before I went to the post. As you can imagine, as an FS-1 wanting very badly to be a senior officer one day, I was worried about the impact this might have on my chances to cross the threshold to become a senior officer. I just did the best that I could. I prepared and I studied and I read and I briefed and debriefed and then in the summer of 1983 we wound up things here and we moved on to Amman.

# BACK TO THE MIDDLE EAST: JORDAN

*Q: You were in Amman from '83 to when?*

YOUNG: From 1983 to 1985.

*Q: Before we get into the workings of things, what was happening in Jordan at the time? How were relations with the United States?*

YOUNG: The state of relations was frankly as good as you could expect under the circumstances. Jordan was a moderate state in the middle of the Middle East crisis. A good friend, and a loyal friend. It had tremendous problems of its own that it had to deal with. Almost the majority of the population there was really Palestinian. As you know, the Palestinians attempted to take over the country in 1971.

*Q: Black September.*

YOUNG: Yes. This was something that the king had to live with. The king was trying to be a peace maker, trying to be the good moderate, trying to be the good soldier in the Middle East. He was trying to be the good friend of the United States and at the same time trying to demonstrate that he was a solid Arab and a good backer of the Palestinians, so he was in a very delicate position. That said, the relations with the United States remained good and I must say that Ambassador Viets's faults notwithstanding, those faults were basically internal, from a substantive point of view he was an extraordinary ambassador. I have never seen an ambassador with a more effective relationship with a head of state as I witnessed Ambassador Viets with King Hussein of Jordan. It was truly exceptional. Hussein trusted Viets more than any other ambassador there and trusted him more, I think, than even some of his own ministers. He relied on him for all kinds of advice and counsel. Viets even looked the part. He was this great, good-looking man with a large mane of silver hair and beautiful complexion. He not only looked the part, but he played it. He was a very smooth fellow, just a top notch professional in his relationship with the host government. He was loved at all levels, not just by the king, but his relationship with the king was truly extraordinary. I've never seen anything like it. I can't speak to this authoritatively, but I'm not sure any of his successors succeeded as well.

Now, to Jordan. We arrived in the summer. We got settled in our house. Then I had my initial walk around the mission and my initial meeting with the ambassador. He acknowledged that the inspectors had written a less than favorable report on the mission and that he basically wanted me to clean it up. That was my job—to clean it up—I understood that and I respected him telling me, "You have a free hand, take care of it." I began to do that right away in terms of all kinds of general services rules and regulations, and administrative rules and regulations, and financial rules and regulations. It just went on and on and on.

I have to tell you a couple of stories to highlight this problem. We arrived at the time the outgoing budget officer was still at post, the one who had had a lot of difficulty with Viets. I might add that when I was in the inspector general's office and the inspectors had returned from Amman, they told me about some of the things going on there. One of the things they said to me was, you know the budget and fiscal officer had a file about five inches thick and on the cover of this file in big black letters were CYA.

*Q: Which means cover your ass.*

YOUNG: That's exactly it.

*Q: You're protecting yourself.*

YOUNG: So, that's what they said. I said, you're kidding. They said, no, he had this file and they showed it to us and we saw all of the things in it.

Back to meeting this fellow who was on his way out. His last name was Hume. I don't remember his first name. He was on his first or second assignment as a budget officer. Now, he went upstairs to pay his farewell call on the ambassador and after that he came down, sat in my office and he said, "Well, here's my checkout sheet. I've done all of the things I'm supposed to do and I can now go and get my tickets." I said, "Oh, how did your farewell call on the ambassador turn out?" He said, "Well, I sat there in front of the ambassador. The ambassador looked at me and said to me, 'You're the sorriest-assed thing I've ever seen as a budget and fiscal officer.'" He continued, "He just laid me out. I listened to him. When he finished, I said to him, 'Thank you very much Mr. Ambassador' and then I took my finger and I pointed it at him, and I told him, 'Thank you Mr. Ambassador, but I'm going to get you one day.'"

*Q: He did?*

YOUNG: I know he did. He said, "I'm going to get you one day." Mr. Hume then collected his tickets and left and moved on to his next assignment. Bernie Woerz was my predecessor, an admin officer who had an outstanding reputation in the Service. He had done just superb work. Well, he left Amman cowed and savaged by the ambassador. The ambassador just ripped him apart in the EER (employee efficiency report) that was prepared on him.

That was how I got started in Jordan. I began to sense that my relationship with Viets was not going to be that difficult. I sensed that it was going to be better. I got terrific guidance and support from the DCM at that time, Ed Djerejian, who was a wonderful guy, a very supportive fellow. When I got to difficult points in something that I had to go to the ambassador and tell him about, Ed was always there to say, well, maybe you might take this approach or that approach. But he never for a moment tried to back away from what we knew we had to do in terms of complying with what the inspectors had recommended. We were quite a group at that time. I didn't realize it until later on, but I just wanted to mention some of the people who were there at the mission at that time. Ed was the DCM. Jim Collins was the political counselor.

*Q: Later ambassador in the Soviet Union, Russia.*

YOUNG: Right. A new junior officer on his first assignment was Bill Burns. Molly Williamson had just left as the head of the consular section.

Brenne Bachmann was the economic counselor. I began to just focus on getting these numerous recommendations taken care of so that we could say that we had complied with the inspection report and had fulfilled all of the recommendations, and we did. I mean it required in some cases for the ambassador to pay back money, which he did. Some of these problems centered around his pressuring the budget officer and the admin officer to agree to paying certain things for him, certain first class travel, purchase of Christmas cards, and all of these things which are clearly prohibited by the regulations, but he pressured them to do it and they did it. Eventually he had to pay all that money back and what have you and he did. We did get things cleaned up. Viets completed his assignment; I don't want to make it seem as if he was pulled out. That was not the case. He completed his assignment and then moved on to await another onward assignment. He was replaced by Paul Boeker who was an economic officer and I think his last assignment was as the head of FSI (Foreign Service Institute), as a matter of fact. A great guy, but no big feats in terms of the rapport and relationship that he established with the king. At that point, Ed Djerejian had moved on and the new DCM had arrived, Skip Gnehm. Jim Collins had moved on as well and he was replaced by Ken Brill. We had that turnover in staffing.

Just to complete the circle in terms of Viets, he returned to the States. There were various possibilities floated as onward assignments for him and for one reason or the other none of them worked out. I was back in the Department one day walking past the director general's office, when I noticed Ambassador Viets in there and I went in to say hello. He called me over, welcomed me very warmly, and introduced me to the director general, who was George Vest at that time. George said, "You know, this is a wonderful man." I said, "I know," and Vest said to Viets, "Before I leave this job, I'm going to make sure that you get a good onward assignment." We chatted there a few minutes and then I left and that was it. Well, these various possibilities continued to float for Viets. One of them was South Africa, I don't know what else. Finally, Portugal came up and that was the one that seemed to click. He was nominated. All of the papers went through. Everything was going very nicely and then when it came time for his hearing, it seems that the information that had been in that famous CYA file was made available to the members of the committee. Dick Viets was never confirmed as ambassador to Portugal and left the Service and that was the end of it.

Q: So, the B&F officer got back at him. How did you read the whole thing? I mean what had gone wrong do you think?

YOUNG: It was a perfect example, in my view, of how autocratic behavior can get you in big trouble and that's what it boiled down to. Viets was good. He knew he was good. He let that go to his head and he thought that he could basically bully his way into anything that he wanted to do with his staff, and that was his failing in my view. A superb officer in terms of substance, but flawed in terms of his ability to listen to the experts who were there to work for him and to make him look good.

Q: Did you have much problem straightening out the administrative stuff or was it a matter of going through and checking off the list that said don't do this, do this.

YOUNG: It was basically working through the list. At that point he had resigned himself to the fact that although he didn't agree with the actions that were required, he had no choice but to go along with them and he did.

Q: How did you find Mrs. Viets?

YOUNG: Mrs. Viets was a lovely lady.

Q: She has quite a distinguished record on her own side during the war in Poland, I believe, or France?

YOUNG: I didn't know that. We just found her a very lovely person. She and my wife got on famously and we thought she was just a warm and loving person, a very caring person. She was madly in love with her husband and just a really good person. We liked her a lot. A little bit unusual in terms of her style. She had a very Bohemian style in her dress.

Q: As I recall and I think I'm right, she had distinguished herself during the occupation of France in the resistance.

YOUNG: I don't know. She was originally Romanian.

Q: Well, then, go on with Jordan.

YOUNG: Well, Jordan for all of its good relations with the United States at that time was a very dangerous place from a security perspective. As a matter of fact, it was considered the second most dangerous post at that time in the world. Beirut was number one and Jordan was number two. I'll never forget that we had bombs going off all over town, all the time. There were assassinations there of various Palestinian and Jordanian officials. They bombed my water truck in the GSO section of the warehouse. I remember when the new security officer arrived, my wife and I went out to the airport to meet him, we greeted him and on the way to his residence we got a call that there was a suspected bomb at one of the residences. So we took off, he and I, to go check that out. Fortunately it was not a bomb in that particular case, but I cite that to indicate the kind of climate that we lived in. We were very careful. Mind you we lived a good life. We went out at nights. We went to restaurants and parties and things like that. We mixed with Jordanians, but we were just very careful.

Now, we had during that time the bombing of the embassy in Lebanon and this had a tremendous impact on us in Jordan. We needed to do something to enhance our own security. We were right on a busy main street, across from the InterContinental Hotel. There was no kind of setback whatsoever. We began to look desperately for measures to heighten and strengthen our security. We tried all kinds of things. We tried additional guards. We tried all kinds of inspection procedures and this and that, and we finally decided that we had to sandbag the embassy and the residence. We got these sandbags and we built a wall of sandbags around the embassy. It was about six feet thick and about two stories high. We did that for both the residence and the embassy. The residence, by the way, was one that we had in 1971 at the time of Black September and there were still the bullet marks all over the façade of that building from the shells that were fired at it during that time. That was really quite something.

The country team decided that we should try to make an interim move from where we were to some other building with sufficient setback until a new chancery could be built for us. The ambassador said to me, "Johnny, it's your job. I don't care what else you do. You've got to do this." So, that's what I focused on. I put the word out that the embassy was looking for a building. Everybody in town came my way. I looked at building after building after building. We settled on a group of buildings. A team came out from Washington to evaluate them. We took core samples of the cement in these buildings to test them for how much weight capacity they could hold and things like that. We looked and looked, but could not find anything after all of the analysis. The determination was that none of the places we looked at would work. The ambassador met with the assistant secretary for security, Bob Lamb at the time, and they had some rather heated discussions and I remember sitting in on a meeting when Lamb said to Boeker, "You find the site. I will build you a new chancery on that site in two years." They agreed on that and we decided we would continue in our sandbagged embassy until we could move into a new chancery. I was then given responsibility to find land for this new embassy.

Once again, the word went out the embassy was looking for land. I had all kinds of people coming to me saying I've got a site here and I've got a site there and my uncle has this and my brother has this and that, and we looked and looked. Finally, we saw a site that was possible in terms of size. It was, if I recall correctly, about thirteen dunums, and a dunum in Arabic measure is over an acre, but I don't remember exactly how much over an acre. This came to about fourteen acres of land or something like that. We could basically have all of this land except there was one little part that we weren't sure about, but the rest of it was all together. We presented this to the Department and to all of the other interested parties and they said, "Well, this looks good." Again, a team came out and we evaluated all of these different sites, including the largest of the sites with this one little piece that was missing. After their evaluation they said we could go with that one site.

It was located literally in the middle of nowhere. It was off of what was at the time the fifth circle. There was nothing out there except rocks and sheep, nothing. I mean absolutely nothing. It was in the middle of nowhere. I made all of the arrangements and we bought that land and I think we paid about eight million dollars for it. I remember signing all of the agreements. Skip Gnehm was the DCM. He was with me when we made the final assignment and got the checks and gave the sellers the check, gave the agent the check. Then we completed the land registration at the office and that was my last major achievement in Jordan in the spring of 1985. I thought that the effort to try to find a transitional building and then the effort to purchase land was going to kill me. I really did. I had never been as pressured in my life as I was during those two exercises. I couldn't sleep. I was just consumed by this because there was so much at stake.

I was so consumed by these two projects, the transition that didn't work out and the purchase of the land, that I couldn't sleep. I couldn't rest. I was tense. It just bothered me so much. When I finally achieved this, I was so happy. Yet there was an element of disappointment in some of this. It came efficiency report time and the ambassador wrote a very nice efficiency report on me. The job that I had in Amman was called a joint administrative operation, and I was the JAO director, so the ambassador wrote my efficiency report. In all of the reports that I had received prior to that, this was at a time when efficiency reports had these little blocks with gradations of ratings, I had always been in the very top block or in the one just below that. I was always superlative or outstanding, which was wonderful.

In this report, the ambassador gave me one a little bit below that, so I was down in the third block and I had never had one there. Yet the substance of the report was extraordinary, because he noted such things as his having given me the responsibility to find this land and my having handled it as well as any minister could have handled it. Really nice stuff, there were good, solid meaty examples in this report. I remember I went to the DCM, Skip, I asked him, "Can you see if the ambassador could change this one block?" I was thinking of the appearance that this would have when people would look at that little checkmark and give more attention to that than to the substance of the report. I was also concerned because the year before I had received a meritorious step increase. I wasn't promoted into the senior service and before Ed Djerejian had left I had spoken to him about opening my window and Ed was the one who encouraged me to open my window. I'll never forget it. He said to me, "Johnny, we have both done very well. We're boys from the streets of New York and Philadelphia, respectively. You open your window. You're going to be fine." I took his advice and I opened the window.

Q: *You might explain what open the window means.*

YOUNG: Well, in the Foreign Service if you want to compete for the senior Foreign Service you have to basically go on notice that you wish to compete. You get six years of being considered for the senior service and if you don't make it in those six reviews then you're out the door. The year I opened my window, as I mentioned, I received a meritorious step increase so I was very encouraged by this. When I got this report from Ambassador

Boeker, I was concerned that the checkmark down at the third box instead of the second or top box, which had been the pattern in my career, might have a negative effect on me. I asked Skip to go to the ambassador and ask him to change it, and he said he did and the ambassador wouldn't change it. He kept it that way. There was nothing I could do. I left, but I was disappointed because I had put such a tremendous effort into buying that land for what was to be the new American embassy.

I was thinking about extending in Amman for an additional year. I had been in touch with Mary Ryan who was the executive director of the Bureau of European Affairs and she had said to me, "If you decide to move out of the Bureau of Near Eastern Affairs, I would love to have you in the Bureau of European Affairs, but I don't have much at the moment in terms of an onward assignment. Whatever comes up you can have." Now, I had never had an offer like that in my career and haven't had one since to tell you the truth. She said, "I don't want you to stay in Jordan. It's too dangerous. I want you to move on." I kind of left things in her hands and I did bid on a couple of things in Europe, but they weren't particularly exciting. Then I got a call from her one day and she said, "Johnny, guess what?" I said, "What?" She said, "Stan Robinson, who is the admin counselor in The Hague, is leaving. He has decided that he would retire instead of completing his assignment. Would you be interested in that position?" The timing was just right for me to move into it after Amman. I answered, "Yes." She said, "You have to bid on it, but as far as I'm concerned, you're my candidate." I bid on the job and that was in '84 for an '85 opening and Mary selected me. I was selected for the job and I didn't say anything to my family. I kept quiet about it.

Christmas of 1984 we went to Egypt and then from Egypt we took a tour around the Nile Valley. On Christmas Day 1984, I informed my family that we would be moving on to The Hague. My son who had become very enamored of Jordan wanted to know, "What do we have to go there for? I'm very happy here in Jordan," and on and on. I said, "This is going to be our new assignment," but he didn't want to go. Later on, he did like The Hague quite a bit. That's how we got to The Hague and I will only add that Jordan was truly a remarkable assignment. Years later, in fact, all of the counselors of the embassy except one became ambassadors. We proudly say we were Viets boys. We learned from him. No matter how you look at it, I'm grateful for what I learned from him, although I wasn't consciously thinking of being an ambassador or anything at that time. I've always had the greatest respect for him.

Q: *Before we leave Jordan, let's talk about the bombings. Who was bombing?*

YOUNG: These were, we believed, definitely radical Palestinian elements.

Q: *Did you get any feel for fundamental Islamic religion while you were there?*

YOUNG: No, there were very conservative types there, but that was not an issue at that point, no. That was something that would come up later on. The king's balancing act was trying to comfort and assure those Palestinians who might stir up trouble in his own country internally as well as those who might come in from the outside and stir up trouble.

Q: *Any relation, as far as you were concerned, with our embassy in Tel Aviv?*

YOUNG: No. We would inform them of course; we kept them informed in terms of reporting and that sort of thing. There wasn't even any talk at that point of any kind of rapprochement. During that time we could move very easily between Israel and Jordan over the Allenby Bridge and we did that almost daily. In fact, we had weekly non-pro courier runs which we would circulate within the mission so everybody got a chance to go over to Israel and sort of have a different kind of environment and shop and do all kinds of things like that. It was very nice. We could take our families as well. We could do these runs independently of the non-pro courier run if we wanted to. We just had to make arrangements beforehand. All of us enjoyed it. I don't know how it is today; I can't speak to it today.

Q: *Any reflections of the Iran and Iraq War when you were there?*

YOUNG: It didn't affect us much at all. I mean, I have to be honest with you, I didn't focus on it that much. But I don't recall that being a major issue.

I would like to cite another little story. One day I was up in Viets's office and I had read a message and I can't recall the substance of it, but I commented to the ambassador, "That was a really good message." He said,

"You liked that message?" I replied, "Yes. I thought it was very well done." He said, "It was well done. Who do you think is the best drafter in this mission?" I said, "Surely you Mr. Ambassador." He said, "No, not me." I thought quickly and said to myself, Young, you better go down the list. I guessed, "The DCM?" He said, "No, not the DCM either." Sticking to the hierarchy, I guessed, "The political counselor?" He said, "No, not the political counselor either." I said, "Well, then who?" He said, "You know that new junior officer that just came up from the consular section, Bill Burns?" I said, "Yes." He said, "He is the best. You keep your eyes on that young man. He's going to go far." Believe me, if ever there was a prediction that came true, that was it. Bill was an extraordinary officer. Everybody loved him because he was so bright and so clever and yet with it all you would never know it because he was so modest and so decent that it was such a contrast with another officer who was there at that time.

We had several junior officers, but the other officers arrived all about the same time. The other one was ready to tell you in a half a minute that he had a degree from Princeton and he spoke Arabic and he did this and did that and on and on. Bill would never say anything. You would ask Bill, where did you go to school and he would say well, I went to a small school in Philadelphia. Okay, La Salle College. Did you do any graduate work? Yes, I did some graduate work; he wouldn't tell you that it was at Oxford University. He wouldn't tell you that he had written and published a book. He wouldn't tell you that his father was General Burns. He wouldn't tell you a lot of things about himself. You literally had to pull it out of him. That was the degree to which he was modest, but when you gave him something to do, he would turn out a piece of work that was just masterful in every sense of the word.

*Q: What happened to Bill Burns?*

YOUNG: He's our ambassador in Russia. Need I say more? Before that, he was the assistant secretary of state for Near Eastern affairs. [Burns later attained the rank of career ambassador and served as under secretary of state for political affairs and deputy secretary of state.]

*Q: You mentioned Molly Williamson. Her name has come up a number of times. Where is she?*

YOUNG: Molly is over at Energy. She has moved up very nicely in the Service and reached the rank of career minister. She has been out of the Department for a while. She was over at Commerce as a DAS (deputy assistant secretary) and now she is an advisor to the secretary of energy.

*Q: Has she left the Foreign Service?*

YOUNG: No, she has not. She's still in the Foreign Service.

# EUROPE: THE HAGUE

*Q: Well, then you went to The Hague from when to when?*

YOUNG: We were in The Hague from 1985 to 1988. I will just add a little note before we get to The Hague.

Just before I left, I remember Skip Gnehm talking to me and saying, "You're going to go to The Hague. The ambassador and I are worried about you." I said, "Oh, really? What about?" He said, "You're going to be there with Jerry Bremer. We're afraid that Bremer is going to eat you alive. You're too nice an admin officer. We're afraid that this could be a problem for you." I said, "Well, thank you very much, but I can't change now. I'll just deal with it the best I can."

I left and after home leave and those kinds of things we arrived in The Hague. We were initially placed in a temporary flat until we could get an apartment or a house that was set aside for us, which all worked out very nicely. We met Bremer. At the time, the DCM was Art Hughes and it was quite a dynamic change, I must say. We had heard about Jerry Bremer and what a dynamo he was. Within minutes of meeting him it was clear he was a dynamo. I mean, he was a man who demanded that things be done and done well and fast and now. He was just incredible. People had to produce or he had no use for them.

Now, in The Hague we had one burning issue at that time and Jerry was sent there to take care of it. It was basically to get the Dutch to deploy Cruise missiles. Everybody else in NATO had signed on except the Dutch, and our goal was to get the Dutch to sign on.

*Q: This was part of a basic strategy. The Soviets introduced the SS-20 intermediate range, threatening Europe, to sort of break Europe off from the United States. And we had countered by putting in both Cruise missiles and Pershing missiles, which are also medium range, as a counter to this. It was very controversial.*

YOUNG: Yes. The Dutch were dragging their feet on it. They hadn't committed and it was Jerry's job to get them to turn around. He was, I believe, forty-three years old at the time, certainly the youngest American ambassador ever assigned to The Hague. As a matter of fact he tells the story of how one Saturday he went on a bike ride with his family and they stopped at a little village not too far from The Hague. They went into this store and they bought something, I don't know if it was water or what, and the fellow asked him if he was American, Jerry said yes. The fellow asked him, well, what do you do here and Jerry says, "I'm the American ambassador." The merchant nearly laughed him out of the shop. He was incredulous. He couldn't believe that such a youngster would be the American ambassador and dressed in jeans and what have you. Jerry looked even younger than he was and he is a good-looking fellow. There's no question about it. He is movie star good-looking. Jerry said he vowed from that day on that he would wear a suit as often as he could to help basically with the image. Jerry was also very athletic and a great jogger. As in his drive to run and direct the mission, he was the same way with his own physical health and he was an obsessive and great runner. The Marines couldn't even keep up with him. I mean, he was just unbelievable. His discipline, his drive; talk about achievement-oriented. He was the shining example of an achievement-oriented type A personality.

Well, we had a good mission there, good people, not the kind of security concerns and challenges that we had in the Middle East, but nevertheless they were beginning to manifest themselves more and more. Missions in Europe and elsewhere were beginning to get instructions to go to the host government and get their cooperation to do this and that, and on and on. Our problem in dealing with the Dutch was that the Dutch felt that we were always overreacting in terms of our security concerns, that we were too excitable on these issues and they had everything under control and not to worry about it. They really dragged their feet in helping us. We were trying to put barriers around the mission and that sort of thing and they resisted us on this and that, and mind you they had had some pretty serious security problems in the Netherlands. A British ambassador had been assassinated there. A Turkish ambassador had been assassinated. The famous Carlos the Jackal was held up in the French embassy, which was literally across the street from our embassy in The Hague. So they had seen some problems over the years, but nevertheless they believed that they had it under control and that we Americans were overreacting.

In January of 1985 the Dutch received intelligence that a terrorist action was going to be carried out in the Netherlands. For the first time, the Dutch reacted to a security threat with the kind of vigor and seriousness and swiftness that we had all hoped for. They moved into action. They went public. They just about closed down the airports throughout the country as they tried to investigate this information. Tourism went down. I mean, it was an incredible move on the part of the Dutch. People were calling us from all over the place. Should I come to the Netherlands? Should I do this, should I do that? So, they really got serious at that point and that was a good thing because we could then ask for their help. We were able to move then to get some barriers around the mission and get flower pots and fences put around. We were on a main street and on a big, historic plaza, and the Dutch didn't want to upset the historic significance of this plaza. They didn't want to do any kind of modernization or anything that would take away from the old pristine way that it had been for literally centuries. But, anyhow, they were cooperating more with us and that was very good.

In the meantime, the financial situation in the State Department was not very good and the Department began looking at closing missions and consulates, and they selected the consulate in Rotterdam for closure. The consulate in Rotterdam had been open for over two hundred years and they decided to close it. The Western Europe office fought it but the Department remained firm and it was closed. Ambassador Bremer told me, "It's your job to close it up. But whatever you do, I want everyone to the extent that we can, the local employees, placed in other jobs. There's one employee there that you must find a place for, no matter what." That was a guard by the name of Ollie. Ollie was an extraordinary guard. He manned the entrance of the consulate in Rotterdam and he was so extraordinary because he had so much personality. He had such an effective way of doing a pat down. Dutch officials and business people frankly resented coming into the mission and being frisked, basically. They didn't like it at all. They thought it was an affront to their dignity and they didn't want anything to do with it. The ambassador had observed this many times and that's why he valued Ollie so much. Ollie would say to them, "Good morning, sir, how are you?" He would go pat, pat, pat, pat and before the person knew it, they had been patted down, brought into the building and they would comment, "That is a really nice guard that you have there." Ollie had just done it all so brilliantly and he would do it over and over again. He was an invaluable asset, because we wanted to keep a positive image of the mission despite the fact that we had an obligation to carry out the security check before letting people in the building. I began to work on a plan to try to find places for these people in the consulate and succeeded in getting them positions either in filling openings in The Hague or in Amsterdam. Some of them decided that they didn't want this and they would just leave the mission and look for something elsewhere.

Matters were complicated because the Netherlands, like many countries in Europe, has very complicated labor laws. You can't just close a building. You can't just declare bankruptcy. You can't just say, well, I don't have any profits and I'm going to close this baby down. You can't do that. You have to continue to pay your employees. Cuckoo labor laws. We had to pay huge sums to people although they didn't want to continue on. They didn't want to be transferred. We paid substantial sums, I must say. I remember one fellow, this is in 1986, we paid $100,000, a huge amount of money at that time, but we had no choice. We had to comply with these Dutch labor laws. They really do handcuff you and restrict what you can do. We finally closed the consulate. We sold the beautiful residence there. One of the prettiest residences I think I have ever seen. Not in terms of size, but in terms of setting on a little lake with a beautiful windmill in the background. It was just spectacular. A fellow by the name of Don Junior was the consul general at that time. I know it was heartbreaking for him to leave that, it certainly was for me, to close it, because there was so much history there. We had to do it and we did it and moved on.

One other important thing that I worked on with Ambassador Bremer was a bilateral work agreement. This agreement would allow the wives of our diplomatic personnel to work in the Netherlands and vice versa for the spouses of Dutch diplomats in the United States. Now, in 1986 there were not many of these agreements in Europe, and we were the pioneers in trying to work one out. We needed some examples of successful agreements which we could then use in encouraging other European governments to sign on. We worked and worked on this agreement. The Dutch can be very stubborn when it comes to something that they consider a principle that should be upheld. On the question of immunity, they were so afraid that if they signed the agreement along the lines that we liked that some spouse working in a bank could rip off the funds of the bank, declare immunity, and never be prosecuted for that kind of crime. We gave all kinds of assurances that this would not be the case, but they wouldn't budge. So we tried all kinds of different formulations in order to retain the immunity provision in the draft treaty and at the same time address the concerns of the Dutch. In the end, we agreed that if there was a problem we would consider a waiver of immunity and at last that satisfied the Dutch. We got the approval on the U.S. side; we got the approval of the Dutch side. I remember the ambassador and I going to the foreign minister, Hans van den Broek, and all of us signing this bilateral work agreement or bilateral treaty, which was a major achievement for the mission. That treaty in turn served as one that we used in encouraging other European governments to sign. So that worked out very nicely.

Bremer was a very highly respected ambassador in the Netherlands. In fact, people said he was probably the best that they had ever had. He had learned Dutch and I can't tell you how popular that was. This was in a country where the people are probably the best English speakers in Europe other than maybe the Danes. They were just unbelievably good with their English. They were very proud that an American ambassador had made the effort to learn Dutch to the point where he could go on television and be interviewed in Dutch; he did it all the time and did it very effectively. Because he was so popular and had such a good relationship, he was able to get the Dutch to reverse and to sign on and implement the request that we had for them to deploy the Cruise missiles.

*Q: Did you have problems at our consulate general in Amsterdam? After the Vietnam War started, they had sort of a perpetual demonstration. I would have thought that this was the last great surge of what the Soviets were able to get in Western Europe. Were you concerned that you would have more of the demonstrations?*

YOUNG: We had our share of demonstrations. We would have them in The Hague and we would have them also in Amsterdam, where there was a lot more activity than in The Hague, but as someone said, the Dutch are fair-weather demonstrators. When it was very cold and what have you, they didn't come out too much, but when the weather was good, it was springtime and young folks were in the streets, they would come out more. Yes, we had lots of demonstrations, but nothing that stopped anything of any importance. We would alert the police or the police would alert us and we would tell people, be careful there's going to be a demonstration today and don't go out for lunch at a certain time, wait, and the like. No great problems as a result of that.

We also had some funny things that happened. One night we had a new marine on duty. At night it gets rather lonely in the mission and I guess this fellow just wasn't used to it all. He was being very conscientious. He was doing his inspection and he came up the stairwell. There was a long corridor as you came up the stairwell and at the end of it there was a window. He came up the stairwell on this particular night and he looked down the hall and saw someone moving. He didn't realize it was his own reflection in the window, and he pulled out his gun and fired. It was unfortunate, but the poor fellow of course paid a price for that and was removed, but that was one thing that happened.

One spring day the Marines were going through one of their exercises, one of their internal hostage things. Someone had left a window open that faced the square. Someone was passing at that point and heard, "Don't shoot him!" and don't do this and that, and "hold him" and this and that, and "call the police." It sounded like a real hostage situation. The person who overheard this on the outside called the police right away and the police came screaming to the embassy ready to break in and rescue this hostage, and on and on.

Another time we had a technician who had come to repair some equipment and he was working late at night. No one knew that he was in the embassy. Suddenly the marine heard screams coming from a far away part of the embassy, so he traced to where this was coming from. He went to the person screaming and there was the technician, blood dripping from his hand. He had gotten his fingers caught in the cross-cut shredder. So, they called the police and this cross-cut shredder was in a classified area. The police came. The ambulance came, took the fellow out, took the piece of finger out and took him to the hospital where they were able to reattach it.

That was the good part. The sad thing was the marine was written up for having allowed the medical personnel to come in and have access to this fellow. Well, we took exception to that and did get the marine off the hook on that particular one, but you can see sometimes these problems that can crop up.

Well, Jerry Bremer completed his assignment there.

*Q: Did you ever get cross with Jerry Bremer?*

YOUNG: I didn't, but I have watched when he has been cross with others. Should we go into that?

*Q: Yes, it's all part of the warp and woof of how we conduct our foreign relations.*

YOUNG: Well, I remember one country team meeting when he asked someone for a report and the person didn't have it and Jerry said, "Well, didn't I ask you for this before?" I think the person said yes. Jerry said, "I'm going to ask you one more time and if you can't do it then I think I'll ask someone else to take care of it for me." I mean boom, shot him down just like that.

The incident I remember the most involved the senior commercial officer, a fellow by the name of Stan Harris. As I said, Jerry wanted us to close down the consulate in Rotterdam as smoothly and as quickly and efficiently as we could and particularly take care of the people. I give him credit. He wanted us to take care of the people. He had asked Stan if he had made arrangements to take care of his commercial person in Rotterdam. Stan had not moved as quickly as Jerry had liked and this meeting took place in Jerry's office. It involved Stan Harris and me, and Jerry wanted to know why there was a delay, because all of the other people had been taken care of. Stan said he wanted to wait to see this and wanted to do that, and Jerry was really furious at what was clearly a delay on Stan's part. He said, "Stan, I told you what I wanted to do and I thought maybe you would have this done by now." Again Stan resisted Jerry's entreaties for him to move swiftly on this. Jerry said, "No, I want this done now and I want you to do it." He literally, physically threw Stan out of his office. Grabbed him by the seat of his pants and threw him out of the office. I was speechless. I could not believe what I was seeing. Stan was considerably older than Jerry. Stan was in his sixties and Jerry wasn't even fifty; he was still in his forties. He threw him out and said he wanted this done by such and such a date. Stan said, "Jerry, I can't believe you just did what you did. Jerry, I can't believe it." In the meantime, Jerry is getting him out the door. He got him out the door and we both left at that point. Stan turned to me and said, "Johnny, can you believe what you've seen?" I said, "Well, what can I say? You know he has asked you to move on this quite a bit and you're not there yet." He said, "That's true, but I can't believe he did what he did. I'm an older man. I remember Jerry when Jerry was a baby basically." That happened.

About three hours later Stan called and said, "I just want you to know Jerry came down to my office and he apologized and told me that he was sorry, that it was over the top. He had crossed the line. He was very sorry. He didn't mean it, but he'd been pressing for action on this particular item and wanted me to do something about it. I accepted his apology and it's fine." Stan was also getting ready to move on to another assignment. He was going to go to London. A couple of months later, before Jerry left, Jerry had a very nice farewell dinner for Stan and they remained good friends. I saw a side of his temper at that point. We got along beautifully and he wrote me just a wonderful efficiency report together with Art Hughes and I'll never forget it. It was the report that frankly did the trick in getting me promoted into the senior Service.

I will never forget when I got word about that. It was a Friday night in September or October of 1986. My wife and I were getting ready to go to bed, and at about midnight, the phone rang. I picked it up and said hello and the person on the other end said, "Hi Johnny, this is Mary Ryan." I said, "Oh, hi Mary, how are you doing?" She said, "We just returned from the White House with the seniors list." I said, "Oh, that's very nice. What does that have to do with me?" She said, "You're on it." I asked, "Me?" She said, "Yes, you're on it." Again I think I asked, "Me?" Because I didn't think it was going to happen. She said, "Yes, welcome to the seniors club." Then she extended congratulations and best wishes. My wife and I just could not believe it.

Anyway, Art Hughes and Jerry Bremer moved on. Jerry moved on to become the director for counter terrorism in the Department. Then we got an interim DCM, John Heimann; his wife was Judy Heimann. They were a team and Judy was on leave without pay while John was the DCM. They had been in The Hague on two previous assignments and were basically returning home, both fluent speakers of Dutch. That was an easy transition for them. They were good folks. They sort of held things together for a while.

So, Heimann was in an interim role. He had come in to await the appointment of a new ambassador. We finally got word that John Shad, who had been the head of the Securities and Exchange Commission, would be visiting several European posts to find out which one he liked the best for his assignment as ambassador. He would be coming out with his wife, who was ill and confined to a wheelchair. He visited Denmark, Sweden, Belgium, and the Netherlands. I made all the arrangements to receive him and take care of him and he looked around and asked lots of questions. In the end, he decided that the Netherlands was his post of choice. Before he arrived, we received a twenty-five-section message with all of his holdings. It was my job to check to see if there was any conflict of interest in his holdings and the U.S. embassy's relationship with the various companies and organizations listed in the stocks and bonds that he owned. There was none. At the time he was considered to be the richest man in the Reagan administration. He was very wealthy.

John Heimann decided he would retire. In his place they sent John Rouse. Rouse became the DCM to John Shad. John Shad arrived. We got him settled in his new house and it became very clear to us right away that this was no skilled diplomat, that this was someone who would require a lot of handholding, a lot of direction if he was going to be seen in a positive light. Mr. Shad was quite a character, to say the least. He would fall asleep at meetings, public meetings, I don't mean just in the embassy. He would also fall asleep in embassy meetings. I'll never forget my next door neighbor, who was a Frenchman, saying to me one evening, "Oh, I just met your ambassador at the Chamber of Commerce meeting. He fell asleep at the head table." That was the kind of start we were off to.

*Q: Was he elderly?*

YOUNG: He was in his sixties at that point. I don't think he had reached seventy; maybe late sixties. Could have been early seventies as well, but he was an elderly gentleman. His wife was terminally ill. She had cancer of the esophagus. She was very nice lady who had achieved in her own right. She had become the first attorney, or something, in some state or college and that made her unique. She'd been the first in something and a very nice lady, but she had her problems. The residence had to provide special care for her because she couldn't eat regular food. She was fed through a tube, and things like that. He would push her wheelchair, for example, in public, but in private, if they were just in the house, he wouldn't have anything to do with it and he treated her very dismissively and not very nicely. He would say to the staff, "You push her, I don't want to push her," that sort of thing. They had separate bedrooms in the residence. We attempted to install some sort of elevator so that she could go up and down and that worked out.

Ambassador Shad didn't really want much to do with substance. A little bit, but not too much. Mind you, the big work and the heavy lifting had been done by Bremer beforehand, but Shad had to maintain the relationship and keep it productive. The Dutch frankly didn't have very high regard for him. He certainly had the access that he needed as an ambassador. My relationship with him was strained, very strained, and I thought that frankly he was going to bring an end to my career. He was very wealthy, but very cheap. He was the cheapest man I have ever run into. He wanted all kinds of things to be paid for by the U.S. government and they were illegal and I couldn't do it. Here we go, Christmas cards once again. I said, no, we can't do those kinds of things and I'm not going to do them. I told him, "Look, when I go to jail you're not going to bake cookies for me. The only one who will bake cookies for me will be my wife and no one else, and I'm just not going to do it." He didn't like that at all. He considered me to be negative because I wouldn't agree to all of these things. He wanted us to buy all kinds of little trinkets and what have you. They got hung up on these things. There was just no money for that and he had lots of money. He could buy trinkets and what have you with his own money, but he was really tight.

The staff at the mission had to write out everything for him. He had to have everything on a card. He read everything. He couldn't do anything extemporaneously. It was really quite a sad state of affairs, I thought. Anyhow, efficiency report time came around and I got a wonderful report from John Rouse, a beautifully written report. I was very happy with it in every sense of the word; I didn't want to change a word. Then it went to the ambassador for his review and I thought well, this is it, because I knew what was coming. The report came back and it had one sentence, "I have nothing further to add to this report," which suited me just fine. I couldn't have been happier because any panel would know that there was something there, that clearly when an ambassador puts that on a report something must be wrong, but at least he didn't say anything negative. I accepted that and we called it quits.

I want to just tell you a couple of things. He had an obsession with video games and Pac-Man. He would go down to the local arcade and play Pac-Man with all of these kids. The DCM and I said we can't have the ambassador down in the arcade playing Pac-Man with these kids. We would go down there and rescue him out of the arcade and take him back to the residence. Then we had to find a Pac-Man machine to put in the residence. Pac Man was one of these computer generated games like Pokemon and whatever else they had at that time. We couldn't believe that this filthy rich man would indulge in this kind of activity with no sensitivity to his position whatsoever and would be caught doing this kind of thing. Well, I said to the DCM, I can't believe it. Here I am, making sixty some thousand dollars a year, which was a lot of money at that time, running around town here trying to find out where I can buy a Pokemon or a Pac-Man machine to put in the residence to keep the ambassador confined to the residence instead of running downtown to an arcade. We did that. Then one night while he was playing Pac-Man in his underwear, he locked himself out of the residence. We had to deal with that mess to get him back into the house. Oh, crazy stuff, just crazy stuff.

*Q: What was there about him that made him so wealthy?*

YOUNG: Oh, he made a fortune in stocks. He was a genius in that regard.

Another thing that happened concerned the secretary of commerce, Malcolm Baldridge. He was killed when he was thrown from a horse. Well, before the body was cold, Shad sent a cable to the president saying that he wanted to replace Baldridge, because he had accepted his ambassadorship only as a kind of consolation prize since there was nothing else available at the time. Well, he sent the message and left a copy on his desk. He had sent it classified. Since I was the admin counselor, the marine brought it to me because they had issued him a violation. I saw the message and I couldn't believe that literally, within hours of Baldridge's death, Shad sent this message to Reagan asking that he be appointed. Well, he never was appointed to that position. He basically sort of hung around as ambassador for the remainder of his time there. I stayed with him until my assignment concluded in 1988, at which time I received a message saying that I had been selected for the Senior Seminar, and that's where I was going to go.

# SENIOR SEMINARIAN

*Q: How did you find the Senior Seminar?*

YOUNG: Well, I frankly didn't know what to expect. I had heard many things about it over my years in the Service. I went with a very open mind, and found as the months in the program evolved that it was really one of the best things that ever happened to me. I got so much exposure from that program in terms of leaders in government and industry that I had the opportunity to meet, along with the other members of the seminar, the places that we visited, and the kinds of issues that we dealt with. It was a very broadening experience. It was also a great confidence-building experience for me. I had risen through the ranks as an administrative officer, and until that program I thought that I would continue along those lines and never that I could possibly do something else that would be even broader than general administration. The seminar gave me that confidence.

*Q: I think this is something that somebody who doesn't know the Foreign Service might not understand, and that is that people who come in as political officers and to a lesser extent economic officers are told they are going to be the leaders, they're going to be the ambassadors. People who come in as consular officers or administrative officers are told basically, "You'll do a fine job and you'll get promoted, but don't get your aspirations up too much."*

YOUNG: That's true.

*Q: That's changed quite a bit, but at the time I went to the Senior Seminar in 1974, 1975 as a consular officer, I was the token consular officer. But it did open things.*

YOUNG: Yes. I was in the thirty-first class, which began in 1988, through the '89 academic year. We had one consular officer in our class. I think we had two administrative officers, myself and Chris Orozco, and the rest were political officers and economic officers.

*Q: Were there any particular things that were noteworthy that you can recall during your Senior Seminar?*

YOUNG: Oh, there were several things that were interesting. One of them was our project before Thanksgiving, where we had to do some volunteer work in the community. I went together with another member of the seminar, David Welch, who is now the assistant secretary for Near Eastern affairs. We went to a soup kitchen, but we worked in different parts of this soup kitchen and I made soup and cleaned floors. It was a shelter for the homeless more than a soup kitchen. They couldn't understand why we were there, why we were doing this, why we were giving our time to this kind of effort. A funny thing happened in terms of David Welch. One of the inhabitants asked him why he was there and David in his very wry, dry sense of humor said that he could not do anything else. The guy asked why not and David responded that he was an escaped killer. The fellow's eyes bulged. He didn't know what he had on his hands there. I had great sympathy for those poor folks and what they have to go through. I felt that my little contribution was just really a drop in the ocean. Nevertheless, we did it and I think the majority of us in various programs ended with a greater sensitivity for the downtrodden. The underclass was one of the themes of our particular seminar group.

We visited a housing project in southeast Washington. The tenants had decided that they would attempt to buy the units they lived in and change the complete makeup of the community. We went there and visited with the woman who was at the head of this community effort to get the tenants to buy these units, which was quite fascinating. You could see that as impoverished as the community was, and as the people in it were, leadership emerged. We were so-called leaders of tomorrow and we could see that in that group, much less fortunate than we, there were leaders. Tammy, the woman at the head of this, was a formidable leader. You could see her at the head of a table of a big corporation directing things. She knew how to get things done and she knew how to inspire and lead and was quite a character. It was fascinating.

As part of the underclass theme, we visited the Detroit police. That was quite a night, or quite a couple of days. The police chief was very well-educated, with a Ph.D. There weren't many around in those days with that kind of training. This fellow was very good, very articulate. We met other people in the mayor's office and in the administration in Detroit. We then went with different police teams and rode shotgun with them in their cars. I will never forget there were a number of calls that we responded to during the night. We rode with them for several hours.

One call was to respond to a domestic disturbance. It was pouring rain that night and there I was, in the back seat. I observed these two policemen respond to all kinds of situations. At one moment they were literally psychologists, the next moment they were peacemakers, the next moment they were marriage counselors. I mean, they just did all kinds of things and my respect for them just went up 10,000 percent. They are just a remarkable group of people, the policemen and what they have to do and how they put their lives on the line every day to protect us and to provide for our security. Anyhow, this particular call was for a domestic disturbance and we went to this home. I remember there was a light on the porch. I could see the rain just coming down in sheets and the two policemen told me to stay in the car. They said, "We're going to go in and check this out and we want you to stay here and when the coast is clear we'll come out and signal to you and then you can come in." I did as they said. I waited, they went inside. I waited and I waited. I listened to the rain and looked at it coming down the window of the car and you know, falling off the roof of the porch of this house.

Finally the door cracked and one of the policemen put his head in and signaled to me to come in. I rushed through the rain, got a little bit wet, went onto the porch and then into the house. When I got into the house, I was stopped in my tracks. I looked across the room and there was a woman with an ice pick stuck in the middle of her head. She and her husband had had a fight and he grabbed an ice pick and stabbed her in the head. The ice pick was lodged in her head. I couldn't believe it. It was just the most horrifying thing I had ever seen. The police called for the ambulance. The ambulance came; they put her in. and they accompanied her to Detroit Receiving Hospital which was another experience that I will never forget as long as I live. They took her to the emergency section and in the emergency section there was blood and gore and things that I don't think I would ever want to see again as long as I live. There was a pregnant woman who had attempted suicide. She had put a gun in her mouth and had attempted suicide and it had failed. That was just a horrible sight. There was also a very large fellow who had been beaten to a pulp and his face looked like it was about four times its normal size. I mean, there were all kinds of problems there. I thought my head was going to swirl off with all of these horrible sights that I was seeing. Anyhow, the doctors and nurses were all running around. I mean it was just like something from TV, and this was years before "ER" came about.

*Q: ER is the name for the Emergency Room, which is a very popular TV program.*

YOUNG: Yes. The two policemen who were with me were just as calm as could be with all of this. They had seen it all and had become a bit numb to it. At one point they said to me, "Do you want to go across the hall and take a look at the psychiatric unit?" I said, "No, thank you. I think I've had enough for one night." We left, but that was quite an eye-opener in terms of seeing what the police go through. I mean I come from the underclass and I understand, but I came from the underclass at a time when there wasn't violence, at least not in my community. We were just poor.

We went to Boston and while we were there, we visited MIT (Massachusetts Institute of Technology). Mr. Deutch was the head of MIT at the time, a very nice man. Greeted us nicely, we couldn't have been happier. Then we were to have a talk with a prominent member of their faculty. I'm not sure if we knew who it was going to be, but anyhow we were told to report to a room at a given time and we did. We went into the room and began to find our seats. There was a gentleman standing up in the room looking out the window and frankly nobody paid any attention to him and he didn't pay too much attention to us. He would sort of glance at us and then glance outside and we all found our seats and sat down. When we were all in, he then turned and faced the class and said, "Hello, my name is David Baltimore." We were bowled over. That was the David Baltimore who was a Nobel Prize laureate for molecular biology. The nicest man, the most humble person you could ever meet. No one would have ever suspected that this great scientific mind would be so modest and that was a good lesson to see how you can have it all and still be a very modest and unassuming person; we liked him very much. He told us that he had never dreamed of winning the Nobel Prize. He thought about science all the time and worked in it all the time and he had this idea and it was like "Eureka." One day there it was and he put it all down and worked on it and that is what got him the Nobel Prize. Quite a remarkable fellow.

We went to Miami, Florida and visited with the mayor and with his staff. When we left, we had a good discussion amongst ourselves that this was a place destined for trouble, racial trouble, and it was just as we thought it would be. We thought it was very revealing that the Hispanic mayor didn't have a single black official in his administration, at least among the people who briefed us and these were all his close advisors in one capacity or another. We interpreted that as a sign of exclusion, as a lack of sensitivity to the black community in Miami. Mind you, we could have been reading a lot more into this than was the case, but that was how we saw it. We said, "That is just not right and this place is going to have troubles." A couple of years later they did; they had riots down there.

*Q: I know they've had recent riots in France, and you see there are conferences of mayors. I watch French TV and high officials in France wonder, "What are we going to do about the problem?" Not one dark face in that group. I mean the French talk about it, but when you get to the political class, this is important.*

YOUNG: Yes, well the French believed that they had no problem, and that the color of your skin didn't matter as long as you spoke good French, and that was it.

*Q: But you look at their political class with no real representation.*

YOUNG: Exactly. Well, now they realize that. We think they do. We'll have to see what happens as a result of this recent experience they've gone through with these riots.

*Q: When you went to the Senior Seminar, did you find yourself getting at all attached or connected to what would be called the black movement? I don't know what you want to call it, but in other words, this whole feeling in the United States.*

YOUNG: The Senior Seminar didn't bring me any closer to that. That has been in my life for a long time. Not as one to lead demonstrations and that sort of thing, but to provide my support in many other ways. That has always been there and the seminar didn't bring me any closer to that.

We were asked to write papers on leadership. I decided I would do mine on what had occurred at my church in Washington, D.C., particularly with the leadership provided by two white priests at what was basically a black Catholic church and one that was dying at that. These two priests, Father Mudd and Father Kelly, were determined that they were going to resurrect this church and bring it back to life, and they did in many ways. They established a number of different ministries in the church and these ministries all reached out to the neighboring community. This church is considered the mother church of black Catholic churches in the District of Columbia. It is located at Fifteenth Street and V and its called Saint Augustine. It was the first black Catholic church in Washington, D.C., first established on Fifteenth Street where the *Washington Post* is presently located. Anyhow, one of the things they did that was so innovative and creative was to ask themselves, what can we do to bring in younger people and to also relate more to the black parishioners of this church?

They went to Howard University and decided that they would try to arrange for a gospel mass where they would take the Catholic liturgy and leave it intact, but imprint on to that the black gospel tradition. They would have the Catholic part intact and the black Catholic tradition which appeals to a number of blacks. They went to Howard University and they found a fellow named Leon Roberts. He was a music director there and a chorus director and they hired him and said, "Would you come over to our church and establish a choir, a gospel choir?" He did. Many of the people they found initially were not members of Saint Augustine at all, but they belonged to different Baptist churches and Methodist churches and so on. Anyhow, Roberts established this choir, wrote music for the choir, and integrated his music into the liturgy, and word began to circulate that this extraordinary thing was going on at Saint Augustine Church. People began to come out to that church, not in the hundreds but in the thousands. I mean it was amazing. From a church that was headed literally, I would think, for closure to one where at this particular mass on Sunday, if you didn't get there on time you wouldn't get a seat.

We first attended this church in 1980. We were living in Chevy Chase, Maryland and we were going to a Catholic church on East-West Highway called Our Lady of Lourdes, very nice, very quiet, very staid, and very geriatric. Our daughter was preparing for her first communion and this lady came over to us one Sunday and said, "Would you like to try something different and a little more lively than this church?" We said, "Sure, why not?" She said, "Well, come with me next Sunday." She told us where to meet her and we met her at Fifteenth and V Street. We went to Saint Augustine for the first time in 1980; twenty-five years later, we're still going there. This gospel mass that I mentioned is still going on. It is a big tradition at this church. The choir that Mr. Roberts started is still going on. They just had their twenty-eighth anniversary. It was just a remarkable example of leadership, of creativity, and of imagination and how you can take a situation and put new life into it.

*Q: Did you get any feel for the interchurch dynamics within the Catholic Church? Were noses put out of joint by gospel masses and things?*

YOUNG: Oh, yes, it created quite a stir within the church itself. I mean there was a traditionalist who said, "My God there is no place in here for this. We can't have this." and on and on. It created quite a bit of dialogue, but these fellows were determined that there was a place for this and they made a place for it and they had the regular usual masses at 7:00 and 9:00 and 10:00 and they had this gospel mass at 12:30 and they continued with it. Yes, it created quite a bit of controversy and the church itself became quite controversial. They had a number of preachers, or priests I should say, over the years, some of whom were quite controversial. One of them was Reverend Stallings, who got a bit, in my view, too carried away with what he wanted to do. He imposed his charismatic style on the church and finally he left and established his own church and then was excommunicated. We had several other rebels there at the church as well. Recently, unfortunately, they were part of a scandal that has rocked the church. One of the pastors there whom we like very much was accused of committing inappropriate acts twenty-five years ago by a woman who is now a professor at a university. This particular case involved a father whom the parish liked very much. He was very dynamic and a good leader, a good priest, but once this kind of thing happened, it was over. It created some division in the church, because he had very staunch supporters and they tried their best to help him. But it was out of their hands and he was eventually asked to leave.

*Q: Well, on with the Senior Seminar.*

YOUNG: We traveled all over the country. It was just an incredible program. As I said, it gave me a lot of confidence. I felt that I was on a par with the other members of the seminar no matter where they came from or what their particular experiences were in the Service. I was getting a little bit nervous because some of my colleagues were getting really great assignments. One was going to Bonn as the DCM, one to Tel Aviv as the DCM, one to the American Institute in Taiwan as the deputy. Those were great jobs. Another was to be consul general in some Mexican post and so on. I was wondering, my God what's going to happen to me? I just let it float. I put it really, as they say, in the hands of the Lord.

I got a call, I think it was in February, from the human resources people, or as we called them, the personnel people. It was the senior assignments division and they were calling to ask if I would object to my name being put on a list for Sierra Leone and I said, "By no means. I'd be crazy to say otherwise."

*Q: You're talking about the ambassadorial list?*

YOUNG: That's right. I said, "Yes, by all means." I didn't say anything to anyone else. I just kept quiet. More time went by and then in late March, I got a call one Friday evening from the deputy assistant secretary for African affairs, Irvin Hicks. He said, "Johnny, I'm calling because the D Committee" which is the committee that selects ambassadors, "met this afternoon and they liked you for Sierra Leone. But the assistant secretary, Herman Cohen, doesn't know you, so they've tentatively selected you, but they're going to leave the choice up to Assistant Secretary Cohen." I said, "Okay." I thanked him. That very day, my mother had arrived in Washington to spend some time with us, so I called Ambassador Hank Cohen right away and mentioned to him what had happened. He said he was aware of it. I asked him if we could meet and he said yes. He said, "What about Monday?" I said, "Well, Monday wouldn't be good for me because my mother just got here and I need to get her settled." I asked, "Can we meet on Wednesday?" He said, "Sure that will be fine. No problem." April 1st, April Fool's Day, 1989, I went and met with Hank Cohen in his office. We sat and we talked and talked and talked about Africa. We talked about running a mission. We talked about a number of things and then he looked at me and said, "I think you'll do just fine. You're going to be my candidate." I thanked him very much and I told him that I would welcome his advice and counsel as I prepared for this assignment and I left and that's how I got Sierra Leone.

I stayed in touch with Hank Cohen. I remember one day we had a talk and he said, "Well, when you go out there, just take it easy. You know, it's a country of marginal interest to us. Nothing ever happens out there. If you get bored, go out to the provinces and visit with the Peace Corps volunteers, but don't ever get in the hair of the DCM. You know this is what happened to me in Senegal." I had to keep that in mind because it's very easy to turn inward when you want things to do. I thanked him very much for his advice and counsel and I also needed his advice on something else. I had met the woman who was coming out of Sierra Leone as ambassador, a woman by the name of Cynthia Perry. Cynthia Perry had tried very hard to get me to fire the DCM she was leaving behind, Gary Maybarduk. She had had some difficulty with him, but she never fired him. She kept him on.

*Q: This is Cynthia Perry who came from Houston.*

YOUNG: Texas, that's right.

*Q: I've interviewed her, but she was a political appointee.*

YOUNG: A political appointee who has done very well. She subsequently went on to another ambassadorship and then another ambassadorship, all because she was a black Republican, but a smart lady, very clever lady, and very capable. Anyhow, I didn't agree to what she wanted and I remember asking Hank Cohen before I went out, "Hank, what should I do? She's given this guy a bad mouth; she's badmouthed him all over the place. I don't know what to do." I had interviewed a number of other candidates for the DCM job. Gary Maybarduk flew back to the States to have an interview with me to basically ask if I would keep him on. I told him, "Well, I'm not sure, I'm interviewing candidates and we'll see how it turns out." I didn't want to commit at that point. I spoke to Hank, who said, "Look, you get out there and you see how things are going. Don't make the decision on the basis of rumors. You get out there and judge for yourself." I did that and it turned out very well. Maybarduk was an excellent DCM and we did very well together. Anyhow, back to Hank Cohen, who assured me, "don't worry, nothing ever happens out there, no problems whatsoever."

Q: *That's usually the kiss of death.*

YOUNG: Well, he didn't know what was going to happen. I mean, it was based on what was known at that time. I prepared. I had my confirmation hearing and after I had my hearing, my wife became ill. She wasn't feeling well. She went to the doctor and the doctor said you must be operated on immediately, I'm not even allowing you to go back home. She was in George Washington Hospital, had an emergency operation and fortunately everything turned out well. We had already made arrangements to pack up the house. I had to pack up the entire house myself, which I had done on one other occasion, but that had been on our second assignment and that was a different situation. I packed up the house, got everything sorted out, and she came out of the hospital and recuperated. We had already rented out the house and all the furniture was taken out, so when she came out of the hospital we needed a place to stay. In good Foreign Service tradition one of our colleagues, a fellow we had come to know in the Netherlands, Jim Marshall, who was our economic counselor there, said, "Oh, you can stay with me." He was a single fellow. We stayed in Jim's house while Angie recuperated.

While she was recuperating, I prepared for the swearing in and for our meeting with President Bush, Sr., who was just a wonderful guy. I mean I'll never forget that meeting. We went in to the oval office in the White House and he greeted us like we had been friends forever. "Hi Johnny. Angie, how are you doing? I understand Angie wasn't feeling well. How are you doing now, Angie?" I mean he was just as warm and gentle and knowledgeable as one could ever expect. He said, "Oh, I understand you have a daughter in school in the Netherlands." I answered yes. He said, "I know that school. Barbara laid the cornerstone for the new building." I said, "Yes, and when I was there I was partially responsible for getting a lot of the materials for that new building duty-free. That was my contribution to it." It was just wonderful. Then he said to me, "Tell me about Sierra Leone." I told him about Sierra Leone. He said, "You know, when I was ambassador to the United Nations, Barbara and I became very friendly with a woman there by the name of Shirley Bujama. Do you know her?" I said, "No, Mr. President, I don't, but I'll make it my business to find out about her and will let you know." He said, "Okay, please do. Please give her my best regards." So, when I got to Sierra Leone, I began to look for her and found her and conveyed his good wishes. I wrote him a letter and passed that on and he wrote me a letter back thanking me for doing that. I thought he was a terrific guy. I liked him very much.

*Q: Well, he was very attuned to the foreign affairs process.*

YOUNG: Yes he was, when you look at his experience. Then I had my swearing in which was the event of a lifetime. I had attended swearing in ceremonies before, but there is nothing like it when you're up on that stand yourself. It was a truly memorable moment and I must have had five hundred people in that room. You could not move in that room. I was so pleased to see that so many people had come out to bear witness to this very special moment in my life. I mean, it was great.

*Q: Did you have any problems with your confirmation hearings with the Senate?*

YOUNG: None. There was one little blip that didn't occur in the hearing process, but occurred when I went up to the office of the inspector general just to number one, pay my respects, and number two, to get from them the inspection questionnaires which I have always found to be a useful tool to sort of take measure of how a post is doing. I wanted to take a set of those with me and of course the IG's office was very proud that one of theirs, I had been in that office, had sort of made it big. At the time the inspector general was Sherman Funk. He was quite a character, but I liked him a lot. I must say I liked him, a man of integrity and courage. He said, "Thank you, Johnny, for coming. We really appreciate it. We're really proud of you." Then he said, "The only thing that showed up was a request from the Senate Foreign Relations Committee wanting to know if there was ever any kind of problem surrounding you." Then he reached down and pulled out of his file. He said, "This was the only thing we had," pointing to an allegation that when I was admin counselor in The Hague I had attempted to get my wife a job there. I said "That is completely untrue." He calmed me down right away and said, "We know it is untrue. We investigated it and found that it was without foundation and we passed that on to the Senate. That was the only thing that came up, but it just shows you that you never know what is out there."

*Q: Did you get any feel for what might have instigated this?*

YOUNG: Oh, I think I know how it occurred and what happened. I never had proof of that and he would not reveal who had made the allegation.

Q: *Was there sort of malice behind it?*

YOUNG: I think what had happened was a position had opened in the Netherlands for a family member and the committee had made its decision. But in the end I recommended for the position a family member who had been at post longer. I felt that the one who had been at post longer deserved an opportunity before one who had just come in yesterday. So I think it was the one who had come in more recently who was upset and drummed up those charges. I think that's what happened.

Q: *What had you learned about Sierra Leone at the time? We're talking about 1989. What was the situation there politically, economically, and what were you getting into?*

YOUNG: Frankly, it was a country that had had so-called multiparty elections, but they were not. They were basically one-party elections. They had some problems in their human rights record, particularly the continued imprisonment of people who had been arrested during the time of Siaka Stevens. Economically the country was in shambles. Corruption was a major, major problem. The military was okay, lacking in equipment and what have you, but not bad. Diamonds ruled; diamonds were the name of the game and that was at the center of so much of the corruption. A country very rich in potential.

At the time there was a major American company there mining something called rutile, which I had never heard of before I got involved. Rutile is a titanium ore. It is dug out of clay, out of earth that looks like clay, and then it is put in enormous washing machines. They look like huge dryers. The machines that dig this clay up and dump it on to trucks and then take it to these washers, these digging wheels, must be about three or four stories tall. They are huge and if you could see the devastation that they do to the area where this stuff is done, it's a horror story, that's all I can say. But it was a very successful operation. Sierra Leone was one of the major producers of rutile in the world at that time. This earth is dug up, put on trucks. The trucks take it to these huge washers. It is washed in water and cleansed. Because of centrifugal force in these washers that also become like spin dryers, the rutile is separated from the sand and the dirt. Then the rutile is put into dryers where it is dried and it becomes a white powder. That white powder is used in a couple of ways. One is in the manufacture of paint, white paint of all things. It is used to make the titanium skins of airplanes. It was a big operation at the time. In 1989, the operation in Sierra Leone was valued at $500 million. That was a huge investment. Originally this plant was put in by Bethlehem Steel. Then I think somebody else bought it and then somebody else bought it and it eventually became Sierra Rutile. It was a consortium of American, Canadian, and I think Australian companies. Sierra Leone was a country with great potential, great possibilities. It was stable politically. It had many ethnic groups and there were some tensions there, but basically when I got there it was a stable country.

Q: *Surrounded by what countries?*

YOUNG: By Liberia, the Ivory Coast, Togo, and Guinea.

Q: *At the time, were there any border problems with those countries?*

YOUNG: Once in a while there would be something, but nothing of great import. The borders that were artificially drawn following the end of the colonial period remained respected and basically intact. At my hearing we thought that one of my colleagues would get more questions than I would, but then I got a number of questions basically on human rights and what I would do in terms of trying to encourage democratization and those kinds of things.

Q: *Well, tell me, when you go to a hearing, you're treading on somewhat difficult things because you can say something that can blow you out of a job if the country to which you are going is too critical.*

YOUNG: I had that later on and I'll tell you about that when we get to it.

Q: *Did you feel there was any problem of answering?*

YOUNG: No, none whatsoever. I had no problem. I don't recall that Sierra Leone had an observer at that point, but I think one of their newspapers was certainly there observing and they report every word you say in these things. It gives the people in the country you're going to a sense of who you are and what you're going to stand for. You can use that to your advantage. I deliberately did that at another post.

# FIRST AMBASSADORSHIP: SIERRA LEONE

*Q: You got out there when?*

YOUNG: We arrived in November of 1989.

*Q: Did you have children with you?*

YOUNG: My daughter was in her last year of high school and that was a major problem to deal with. She had previously been in high school in The Hague and then she'd been in high school in the States for the year. We were only in the States a year. We were fortunate to find a family in The Hague, a family we had known when we were there that agreed to house her and allow her to attend the American School of The Hague to finish her last year, which was good because she could then reconnect with some of her friends. Our son was already in university at that point, at Brown University.

So we arrived, my wife and I, the day before Thanksgiving 1989 and I remember the DCM invited us to his home for Thanksgiving. We, of course, were met by the Sierra Leone protocol people, who treated us very nicely. The arrival was a bit scary because just before we arrived there had been a helicopter crash. Helicopters were used to carry people from the airport across the channel to the main city of Freetown. The ferry service had basically broken down and was in a state of disrepair. When we were whisked off the plane and into these helicopters, I thought oh God, will we ever see the light of day again? It worked out nicely and we didn't have any problems with the helicopter.

Sierra Leone has a very special place in my heart and in my history. I mentioned earlier that I was born in Savannah, Georgia. The woman who was my mother and my biological father and all of his siblings were not born in Savannah, Georgia. They were born in a place called Lady's Island, South Carolina. Then from Lady's Island the family migrated to Buford and then from Buford to Savannah. Now, Lady's Island and Buford are part of what are called the Sea Islands off South Carolina and Georgia, and there are some in Florida as well. The interesting thing about these islands, the ones in South Carolina in particular, is that they were populated by slaves from Sierra Leone. The slaves were sent there to grow rice when cotton was no longer viable. The language they spoke was Gullah in the U.S., and if you look at Mende or at Creole, the language spoken as sort of the lingua franca of Sierra Leone, you will see they are identical. There is a definite link between those two. And, of course, rice culture is also another link between those places.

I mention that as a bit of background. When I got to Sierra Leone and I had my presentation of credentials, I called the president's office and asked if I could bring my wife to the presentation of credentials. He said, "We normally don't do that. This is for the ambassador only, but in your case I'll make an exception." So, my wife was there with me. It was quite an elaborate ceremony where the president and all of the ministers were present. I walked in and my wife took a seat and then I went through all of the pageantry of presenting the papers to him and he received them and made a little speech and then I made a little speech. As I was walking out I heard one minister say, "Welcome home brother." It was very nice and it added to the moment. I'll never forget it. That's how we got started in Sierra Leone.

*Q: Well, let's talk a little about your impressions. What was Freetown like?*

YOUNG: When we arrived by helicopter, we couldn't see very much of Freetown simply because it was by helicopter and it was at night. We couldn't see anything and I wondered what it looked like. I had read wonderful descriptions of what it looks like from the sea, how pretty it is and what a magical looking place it is until you get up close and you see how run down it is. We were taken to the residence. We got out of the car and I remember we looked around and we thought, oh, what a nice house. This is not so bad. The residence was located in a spectacular location. I couldn't even tell at that point how spectacular it was and I had to wait until the next morning to get a real sense of what it was like. I was told next door was an apartment building that belonged to the embassy. It had, I think, about six apartments in it, a nice looking building. The grounds were very nice.

Now, before I had gone out to post I had learned that my predecessor, Ambassador Perry, on her own initiative had made a number of improvements to the residence. She knocked out the walls of a bedroom to make the kitchen larger, more appropriate in size for what was needed for a residence. She took another room and knocked a wall out and made a combination, a sort of little family room off of the bedroom. She had built little waterfalls and all kinds of things in the garden. It was all very nice. Mind you, the bureau of foreign buildings was quite upset with her because none of this was done with their approval and they never had the funds for it. She just did it. They were quite annoyed. I think the inspectors even tried to get her to pay back the funds that she expended in undertaking these projects, but she'd have none of it and she never paid anything back. I was very grateful and it was in good shape by the time I got there. I could only think, my God, if I had tried that they would have put me in jail, not only in the jail, but under the jail. I was truly grateful for all of the nice little changes that she had made.

The next morning when we got up, I could see that we were on top of this hill with a magnificent panoramic view of the Atlantic Ocean. It was just a splendid setup. The house was nice. The garden was built up along the side of this hill in kind of a terraced style. Nice rooms, just a nice residence. Then as I drove around town, I could see other nice houses. It was very tropical, very lush. You could see though that in the government buildings there wasn't much care, and that they needed a lot of attention. Things were falling down and breaking down. You could see all of the old mildew and where moss had eaten things up and that sort of thing. The glory days had long passed, but yet you could see the potential was there if only they had taken care of some of these buildings. The embassy itself was located in a large office building; well, it was large at that time. We owned the entire building. I think it had about four floors if I'm not mistaken. It was right on the corner of a very historic point in town.

At that point there was a roundabout, and in the middle of this roundabout was this absolutely enormous cotton tree. I mean, absolutely huge. Many things were centered around this cotton tree. It was like a center with spokes from this tree leading to the courthouse and the ministry of this and that, and what have you. It was quite nice. The impression in all of this lush vegetation and these lovely trees and flowers was of buildings that had seen much better days but were really deteriorated and falling down.

I began my series of calls on various ministries and ministers and found that to be very interesting and worthwhile and discovered a cadre of very talented people. Sierra Leoneans were really quite smart.

*Q: Where had they gone to get their education? Had many of them gotten their education in England?*

YOUNG: Remember that at one time Sierra Leone was the key location. There were two prominent universities in English-speaking Africa; one on the east coast in Uganda, Makerere University, and the other was in Sierra Leone at Fourah Bay College. These two schools were very important in training the first generation of leaders following the end of the colonial period at the beginning of the 1960s. They would train their own at Fourah and then from Fourah they would then go to Manchester or University of London or Cambridge or Oxford for graduate degrees. In many ways it was very similar to what we had in the United States in terms of the training of blacks up until the time when mainstream universities were fully open to black candidates. Blacks would train initially at historically black colleges, let's say in the South, and then from there they would go to the University of Chicago or Harvard or Wisconsin to get graduate degrees. It was a similar situation in Sierra Leone. Fourah College played a very historic role.

*Q: Was Sierra Leone's relationship with England somewhat analogous to the relationship that we had with Liberia?*

YOUNG: No, not quite. There are some similarities. What happened was, following the international ban on slavery, a place was needed basically for people to be sent when they were picked up on the seas and freed.

*Q: They were very active in picking up slaves and taking them back to Africa.*

YOUNG: Right, so they took them to Freetown. They had this land that they governed and ran in Sierra Leone. These people were from Portuguese-speaking places, French-speaking places. In Freetown you had all of these different mixtures, so they created a new language of their own to understand each other and to communicate. They created Creole, which is a mixture of English, Yoruba, Portuguese, and French. It is a mixture of all of those put together, and Sierra Leone is the only place where you have it. That's how that came about. The place was "free town;" that's how they got the name Freetown.

*Q: Let's talk about what was on your plate when you got there.*

YOUNG: At the top of the list, democratization, economic reform, and political reform. This is what we wanted to push the government to do, to reform itself to become more democratic.

Now, at that time the Berlin Wall had just fallen. October of 1989, it had just fallen. The full impact of that wasn't appreciated at that point. We knew that the ramifications were going to be felt around the world, but we didn't know the extent. It was really in 1990 with the end of the Soviet Union that there was a tremendous impact on Africa, because we completely changed our interest in the continent after that. Russia changed its interest in the continent. The competition between the United States and the Soviet Union subsided and we basically cut the knot and put Africa adrift. I thought that was a major, major mistake. Sierra Leone didn't have money, it didn't have food, it didn't have the means for development and we weren't interested. At that point, 1989 to 1990, the United States decided it was a whole new paradigm, a new world, new reality, and we were going to only focus on democratic countries now. So, I asked the question, how were these countries to become democratic overnight? They had no history of democracy per se.

*Q: Well, supposedly Sierra Leone had been independent for thirty or forty years?*

YOUNG: Since 1961.

*Q: So, in a way, did you feel that it was a bit presumptuous for us to go and say we want you to be a democracy.*

YOUNG: True, but that's what we were saying at that point, particularly after the dissolution of the former Soviet Union, because that was the end of the bipolar competition. It wasn't a question of well, this African country is on our side and that one's on our side, and what have you. It was just a whole new ballgame. It really made things worse for Africa. I don't think it made things better for Africa. Now, we began to talk about focus countries and all kinds of things like that. One of the focus countries was Zimbabwe.

*Q: At this point, we're talking about Zimbabwe under Mugabe, which is an absolute disaster.*

YOUNG: Well, of course it's a disaster. But I'm just saying, we thought Zimbabwe was going to be a model that we could show the rest of Africa at the time, and it didn't work out that way at all. Some of the other ones that we had picked out as models didn't quite work either. Zaire and some others didn't work out as well. I arrived in Freetown in November of 1989. Most of November was taken up with introductions, in learning the lay of the land, the issues, and that sort of thing.

Christmas Eve 1989, we got a report that there was an incursion carried out by Charles Taylor into neighboring Liberia, up by the border with the Ivory Coast. I got an instruction to go to the president, who was Joseph Momoh at the time, and to elicit his support in weighing in with President Doe of Liberia to bring an end to this as quickly as possible. I went to the palace; there was nobody at the palace. No one knew where Momoh was. No one knew where any minister was. It was Christmas and all of the ministers had gone to their villages. Everybody had gone to their villages for the holiday. There was nothing I could do until after Christmas. I think it was the day after Christmas that I got my meeting with the president and he was a very helpful man. He said, "Well, I will do my best. I will certainly encourage Doe to get this sorted out quickly. If not, this will be trouble for him, it could be trouble for the region. I know that boy," that is what he called Charles Taylor, "I know that boy Taylor. He came here to Sierra Leone. He tried to launch his coup from our country, but I denied him that privilege. We put him in jail." Taylor had come from the States where he had been in jail for a while, then he got out of jail and he floated around and went to different places. Momoh said, "So, obviously he got the approval of the Ivorians to launch this incursion to begin his coup from the Ivory Coast," which is what he did. I did my job and we left it and concerned ourselves with things Sierra Leonean, as we watched the war. Taylor made inroads into Liberia by taking town after town. As he did so, reports of atrocities and that sort of thing would surface and he moved closer and closer. We didn't bother too much about Liberia. But we watched very carefully as events unfolded there.

Ambassador Jim Bishop was in Liberia at the time and was preparing to conclude his work there and then Peter de Vos was to replace him as ambassador. I don't remember exactly the timing, but it was sometime before the summer of 1990 that Peter de Vos was nominated and approved for Liberia. Bishop came out and Pete de Vos came through Sierra Leone and was getting ready to go to Liberia via a very small, chartered plane. That was the only way you could get in and out at that point because the war had grown in such intensity that there were no longer commercial flights to or from Liberia.

I'll never forget this particular incident. Pete de Vos was all ready to go. He had spent a few days with us. We were sending cables back and forth. We were observing this situation that was growing in intensity as the fighting grew closer and closer to the capital city. We then began to talk about possible evacuations and things like that, but no evacuation had been made at that point. Pete was all set to go. We rented the plane for him to go to Monrovia. We took him out with an embassy car. Just before he got on the plane we got a telegram that said, "You cannot go to Liberia until you have been sworn into office." We thought, "My God how are we going to do this?" We needed to get him there as quickly as possible.

We got him on the radio by getting the driver on the radio and we put all of our heads together and I said, "Well, we're going to have to do this swearing in via two-way radio." We spoke to Pete and we said, "Do you have a Bible with you?" He said, "I don't travel with a Bible." We said, "Do you have anything that could substitute for a bible?" He said, "Well, I have my address book." We said, "Take that address book out and put your hand on the address book, raise your right hand." I think he got the pilot on the plane to hold the address book for him and he put his hand on the address book and then to the consular officer, Allen Latimer, I said, "Allen, here's the oath you've got to get him to repeat it over the phone and then we can sign it and certify it and send it out to him and he can sign it and he'll have his copy in the works," and that's how we did it. It was a riot. An officer in a holding pattern in Sierra Leone at the time, Charles Gurney, wrote a cable on this that became a classic, describing how Pete de Vos was out in the middle of this field. There was a man passing with goats and looking at him with his hand on this address book and his other hand in the air, you know, listening to the radio saying, "I, Peter de Vos, do solemnly swear" and so on. It turned out well and he went on to Liberia.

Now, the intensity of the fighting just continued to accelerate. The government forces appeared to be losing and Charles Taylor's forces made headway and they headed straight for the capital city. They were held off and didn't quite make it to the presidential palace. Now, we're up to about May of 1990. I was going on R&R (Rest & Recuperation travel). I wanted that R&R very badly for several reasons. My daughter was graduating, she was going to her prom, and we needed a break as well. We needed also to get her situated in the States for university and things like that. This was a very important time for us.

We arrived in The Hague, where we had made arrangements for a very nice house that came with a car. It was a house-sitting arrangement that was just the most perfect one I have ever run into and it came with everything that you could possibly ask for. Since we had lived in The Hague, we had lots of friends there and the night we arrived. We were with our friends and had wonderful food and wine and caviar in the works. It was a night made in heaven. We couldn't have asked for better. Good conversation, good jokes, it was just wonderful. Lovely home, car, a happy daughter, what more could you ask for? So, my wife and I arrived home at about 2:00 in the morning and the phone rang, it was Deputy Assistant Secretary Irvin Hicks. He said, "Johnny, I'm calling because the situation in Liberia is looking pretty bad. It looks like we may have to evacuate and if we do we're thinking of doing it through Sierra Leone although Sierra Leone has very little in the way of infrastructure to support this kind of thing. I know why you went to The Hague and we know why you're there and we understand that. We're not asking you to leave now. But if the situation gets much worse, we may have to ask you to return." I thanked him very much and went to bed.

The next night we went somewhere else and had another one of those great nights in The Hague, and when we returned home, the phone rang at 2:00

in the morning and it was Irv Hicks once more and he said, "Johnny, I'm sorry, but you've got to get back to post. The situation is just getting too bad and we have already sent military people to Sierra Leone and you've got to get back there and you've got to keep them under control." I was upset because my wife's birthday was on June 3 and on her birthday I returned to Sierra Leone. As our plane hit the ground and as it was taxiing in I could see part of our problem already. The military people had already strung out all of their tents and equipment at the airport and that sort of thing, but that was not what we wanted. We wanted a less visible footprint than that. That was the first thing I had to do. We got it sorted out in very quick order.

Q: *How did you sort it out?*

YOUNG: By speaking to the head person there and also to their leader in Europe in EUCOM (U.S. European Command).

Q: *What kind of troops were these?*

YOUNG: These were Marines.

Q: *Were they off one of our carriers?*

YOUNG: That came later on. These were flown in. So in June the decision was made that we would evacuate Liberia through Sierra Leone. We had tried two evacuations, one out of the Ivory Coast with several planes, but we found that the government of the Ivory Coast was very unhelpful.

Q: *At the time, you mentioned that Sierra Leone had not helped Taylor, but the Ivory Coast did. The Ivory Coast had such close ties with the French. Did you get the impression that the French were meddling?*

YOUNG: Not initially, we didn't. We learned later on that Charles Taylor had business relationships with French President Mitterrand's son, but that didn't come until later. We decided to evacuate. As I said, I returned. I went to the president and asked for permission for our planes to land and to evacuate people through Sierra Leone and he said, "You have it, do whatever you have to do." Over the next months, we evacuated 2,400 people of forty different nationalities in one of the longest naval evacuations at the time.

I want to highlight a particular incident that occurred. When a decision was made to evacuate, the Defense Department said that they were going to come in with ships behind our embassy in Liberia. They would just come right in onto the shore behind the embassy and take people out that way. Ambassador de Vos said, "You can't do that." It was impossible because the government had put these huge boulders all along the beach as a breakwater. They had done so years before any fighting, so it wasn't an immediate measure that was taken. Defense said no, we have it all under control, we'll take care of it. Ambassador de Vos said again, "No, you can't do it." They had this back and forth and de Vos finally told them, "Okay, if you come in that way, the moment you set foot on Liberian soil I relinquish my responsibility as ambassador and turn the responsibility for the Americans and for this mission over to you." That got their attention and they backed off and thought about a different approach. That different approach entailed the use of helicopters.

They decided that they could use the basketball court of the embassy compound as a helicopter pad. They could position the helicopters in Sierra Leone, Huey 53s, and then send them over and take out the people that way. The big question was how do you secure helicopters in the middle of a war zone, because there was a war going on all around the city in Monrovia. So we got the word out very clearly that we were going to evacuate by helicopter and that the helicopters would be carrying sharpshooters, and that if anyone fired on these helicopters the fire would be returned with the intent to kill. This obviously worked because in all of those flights we didn't lose a single person, because not one of those helicopters was fired on. It worked very well. From the ambassador's residence I could watch the helicopters as they came in, and I saw them land and take off. People would come in. They would be discharged and then sent on commercial flights to wherever they were going. I think we evacuated four hundred Lebanese alone. It is amazing when you have this kind of problem, you find people from everywhere. We even had one Iraqi. Keep in mind this was 1990, when Saddam was a big problem, so we didn't know what to do with this Iraqi. In the end, we did the right thing. We evacuated him, brought him to Sierra Leone and put him on a plane, and he went on his own, which I think was the right thing to do.

*Q: This must have been essentially an administrative problem for you, making sure that the right people got on the right planes and all. How did you do that?*

YOUNG: We put everybody in the mission to work. We had a little bit of TDY (temporary duty) help; the consular people had sent in some additional people as well. We managed. We worked it out with the local airlines. In some cases they had chartered flights. For example, with the Lebanese they took a whole planeload out.

Before the evacuation, and shortly after Pete de Vos arrived in Liberia, the first peace talks to ever take place in trying to resolve the Liberian problem occurred at the American embassy in Freetown. We included people from the Charles Taylor faction and people from civil society, basically from the churches and the chamber of commerce and Liberian government officials as well. Those talks didn't succeed, because Taylor really didn't empower his people to decide anything. Despite what he was saying at the time, that he really didn't want to govern Liberia, Taylor didn't empower his people to do anything; so the talks didn't go anywhere in the end.

*Q: What were you getting about Charles Taylor and his crew, what were your impressions, and what were you hearing about them?*

YOUNG: We weren't getting lots of information from Charles Taylor, because he was making his push from up by the Ivorian border and moving closer and closer to the capital city. What he had said initially about not wanting to assume power was not credible, because it was clear that his goal was to take over the presidency. His troops were very efficient. We were beginning to get reports of atrocities in villages. It was beginning to surface that he was ruthless, that he would take over villages and also exploit them economically for whatever resources could be found in the villages that his troops subdued, and he just continued his press onto the capital city.

In Freetown we continued to monitor the situation and to help in whatever way we could. The evacuation of Liberia in 1990 was quite an exercise for us, but in the meantime we continued to have a normal bilateral relationship with the government of Sierra Leone. The government was trying to reform itself. We were pressing them on reforming the economy and in terms of making it possible to have multiparty elections at some point. We were pressing them on human rights as well, although the human rights problems really stemmed from actions that had been taken by the previous president, Siaka Stevens. President Momoh was not accused of any human rights abuses, but he never released from prison those persons who had been incarcerated by Siaka Stevens. The press was relatively free and we didn't have many problems in terms of the press. The biggest problem was really the one of corruption. The country was deteriorating rapidly. It had no benefit from its resources. The money coming in from the diamonds and from other resources was basically being squandered by the various people who could get their hands on the funds. As I said, our relationship was normal, the government was helpful, and it continued to plod along. They would come to us and plead for food assistance. I would go to our government and ask for aid. We turned our backs on Sierra Leone at that point. We knew the situation was bad. Infrastructure was bad, economically it was bad, politically a one-party state, but still stable, not too many problems in terms of human rights; but we turned our backs on it. We said we didn't want to help. We pulled out the AID mission before I arrived there. And we didn't want anything to do with it. We said, well, it's a new world now. The Berlin Wall has fallen, the Cold War is over, the former Soviet Union has disappeared and we have a new paradigm now and we're only going to help a certain number of countries that are clearly democratic.

*Q: What about saying okay, we got Liberia and we have a responsibility, but you Brits have got Sierra Leone, that's your problem? Was there any of that attitude?*

YOUNG: The British were very helpful and they remained considerably more loyal to Sierra Leone than we did. I mean, it was a former British colony, so I guess there was a greater natural inclination for them to do that. They didn't abandon the country, they continued to help, and they were very concerned. I think they would have done more if we had indicated that we were willing to do more.

Now, I must add something that will indicate the extent to which the government of Sierra Leone was helpful to us. Following Iraq's invasion of Kuwait, we put out the word to get cooperation from partners all over the world to form a coalition. Our ambassadors all over the world went to their host governments and attempted to get them to sign on to this coalition. I went to the government of Sierra Leone and I explained to President Momoh what we wanted to do. I told him it would be good if Sierra Leone could be seen as contributing to this effort and he said, "Okay, I'll see what I can do." He put together a twenty-six-man medical team and sent them to Iraq as part of the coalition effort. Sierra Leone and two other black African countries, Senegal and Niger, were the only sub-Saharan countries to do anything whatsoever for the coalition. No one else in all of Africa lifted a finger to do anything. They gave some lip service and that was about it. Now, we know a twenty-six-person team is not enormous, but it was significant symbolically and it was very important and it wasn't forgotten. That is indicative of the kind of support that we got from that government, but despite that we kept our distance from helping Sierra Leone, because there were other places that were sexier and more attractive at that time. This was a small country and we figured oh, well, no big deal to us. War had not broken out in Sierra Leone yet. The war was going on next door in Liberia, so we never thought in terms of, well, let's try to help this country and maybe we can make it stronger so that this situation would not spill over from Liberia. We weren't thinking in that way at all. We were just thinking one country at a time.

*Q: Was anybody explicitly spelling this out for you back in Washington?*

YOUNG: They just weren't interested.

*Q: It was more a matter of indifference as opposed to somebody saying we've got priorities and you're not one of them.*

YOUNG: That was the story. I mean that was it plain and simple: it's a new ball game now and Sierra Leone doesn't figure into our priorities. This despite what was going on next door, but not in Sierra Leone itself, at the time.

*Q: Did you get any feel about the attitude not only of the Africa Bureau but also of the NSC and the White House towards sub-Saharan Africa at the time?*

YOUNG: Well, I was after aid. I was after plain and simple food; that was what I wanted for that country. That was what they needed at that time. They needed military assistance as well, because their military was in pretty bad shape although we continued with our military assistance program, which paid off very handsomely later on. We continued to provide some assistance there because we thought that the military in Sierra Leone was fairly good relative to what else was in the region. They were disciplined and well-trained, not well-equipped, but as good as could be expected under the circumstances. As I said, I wanted food. They were starving and couldn't get any help from AID or from the State Department. At one point I went into the Department of Agriculture and sought out a fellow I had met in The Hague. He was the Ag attaché in The Hague, Bud Anderson, a wonderful man. He had then become the administrator for the Food and Agricultural Service, and I went to him and said, "Can you help me? Can we get a shipment of PL480 rice or grain of some kind, food, so that we can have it delivered to Sierra Leone, monetize it and then put the money in development projects?" He said, "I'll see what I can do." In the end, he followed through and I think we had a shipment of about five or six million dollars worth of rice that staved off the hunger and desperation for a while, but things just continued to get worse. That was the last time that the U.S. government provided food of any kind during my time there.

I'd like to make a couple of other points about the war. At one point, when the situation was getting so bad and we feared for the lives of American citizens in Liberia, we brought in the Marine Amphibious Ready Group (MARG). I think it had about six ships. They were anchored off Sierra Leone, close to Liberia, with five thousand Marines on board, so that if need be they could go in and evacuate. That wasn't necessary, because the evacuation was carried out by helicopter in the end, but that group remained off the coast of Sierra Leone and Liberia for months until it was finally directed elsewhere. I could only think that if we had employed that group to go in and put an end to the fighting, which they could have done easily, we would have saved Liberia. We would have saved the world so much suffering, not only in Liberia, but in Sierra Leone as well. There was no will whatsoever to do that; just the thought of it was anathema to the folks in Washington, who didn't want to hear anything about any kind of American intervention. This was an internal matter in Liberia and, by God, the Liberians were going to sort it out and we were not going to get involved.

*Q: Doe and the way he came in, with the slaughter of the cabinet and all that, had left such a bad taste in peoples' mouths. The name of Doe was sort of anathema anyway; this was a problem because whatever we did would have been essentially in support of Doe.*

YOUNG: It would have been, but there are various types of devils. When you look back on Charles Taylor versus what Doe did, it is like night and day. I never thought that I would live to say that, but that is an absolute fact. As horrible as Doe was, and despite the many bad things he did, his deeds were not at all comparable to the atrocities and the evils committed by Charles Taylor. Anyhow, I wanted to make that point about the Marine Amphibious Ready Group being there, being prepared and having all of those resources available; but there was absolutely no will whatsoever to introduce that force into Liberia to end the problem there.

*Q: Could they do any R&Rs in Sierra Leone?*

YOUNG: They could have, but no. They did serve as a supply center. Supplies, for example, for the military who were stationed in Sierra Leone would be sent from Europe to the MARG and then from the MARG to Sierra Leone, particularly mail and food and things like that. Because we had all of these helicopters based in Freetown and the men who took care of them had to be fed and given their mail and so on. We had military people and we had our embassy in Monrovia that also received supplies and other equipment that way as well.

I remember the embassy in Monrovia needed a new generator. The generator was purchased and flown to the MARG, then the helicopter was supposed to pick it up and fly it from the MARG to Monrovia. The helicopter picked up this 15,000 pound generator, I mean a real behemoth, and lifted it up, up, up and then the helicopter tilted slightly to the side, a little bit more to the side and dropped the generator, which sank to the bottom of the sea. It was quite a loss, but unfortunately these things do happen. The pilot was subsequently court-martialed, which is what the military do in situations like that.

So, we had the evacuation where we took out 2,400 people of over forty different nationalities. They were taken out by what I think are called Huey 53s, those big helicopters. Those helicopters would land at a facility near a big hotel in Freetown, disgorge their passengers, and then the passengers would be taken to buses and what have you. Then they had to go over the channel to get their planes to leave Sierra Leone. One of the funny things that occurred was among the children who lived near this helipad. Across the street from the helipad there was a fence and these kids would sit on this fence and as the helicopter passed overhead, the downdraft was so powerful it would blow them all over. It would knock them all off the fence. They found this the greatest game. They would just sit on this fence and wait for the helicopters to pass over and then they would all get rolled over, just like ducks. It was really cute. They would just wait and wait there. They thought that was just the funniest game. I thought that was cute, too. It is one of those images I think I will always remember.

In 1991, about March, things had quieted down; the big part of the evacuation was over. The group that had come in to do the evacuation left Sierra Leone and we had smaller commercial planes to go back and forth at that point. The airport in Liberia was not open, but there were small aircraft that would go in and take people out. Once in a while I'd get a call from Ambassador de Vos: "Johnny, you've got to help me get this man out." It was often somebody in the government who was considered a destabilizing person to have around, so we would get him out and get him to Europe or the States or whatever the case may be. We had several cases like that.

I'll never forget one of them. Pete called and said, "Oh, you've got to help me get this guy out," and we got him out and he was one of the worst killers going. If he had stayed there he would have been a really destabilizing force, so we got him out. I remember looking at him and saying to myself, "My God, he really doesn't look like a killer. He looks just as normal as anybody else."

Gary Maybarduk was the DCM in Freetown at that time; it was 1990. We had worked so hard on Liberia. It was almost to the detriment of our bilateral relationship. There was so little that we could do with it in terms of any kind of support from Washington; we just did the best we could. We had our self-help projects and things like that. We tried to give some support to civil society—projects that would encourage democracy, the press, and little community groups to help themselves with various little projects to improve health and sanitation and water. That was very useful. We had a very active Peace Corps program, and that worked very nicely. Our efforts really were on Liberia, and my deputy and I looked at each other one morning and said wow, it is quiet at last. We were feeling very good. Then we got a report in, I think in March of 1991, that rebels had crossed over into Sierra Leone from Liberia. Initially we said oh my God, but we didn't think that it would really get worse. We thought that the government forces would be able to put it down and that would be the end of it. Well, that wasn't the end of it, because the government forces were so badly equipped. Although they were not too badly trained, they just didn't have equipment. The rebels were much better equipped, very disciplined and undisciplined both, and they began to make inroads into Sierra Leone.

*Q: Were these Charles Taylor types?*

YOUNG: Definitely. I left out a key development that occurred prior to this point, and I'd like to go back to that. The Economic Community of West African States (ECOWAS) became involved in trying to bring about peace in Liberia and trying to bring an end to the problem there. They had put together a peace force, stationed in Sierra Leone, and it agreed to go into Liberia and try to bring about peace. They would try to do it militarily. These forces were made up of Ghanaians and Nigerians, and I don't recall some of the other groups from Africa, but they were headed by a Nigerian and subsequently a Ghanaian. It was basically between the Nigerians and the Ghanaians as to who headed up this group and they went in. From Sierra Leone they went in and stopped Charles Taylor's forces from advancing further into Monrovia. Taylor was near the presidential palace, almost had the prize in his hands when this ECOWAS peace force went in and stopped him. He was furious, absolutely furious. He made it known that he resented President Momoh's allowing these forces to come into Liberia and to basically stop him. He said that he was going to overthrow the government of Sierra Leone and he was going to get back at them. He made that public; it was clear at that time. Anyhow, ECOWAS went in and kept him from assuming power. That should be kept in mind because later on, his forces did exactly what he said he wanted them to do at that point.

Anyhow these rebels crossed over from Liberia and entered Sierra Leone. They began to take over points held by the Sierra Leone military. The fighting went on and increased as the months went by. The military officers who were trying to stave off the rebels complained to the government that they didn't have supplies, they didn't have medicines or food and on and on, and the government ignored them. I wouldn't say the government ignored them completely, but it didn't respond sufficiently to their pleas for assistance, which is key. Anyhow, we monitored the situation. We asked Washington to help this government, but the help was not forthcoming. The Sierra Leone forces struggled as best they could to deal with this problem. It was like a festering sore that was sort of stanched, but would just open up from time to time. That went on for some months.

Then, at the end of the quick Gulf War, two things happened that gave Sierra Leone recognition for what it had done in becoming a part of the coalition. First, we got word from the military that they had something like sixty forty-foot containers of meals ready to eat, or MREs. I said I would take them and this would be a nice way to say thank you to this little country that helped us during the Gulf War. So they shipped the sixty containers to Sierra Leone. We arranged to have those MREs distributed to churches and it was a big success. That was the number one thank you. Number two occurred in March of 1992. We got word that the chairman of the Joint Chiefs of Staff, General Colin Powell, wanted to visit the three African countries that had contributed to the coalition effort and thank them personally for their support. This was going to be his first trip ever to Africa. Those countries were Senegal, Niger, and Sierra Leone. He was also going to make a stop in Nigeria to encourage the government there to reform itself and to change its ways. He went first to Senegal. You may not recall, but Senegal lost an entire planeload of its soldiers during the Gulf effort. One of their planes went down with their soldiers and they lost everyone. I think it was ninety some soldiers. It was quite a tragedy. Anyhow he went to Senegal, had a good visit there, and then he came to Sierra Leone, where he was welcomed like the king of England. The Sierra Leoneans were just absolutely ecstatic that he came. He had a terrific visit. The government loved him, the people loved him. He liked the people and the country. We showed him some things that he wasn't aware of. One was an island where slaves were kept after they were captured and before they were shipped to the New World. That New World in terms of Sierra Leone meant they were shipped basically to the United States or to Cuba or to the United States via Cuba. In fact, it was from this island that the ship The Amistad left.

*Q: Oh, yes, the famous mutiny and takeover.*

YOUNG: That's right. A Sierra Leonean by the name of Sengbe Pieh led the mutiny on the Amistad. That was when it left Cuba for the United States and, if you recall, John Adams came out of retirement and argued their case. It was one of the first civil rights cases before the Supreme Court, and he won. The mutineers were set free and it really was a great moment, I think, in American history. Anyhow, we showed General Powell that island. We showed him other things and he was prepared to move on to the next phase of his trip when there was a report of an attempted coup in Niger. He canceled the Niger trip and stayed with us an extra two days. We just had a wonderful time with him.

One of the things that we did was arrange for a dinner, just a very private dinner at the residence. We had Denny Bray and Art Lewis, who had been the American ambassador to Sierra Leone prior to Cynthia Perry. He also happened to be the first cousin of Colin Powell. So it was a very nice evening. We wanted to do a Jamaican meal for him because he has Jamaican ancestry. We found all of the ingredients and we wanted to prepare this one Jamaican specialty called salt fish and ackee. We got the salt fish and we found an ackee tree. Now, this ackee tree is very interesting. It produces a fruit that looks like an opened avocado inside. We had a Jamaican friend there who knew how to make this dish and we asked her to make it for us. She said yes, I'll do it, but you have to get the ackee. She told us where this tree was and we went there. Now, you have to allow this ackee tree to open by itself naturally, you can't force it open. If you force it open and eat it, you die instantly. It's a deadly poison. The Sierra Leoneans don't touch it at all. They don't bother with it one way or the other. While I was observing, a fellow was collecting these ackees that had opened up naturally and had fallen to the ground. This little Sierra Leonean man came over. In Creole he asked what we were doing with this fruit from this tree. Our fellow said, "We're going to cook them." The little man said, "If you cook them tonight you'll have some dead people later on this evening, because we know this tree as being just a deadly poison." But it is not poisonous if you eat it the proper way, allowing it to open naturally and then scooping the fruit out. It looks like scrambled eggs when it's cooked. At dinner, we had ackee and salt fish, and rice with peas and jerk chicken, and just a wonderful evening of relaxation and good conversation. It was really very, very special. And no one died.

*Q: If I had heard the story I think I would have thought twice about serving it.*

YOUNG: Yes, I know, but that was Colin Powell's trip to Africa and our first time meeting him. I'll tell you something else he did that indicated to me that this is a very special man. We had had a photo-op for the diplomatic corps and for other VIPs with Powell because he was such a well-known celebrity. He had gotten us through the Gulf War and of course was known all over the world. I remember asking him. "Why didn't you retire and make your money the way Schwarzkopf did?" He responded, "I'm a military man. I am committed to my profession. I'm committed to the government. I plan to serve my full term. I'm going to retire in a couple of years. If there's money to make, I'll make it. If not, I won't worry about it." I thought that was wonderful.

Then, after this photo-op for the VIPs and the members of the diplomatic corps, I got a call from the woman who ran the British Council. This is equivalent to our United States Information Agency. She was a single parent and asked me if I would ask the good general if she could come over with her children and take a couple of pictures. I said, "Well, I'll ask him." I asked him and he said, "Sure, have them come over." They came over to the residence and we introduced each other and we began to take pictures. She had a little girl who was eight years old and a boy about twelve years of age. They took pictures with General Powell and I thought it was all over, but he said, "Just a minute." He took off his jacket with all of the medals on the side and he put it around the shoulders of the little girl and said, "Now isn't that better, let's take some more pictures." That was a really sweet, touching, personal thing. There are not many people who would do that, who would be that thoughtful and kind. I thought to myself, this is a really special, great guy.

*Q: Now, did the question of the Sierra Leone military and of the Taylor incursion come up when he was there?*

YOUNG: It didn't. I mean, he met with the military. The military fellow described their problem in the north as dealing with some rebels who had come over from Liberia, but it was never regarded at that point as a major threat to the country. I mean, if we thought it was a threat to the country, we wouldn't have even allowed Powell to come in. It seemed to be just a local problem way out in the north or west somewhere, and the government figured it had contained it at that point. That was in March of 1992. So Powell had a very successful visit. It couldn't have been better, really.

Then in April of 1992, for Easter, my wife and I decided to visit some of our former posts in West Africa. We went to Guinea and Senegal and then Gambia. We had a very nice time, just loved it. We returned home on the 26th of April and before going to bed that night, we were talking about the trip and about our good fortune and being in Sierra Leone and how well things had gone. We said, you know, we've been very lucky. This has been a fascinating assignment in a poor country, with wonderful people, but we've been blessed. We haven't had any coups. The government had been helpful and we had been very lucky. We kissed each other and went to bed.

The 29th of April, 1992, I went to the office as usual. We were beginning our work and it must have been around 9:00 a.m. or so. I think we were getting ready for a country team meeting. We heard what sounded like gunshots. Someone said, "Oh, what's that?" We heard it again. I went over to the window and looked down on the road below and saw a motorbike going around this big tree called the cotton tree that was in front of the circle on which the embassy was located. I said, "Oh, that's the backfire from this motorcycle going around the cotton tree." Then we heard it again and with greater intensity and greater thunder. Then I looked down the street and could see the fire spewing from the barrels of these big guns that were mounted on trucks. I yelled to everyone to hit the floor and get under their desks, and that's what we did. It was clear immediately that there was an insurrection underway. I got on the phone immediately to call the president and he said, "Oh don't worry, these are just young military boys discontented, don't worry about the situation. We have it under control. It's okay." So, we called our people right away, told them don't move, stay where you are, try to get to a protected area in your residences, and what have you. My secretary, Lupe, was a woman of incredible skill and talent, but even more noteworthy was her calm. She called my wife and in the calmest way possible said to her, "Mrs. Young, this is Lupe. I'm calling because we seem to be experiencing a little bit of a problem at the moment. There seems to be some gunfire in the street." I mean, just calm like that. She said, "I just want you to take it easy and try to protect yourself and go to a safe area." My wife asked, "Well, where are you calling from?" Lupe said, "I'm under my desk at the moment on the floor. The ambassador told us all to hit the floor." I mean, she was calm like that, and then my wife called the other wives in the area and had them all come over to the residence. So they were all congregated there at the residence.

For the next several days we remained at the residence. And it goes to show that you never know how things will work out. The DCM happened to be sick on that occasion. I had changed DCMs by that point, and the new DCM was Frank Urbancic. Frank was sick that day, and when this incident occurred he couldn't get to the embassy. We had to carry on without him. For the next couple of days, we were trapped in the embassy. We couldn't go anywhere. We heard gunshots and fighting all night long. During the day, I continued to call the president and he continued to give me assurances that everything was okay. But when I began to call and call and couldn't get an answer, I knew that it was over, that he had fled and someone else had taken control of the government. Then later on it came over the radio that it had in fact happened. I then got a call from the man who was the head of the Ministry of Interior, a feared fellow. He was in hiding and was calling to see if he could seek refuge in the embassy. I wanted to let him in to save his life, but I realized that that could possibly pose a risk for us, because the folks who were leading this effort were after him. I cabled Washington for guidance on what to do and they advised us not to take him in. I didn't, and unfortunately later on they found him and shot him.

A couple of things happened during that first night. One, my secretary slept on the sofa and the DCM's secretary slept on the loveseat, while I slept on a chair and put my feet on a hassock. All night long we heard the rat-a-tat-tat and boom boom of machine guns. The DCM's secretary, Jenny Leon Gariro, was a woman who had come into the Foreign Service rather late after raising eight children and had had one previous assignment, I think in India somewhere. She had an incredible wit. There we were at 2:00 in the morning, a small lull in the sound of gunfire, and she said out loud, "This is what I always dreamed about in joining the Foreign Service, sleeping with the ambassador." We had such a good laugh and it was such a nice way to break the tension of the moment.

Anyhow, things were still very tense the next day. I think it might have been on the third day, I put the word out that we wanted to meet the new head of the government, whoever it was. Kiki Munshi, the public affairs officer, went out and put the word out that this was what the American ambassador wanted. We got word back that they would be prepared to do it and we agreed on the time. The venue was going to be the embassy and we also invited the other Western embassies as well. We invited all of the embassies that wanted to come. That took place, I think, at about

5:00 or 6:00 p.m. on the third day. The new leader was a fellow named Strasser. He was a young fellow, twenty-some years old. He had been one of our International Military Educational and Training (IMET) graduates. I think that had a very good positive impact on him in terms of what I said to him. He came in with his folks at 5:00 and I had the people from the embassy there and people from the other embassies as well. They explained to us that they really had had no intention of taking over the government, but the government wouldn't pay any attention to their pleas for assistance. They came to town to basically address the government, but when the government wouldn't pay any attention to them, they decided they would just take over. It was almost really by accident that this happened. If President Momoh and his group had paid attention to these fellows, perhaps this wouldn't have occurred, but it did. I told them we were very sorry that there had to be a change in government as a result of fighting and the killing of people. I pleaded with them not to take any retaliatory measures against those persons suspected of being involved in this. I begged them, pleaded with them, in the presence of these other diplomats. I think it had a positive impact. I told him that we were thinking of possibly evacuating. I wasn't sure, but if that happened we were doing it because we thought it was in the best interest of our people to do so. Then they left.

We subsequently had a country team meeting to discuss what we should do. We decided that we would evacuate, that the situation was too unstable and too impenetrable at that point. They hadn't decided who was going to be in the leadership of the new government. We thought that this could be the beginning of further tensions within this group. The Department agreed and we got the word out that we would evacuate. We managed to get all the volunteers in, all the missionaries, anybody who wanted to go, we got them out within forty-eight hours.

*Q: Where did they go?*

YOUNG: They went to Senegal by plane. And at the time of the coup, something occurred. We had a military medical team in town. They were looking at eyes and teeth and mouths and everything else. In fact, when it happened, the military team wanted to pull out and leave us there. I spoke to the head of the European command, or EUCOM, and told him we could not have this. If we were going to be evacuated, we all had to go together. He gave the order to keep the military there and we would all leave together. He would send in whatever additional resources were needed to take out the other Americans as well, but the military, they were ready to pull out and leave us all there. I was shocked that they would basically put their tail between their legs and take off. We did it on a first-come, first-served basis and they helped us. The new government regretted that we did that, but I told them we had no choice. Our first concern was the safety of our nationals and that's what we had to do.

I also made some decisions that were not in accord with the emergency evacuation plan in terms of who would stay and who would leave and that sort of thing. For example, I kept the Peace Corps doctor. All of the other Peace Corps folks, including the director and the other associate directors, all left. I kept the GSO, but not the admin officer and I kept the public affairs officer, Kiki Munshi. That's the way it went. We managed, and we just did everything. We all flipped around and did all kinds of jobs. We had the Peace Corps doctor doing political reporting and on and on. I mean, we just did what had to be done. Just a couple of days after the coup the DCM was able to get in.

*Q: Did you feel that the Momoh government was sort of oblivious to the military problems? Was it just not responsible? How did you find it?*

YOUNG: I just think that they were strapped for cash. They were strapped for supplies and they didn't give the military the attention they needed. I mean they were people who had been wounded in the fighting to try to keep the rebels at bay, but they hadn't been treated, couldn't be treated, because the government had nothing to treat them with. Some of the ones who came on this journey to put their petitions before the government were still wrapped up in bandages from wounds that they had incurred in fighting the rebels. The government just was not serious about listening to what was coming from its military people.

*Q: Was there such a thing as a presidential guard as part of the army?*

YOUNG: Yes, they had that.

*Q: Were they supporting the president?*

YOUNG: They were loyal to the president, definitely, yes.

*Q: Did atrocities appear at all?*

YOUNG: Just before the coup, I remember there were reports beginning to surface of atrocities in the area where the rebels had been fighting the government forces. A Peace Corps volunteer came to us one day and said, "Oh, ambassador, you know I saw something I've never seen before. I saw a child soldier and he had a machine gun. I was scared to death with this little boy and a machine gun."

This scene occurred not too far from Freetown. This was the first time anyone had seen a child soldier in Sierra Leone. That was the beginning of something that would really manifest itself quite a bit in Sierra Leone in the coming years, as well as the atrocities. The Sierra Leoneans were a very peaceful, gentle people. They never engaged in atrocities and pillaging and burning villages and all of these kinds of things. They were poor, but just very nice folks. The first signs of these kinds of problems were seen before the coup occurred.

*Q: When you say atrocities, I think later we heard about children with amputations.*

YOUNG: That's right, yes, not only children, I mean adults, babies, it was awful.

*Q: What was motivating this?*

YOUNG: This came from Charles Taylor. These are the kinds of tactics. The man who was leading the rebel forces at that time was a fellow by the name of Foday Sankoh. No one had heard of this fellow, no one knew him. They knew that there had been a Foday Sankoh who was a military man and had been put in jail. No one knew where he was or what he had done, but he had obviously gone over to Liberia and lined up with Taylor and then had crossed back over. Sierra Leone had no history whatsoever of the kinds of atrocities that occurred basically for the next decade while that war was underway.

*Q: What developed? I mean your people left; they went to . . . .*

YOUNG: Senegal and then from Senegal they went home, went to the States or wherever they were going.

Q: *What happened at the time you left?*

YOUNG: Until the time I transferred?

Q: *Yes.*

YOUNG: Well, we continued our work with the new government, trying to establish some kind of rapport. That was the only alternative. The new government was young and confused. Despite promises that it was going to be different and they were going to lead the country in a new direction, it became apparent to us rather quickly that this was going to be more of the same. The first thing they did was confiscate all of the fancy Mercedes and BMWs that they could put their hands on. Then they took over the fanciest villas. Then there were shipments of liquor to the villas, and the girls, and on and on. It was the spoils of having taken over the government. It was clear that these were not serious people in terms of governing a nation. They were falling into the traps people often fall into when they get into a position of power. They want all of the things they think go with power, the fancy house and the cars and the girls and the booze and the food and everything else. We could see that.

Some of them were Catholic. I went to mass one Sunday. Several of the top people in the new government pulled up in their BMWs. They hopped out in their military uniforms carrying their machine guns. We had a Catholic priest who had been there for forty some years. He stopped in the middle of the mass and told them, "Get these guns out of this church. There is no place for guns in this church." The fellows listened to him and they took the guns outside and he said, "Don't bring any guns into this church." Then he continued with the mass. After the mass I said, "Father, I'm amazed that you addressed those fellows the way that you did." He says, "Oh, sure, I know them all. I remember when they used to piss on the side of my cassock." He did, he knew them all from the time they were babies. It was clear that this was not a serious group and that this country was going to be in for trouble as it sorted itself out.

*Q: Obviously you were reporting back what you were seeing. What was the response from Washington?*

YOUNG: Oh, the response in Washington wasn't too enthusiastic. They basically wanted stability. They wanted us to encourage the government to do the right thing, to hold elections as soon as possible, to not embark on any programs of killing. It was the standard stuff that you get: have elections as quick as possible and then turn over the government to civilian rule, and those kinds of things. It was the standard.

*Q: What was the feeling? It sounds like a bordello gone wild or something like that. How did they respond to your message?*

YOUNG: They were beginning to learn quickly in terms of responding in a way that provided positive answers. They said they planned for transition to democratic governance and those kinds of things, and what they were going to do and so on. They weren't going to tolerate corruption and this and that. I met with a group of Lebanese businessmen and the Lebanese business people in Sierra Leone were quite a force to be reckoned with. I mean, they controlled a substantial part of that economy. They said, oh, yes, we met with so-and-so-and-so, the new president, and the new minister of the economy, and on and on and they refused our offer of assistance. Assistance really meant bribes and the head of them said, "Well, that's okay. Give us two months. We'll have them just where we want them." They were right.

Anyhow, things were calm for the following month and I began to press to try to get the evacuation order lifted so that people could return. I was leaving in July and I wanted my wife back so that we could say farewell and leave together. There was resistance to this in Washington, because at the time I think there was a ninety-day rule or something like that. They were not going to look at you until ninety days had passed and then they would make a decision if they should lift it or not. In our case, they lifted it after I think thirty days and my wife was able to come back and we concluded our assignment there and then moved on to Washington.

# WASHINGTON: CAREER DEVELOPMENT AND ASSIGNMENTS

Before I left, I received a telegram from Ed Perkins, who was the director general of the Foreign Service. He said, "Johnny, I have a key position in my office that I will be filling and I've looked around at people for this position and I've decided you are the perfect man for it, to be the director of career development and assignments." I sent him a message back saying thanks very much, but no thanks. The last time I was in Washington in personnel, I developed high blood pressure and haven't gotten rid of it since. I don't want to go to Washington; I really want to stay in the field. He cabled back and said, "No, I want you for this job," and I said, "No thank you." Then I tried to get the support of my friends in high places like Mary Ryan and Ambassador Hicks and a few others to weigh in on my behalf with the director general and they said, Johnny, forget it. He wants you for this job, you should do it and that's that. That's how I ended up as the director of career development and assignments. Perkins called me up and said, "Johnny, you take this job. I assure you I'll take care of you." That was that, and I transferred to Washington. Before I had even gotten to Washington, Perkins was transferred out of the job and moved to the United Nations, and Genta Hawkins Holmes replaced him as the director general of the Foreign Service.

*Q: So, you started that job in '92?*

YOUNG: In 1992.

*Q: For how long?*

YOUNG: Two years.

*Q: How did Ambassador Holmes operate?*

YOUNG: She was, I would say, very informal. She was very laid back, relaxed. I think she listened most of the time to her various section chiefs, but if she had it in her mind that she wanted something done in a particular way or that she frankly didn't like a particular person, you couldn't change her mind. I witnessed this and couldn't understand it, but she was unshakable if she didn't want to support a particular person. Before I went to that job I found out that I suddenly had hundreds of "friends" that I never realized I had. Literally, it was in the hundreds. You know, they all congratulated me and this and that. "I'm going to stop by to see you," and the Christmas cards, and on and on. It was a wonderful job, I must say, I liked it very much.

Before we returned to Washington in 1989 we had sold the house that we had lived in on Leland Street in Chevy Chase, Maryland. We couldn't upgrade in the same neighborhood so we moved to a nearby neighborhood in Kensington, Maryland.

*Q: Talk about your job. What were the responsibilities? What did it involve?*

YOUNG: The Office of Career Developments and Assignments had responsibility for assigning all of our Foreign Service personnel and for providing career counseling to all of our personnel. The assignments were carried out by chiefs of geographic divisions and we also had counselors for all of the various specialties in the Foreign Service. An assignment was worked out in conjunction with the assignment chiefs who worked for the bureaus, who basically represented the bureaus' interests, and the counselors who represented the employees of the Foreign Service. The goal was to work an assignment in such a way that you had agreement among these elements and then an assignment would be made. I had about a hundred people working for me between the assignments offices and the counselors and the senior training division. All these different offices were part of career development and assignments. When I was there people were saying, "Oh, this office is too big and the Department is looking for ways to cut it." A huge reorganization was underway while I was there. Fortunately, it was concluded after I left and I think they reduced the office. Now the office is even bigger than it was before. They realized that if you are serious about career counseling and about assignments, there is just a certain way you have to do it.

*Q: Of course, unlike the normal civil service and most other businesses, assignments are almost the depths of our organization, because it's not resources, it's people. We have about 200 posts to staff and to get it right, there's no way you can get around it.*

YOUNG: Exactly. Yes. There were various discussions of how we ought to do it like the military and so on. Well, that would be fine if we had the kind of disciplined service like the military. We could do it with fewer people and we could say to someone, you're going to X post and case closed, but we have become a service that has become more family-oriented, more family friendly, and we try to work out assignments in a way that is beneficial to the employee in terms of his personal needs and requirements, the needs and requirements of his family, and the needs and requirements of the Service.

It takes human resources people to get all of this sorted out. You have competing interests: the interests of the Service, of the employee and of his family, and professional needs. In addition, we were going through a period where we were expanding posts. We needed people to fill these new posts in the former Soviet Union. And we were closing posts to get resources to open up these new places. It was quite a juggling act to make all of this come out. We were not getting any additional people at all to help us with this.

*Q: Especially money-wise during this time.*

YOUNG: Oh, it was awful. It was dreadful. This was the time when we decided not to take in any junior officers this year and to cut the numbers. This was when we really went on a huge diet and reduced the intake of junior officers and other officers as well. It was not an easy time.

*Q: I come from an era where you put in your wish list due on the First of April, known as the April Fool's Report, and you were assigned somewhere and you had to go. That is for most of us. Those who knew better would negotiate and work it out through some of the old boys' network and all. If you weren't smart, you just submitted. I've got the feeling now that positions are negotiated, as if an officer appears with his or her lawyer. How did you find it at the time? Did you find it was hard getting people to go to places?*

YOUNG: Yes, it was hard to get people to go to places they didn't want to. We used to tell people that they should be known in the offices that they want to be assigned to, but we didn't encourage strong lobbying, as is the case today. Today the lobbying effort is intense; it is just unbelievable. I'm no longer in the Foreign Service and I continue to receive requests from people begging me to write letters and e-mails to various offices and individuals to support them for the various jobs that they're bidding on. The bidding process is more intense. I think it's more stressful, more automated, certainly in terms of making sure the round pegs fall into the round holes and that sort of thing, but the personal involvement and lobbying is considerably more.

*Q: Let's break this down into various parts. What were your impressions of junior officer recruitment, just plain junior officer recruitment and also the effort to recruit minorities. When you got there, what was your feeling of how we were dealing with all of this?*

YOUNG: Well, this was my second time in personnel. When I was first in personnel from 1979 to 1981, I was a counselor for admin officers. I was the deputy to Mary Ryan in counseling administrative types. They were not all administrative officers, but just administrative types. When I returned in '92 it was as director of the office, and things had changed considerably. We were still getting high-quality, top-notch junior officers. I certainly didn't see any problem with the quality of officers. Junior officers, however, during this later period in '92 to '94 were certainly more outspoken in terms of what they wanted and what they didn't want, what they would do and wouldn't do, and their rights and prerogatives, and that sort of thing. That had changed a lot. It was not a question of the new recruit receiving his orders and marching off to duty. No, they came in with their list of demands. It was just unbelievable. I could not believe some of them. They come in knowing everything and wanting everything.

In terms of minority recruitment, the emphasis had shifted quite a bit. Back in that '79 to '81 period, we still had a minority entry program and a mid-level program that could bring minorities in at the mid-level, which ended very quickly when the Republican administration came into power; that was the end of that. The program was the source of some minority talent that we got into the Service. All of that had ended by 1992. The efforts to recruit minorities had shifted to programs initially like the Foreign Affairs Fellows Program, which subsequently evolved into the Pickering Fellowship. That was one tack that seemed to be working. There was certainly a great effort, but the goal was to find a way to get minorities interested in the Service without breaking the law. A great emphasis was placed on the Diplomat in Residence Program, using the diplomats in residence as a recruiting tool to encourage minorities to study the right subjects in school and to prepare for taking the Foreign Service exam. I think there is still a great emphasis on the persons in those programs as a recruiting tool for the Service, and it has worked.

*Q: By the time you were there in the '92 to '94 period, had things sort of leveled off, so that there was no longer a particular program for getting female junior officers to come in?*

YOUNG: That was not an issue, no.

*Q: Because at one point it was a major issue.*

YOUNG: Yes, if you were to look at statistics of how many women were entering the Service in '79 to '81, you would see the contrast with how many were entering during the '92 to '94 period, not because of me but because it had changed considerably. In 1992, we were anxious to find good opportunities for women officers so we could give them an opportunity to compete with their male colleagues. We needed to make up for that.

*Q: On assignments, did you find there were people trying to go around the system? I mean you all would come up with the idea that X should go into Y position because it makes sense and somebody's got to fill Y position, but X would then go off and say I don't want that, I want Z position.*

YOUNG: I always looked at it in terms of people being along the bell curve. You had those on one end who really didn't need the system, they were so good and so well known and so popular and so highly visible that people were fighting to get them. Those people would always be taken care of. On the other extreme, you had the poor schlub that nobody wanted, nobody fought for, or nobody would take. You had to really beg people to take them. Then you had the people in the middle, which is where the majority of us fell, and we had to get all of that sorted out.

*Q: Well, did you find during this period, as it straddled the Bush I and Clinton presidencies a bit, that political appointees were a factor in reaching down and pushing people for assignments?*

YOUNG: That didn't affect my operation really, because we were dealing with career positions. We might have had one or two exceptions to that, where maybe some ambassador decided he was going to put a political appointee in a position that would normally be held by a DCM or something like that, but that rarely happened. All of the positions we dealt with were career positions except at the ambassadorial level, and that was really a matter of what the White House wanted to do.

*Q: Certainly the director general and above.*

YOUNG: Yes.

*Q: What about discipline matters or selection-out problems? This was a period, if I recall correctly, when all of a sudden sexual harassment became an important issue. Everybody was thinking, "Oh my God, am I being sexually harassed, or am I a harasser?"*

YOUNG: The sensitivity about that subject was on everyone's mind. When I was director of career development and assignments, I decided that because of this sexual harassment business, I would not meet with any female officer in my office with the door closed. I always kept the door open and that was how we had our talks. I had a number of women on my staff. Suddenly you have a female colleague who decides that she's going to have a makeover or something like that and she would come in looking very different. I would reserve comment and not compliment them on how nice they looked or anything like that. You just never knew how it was going to be interpreted. I was very aware of that. At that time it was a big issue.

*Q: What were your biggest problems?*

YOUNG: Fights with the bureaus over their choices for positions based on favoritism, based on the old boys' network and that sort of thing, versus our perception of what a candidate needed and who should have that job. We had those problems to resolve. Those were the biggest problems. Then you would assign someone to a position and suddenly for medical or personal reasons the job would fall apart at the last minute and the person couldn't go, and then you had to scramble and find someone else. Those kinds of things happened. Problems of bringing people out, breaking assignments because of problems at post. At one post, we had to suddenly take this man out, and he was brought out in handcuffs because of terrible allegations of child abuse. So, we had all kinds of problems. Also, there was one ambassador who allegedly slugged his political officer and denied it.

*Q: Well, there are policy disagreements.*

YOUNG: The ambassador denied it. One day Jim Whitlock, who was the counselor for political officers, came running to my office. He said, "I have so-and-so on the phone." I asked, "What's wrong?" He said, "Well, he claims the ambassador just slugged him." I replied, "Oh, well, tell him don't do anything. Just cool it." Later on the fellow calmed down. He never retracted his story, but the ambassador never admitted that he did it. So we never knew where the truth lay in that particular case.

*Q: Did you find yourself having to deal with clubs like the Soviet club, the German club, the Italian club?*

YOUNG: We knew that those existed. I would look at those as part of the old boys' network, but that was another kind of network. No, we didn't have problems of that type. The bureaus were the managers of those situations.

*Q: Did you have a problem over staffing what became known as the Stans, the former Soviet Republics? Some of those places were horrible. I spent three weeks in Bishkek as a retiree, but talking to the consular service in Kyrgyzstan. They were essentially in a run-down cottage.*

YOUNG: They were, but these were pioneers. The people who went out there were pioneers. They were the same as the ones who went to Francophone Africa and set up posts in those places in the 1960s. These were the trailblazers. These people were wonderful and they did a fantastic job. The kind of esprit de corps we had was unbelievable and they volunteered.

We forced no one into any of those assignments. The people who went out there did well by the Service and they did well by themselves also. In the end it helped many of them in their careers. This happened so suddenly and you had them all at once. Where were you going to get people? Where were you going to get an Azeri speaker and a Kyrgyz speaker?

*Q: I know that a number of my friends who by this time had retired were brought back in the Service to open up posts. Did you find yourself using retired officers as a real resource?*

YOUNG: Maybe they did, but that was not my bailiwick. Another office used WAEs (When Actually Employed), but I didn't. We just dealt with the people we had and we pulled them from all over, and they went and truly did the Lord's work in opening these places and living in such dreadful conditions.

*Q: Did you have any problems with political ambassadors trying to change their staffs? In other words, political ambassadors come from different fields where they are used to having control of people around them. Was this a problem for you?*

YOUNG: It was. I mean that is always a problem. That was nothing new. I think that we do a better job of preparing political ambassadors before they go out on assignment these days than we did. So you don't have that kind of problem as much as you did perhaps in the past, with them saying well, I want so-and-so out of here. Just a wave of a hand and they're gone. We had some of that. I can't think of a particular case right now that was especially egregious, but we did have them, definitely.

*Q: What was the spirit of the State Department from your perspective? What were you getting from the officers you were seeing during this particular time? With the cutting down of funds when the Clinton administration came in with very much a domestic outlook, and Warren Christopher not being a dynamic leader. I mean, he was primarily the president's policy advisor.*

YOUNG: He was good in that sense, but he had no interest in leading and managing the place.

*Q: It did not seem to be a terribly inspiring time at the beginning.*

YOUNG: At the beginning it may not have been, but there was a great deal of admiration for Clinton and for his administration. Secretary Christopher was highly respected, but he was not an inspirational leader at all. I think there was a sense of a kind of drift. We were just treading water, and that was about it until he left and then Madeleine Albright came in and things changed.

*Q: During the time you were there, did the Balkans present a particular problem?*

YOUNG: From a staffing point of view, we were more concerned with people coming out and where were we going to place them. People were being evacuated out of the Balkans then. I remember the siege of Sarajevo and Belgrade and so on. In fact one of the fellows who closed down Zagreb, Mike Einik, came to work for me following the closure of Zagreb. We were busy trying to find places for all these people who were coming out.

*Q: Were there any other issues we should talk about during this period?*

YOUNG: Well, we covered I think most of the issues. I was there for two years. My first deputy in that job was a woman named Lange Schermerhorn. She was wonderful and such a wise person. She was fair and witty and smart and I liked her very much. My only problem with her was that she was a packrat. I mean, you would go into Lange's office and look around and say, my God I've never seen so much paper and piles of stuff in my life. Yet I would say to her, Lange, do you have that note that we got from the director general and she'd go right over to it and say, "It's right here." She was just wonderful. I liked her a lot. She was replaced by a woman named Phyllis Ritoud, who was a good consular officer, a different type altogether, and just the opposite of Lange in terms of the tidiness of the office. Everything was in order. Phyllis was very effective, with good judgment as well. I got along with both Lange and Phyllis very well. Genta Hawkins Holmes was the director general and Peter Burleigh was the principal deputy assistant secretary.

As I said, if Genta didn't like you, you might as well hang it up. I thought she was very good in many ways and did an excellent job. But there was one thing that I could not understand for the life of me. It was amazing how she did her job as director general, because Dick Moose, the undersecretary for management at the time, constantly looked over her shoulder and just about ran personnel from his office. He treated her just horribly, I mean with the greatest disrespect, even in public meetings. She took it, and Genta was a woman who could out curse any sailor that I have ever run into. Yet she would smile and just do whatever he wanted. I remember once Peter Burleigh and I were talking about it and he said, "You know, first of all he knows better. He would never speak to me in that way and I can't understand at all why he treats her that way." I thought he treated her just dreadfully. If it had been at a lower level, I am convinced that she could have filed a suit against him and would have won, because we all saw it. It was just absolutely awful. I think she probably knew that he would have a big hand in anything she wanted following that job and in the end she got something very nice, because she became ambassador to Australia. I guess we endure what we must in order to reap what we want.

Peter, I thought, was an absolutely marvelous deputy. He gave Genta and all of us good advice. I found that he was always fair and decent. He was just a wise, well-balanced deputy director general. He was just terrific and knowledgeable, just a good, solid man. Unfortunately he was very badly treated in the system He was designated as ambassador to the Philippines and we were all so happy for him and he was happy. He had his hearing. Everything went well. Then Senator Grassley, I think it was, put a hold on his assignment and it wasn't about Peter; it was about something else.

*Q: Grassley from Iowa.*

YOUNG: Yes and as I said it wasn't about Peter, it was about something else. This went on for months and months. In the meantime Peter began working on a project of "right sizing." I think that is what it was. This was going on for months and the man didn't have a regular job at that point. Somebody had replaced him in personnel and the new director general had come on, and so on. Richard Holbrooke had been nominated to be our ambassador to the UN and there was a hold on Holbrooke. Actually, Holbrooke was held first. This went on for months and months and in the meantime, Peter's nomination had not come up for a full vote by the Senate. Then the Department began to negotiate with the Senate to get Holbrooke broken out so that he could be confirmed and go to the UN. After all of these negations, I think it was Grassley who said, okay, I'll lift the hold on Holbrooke and that's when he put the hold on Peter's assignment and that went on for months. After nearly a year there was no indication that it was going to be lifted. It wasn't against Peter, it was just a matter of principle because there was something that Grassley wanted from the Department. I don't know what it was, but he was holding the Department hostage for something and as a result he kept the hold on Peter's assignment. In the end, Peter said I've had enough. One morning he went down to the retirement office, filled out the papers and left, and has retired to Florida where he lives a very happy and contented life. So, that's what happened. It was awful, terrible.

Now, Peter had been ambassador to Sri Lanka and had done very well there. I mean he was going on his second ambassadorial assignment. Before I left, Genta took very good care of all of us. I had been recommended to be ambassador to Luxembourg and the secretary agreed. My name went over to the White House and it sat in the White House for three months waiting for a decision by the president. The word kept coming back, well, maybe, maybe not, we think it's going to be a political appointee.

*Q: It's almost always political.*

YOUNG: Almost. Once in a while, I mean, we had Ed Rowell there and that worked out, but we just didn't know and I didn't get optimistic about it. In the meantime, I was considered for other prospects and those prospects did not work out. So, in the end I was asked if I would be interested in going to Togo and I said that would be interesting. I have the language and it's in West Africa, so why not. I put my name in for Togo, which worked out and that was how I got to Togo in 1994.

# AFRICA AGAIN: AMBASSADOR TO TOGO

*Q: You were in Togo from '94 to when?*

YOUNG: 1994 to 1997.

*Q: At the time what was happening in Togo, and how were the relations with the United States?*

YOUNG: Relations with the United States were fair; they were not great. We were not too pleased with Togo, because since the fall of the Berlin Wall and the end of the Cold War we had a whole new paradigm for our relationship with countries in Africa and in the rest of the world as well. Democracy was the name of the new game. We wanted Togo to move in a more democratic way and to reform its economy. It wasn't doing any of these things. The ruler at that time was Gnassingbe Eyadema, who had come to power in a coup in 1967. Other than Joseph Mobutu of the Congo, who was still around then, Eyadema was the longest serving head of state in Africa. That meant that by sheer tenure or longevity he enjoyed a considerable amount of respect from his fellow African leaders despite the fact that some of them were changing and reforming and moving in the right direction. He was not. My mandate when I went to Togo was to try to get the country to change, to reform, both politically and economically.

*Q: What was Eyadema doing in Togo? I mean, with his people and with the economy?*

YOUNG: One word: nothing. He was doing absolutely nothing and the people were very frustrated as a result of that. Togo had been a model of development and stability at one time during the late '60s; rather I should say during the '70s and '80s. It was a vacation spot; French and other nationalities would fly in from all over to enjoy the beaches and the resorts. The hotels were first class. It was famous for being a nice little place of stability. At the height of Togo's fame, many other countries in Africa were moving towards the left and towards socialism and Communism and things like that. Togo remained stable and it was very pro-democratic, very loyal to France and to the United States. Eyadema came to the U.S. and was welcomed by our president and was welcomed at famous universities that gave honorary doctorates and things like that, because he was considered a good soldier in the war with the Communists. That worked too well for him at that time.

Then when he began to lose favor, the aid and support weren't there anymore. The country began to decline and it continued its downward slope. The European Union had begun to make its economic assistance conditional on reform, so they had reduced the amount they were giving. The French had reduced the amount they were giving, although they were still the principal country contributing. The Germans were basically doing the same as we were doing, as well as the Italians and all of the others. Of course there was nothing forthcoming in terms of any kind of development assistance from other African countries, even in the name of African solidarity. Eyadema wasn't doing anything.

We arrived. It was clear to us when we took a glance around that this country was fading. It had had a glorious past and now it was into a dowdy, seedy future. The buildings were shabby and hadn't been painted, mildew and moss were growing on them. The number one hotel in town had great prospects. You could tell it had been a grand hotel at one time. It was the largest skyscraper in town, with about fifteen or twenty floors. They had about six or seven upper floors that were not even constructed and had never been finished. The elevator didn't work. The water didn't work. Just all kinds of problems, yet Togo continued to reach out and present itself as a place that was perfect for international conferences and gatherings and meetings of that type. The other big hotel in town had a similar situation. You could see it had a glorious past at one time and was struggling just to keep its head above water.

Shortly after I arrived, I presented my credentials to President Eyadema. He allowed me to bring along my deputy, which was very nice although the deputy sat in an outer room. We had our tête-à-tête after the presentation of credentials. I looked at him and I said to myself, you know, you look just like you have been described in various narratives—as a snake. I mean, he looked like a snake. He had these slanted eyes and the whites were not white, but sort of orangey looking, with penetrating black centers to them. Very well groomed and coiffed, but there was just something about him that was slippery and it came through. A very clever man.

Over the course of my time there I was invited to many functions. It used to break my heart to go to these things, but I had no choice. I was the representative of the U.S. and I was expected to be there. I used every opportunity possible to make known what we would like to see in that country. We would go to these dinners. Eyadema loved hosting various leaders who would come to Africa. Because of his longevity, they came and paid respects. They paid deference to him and he was a good intermediary from time to time.

At one point he was particularly helpful to us. The French loved him. They loved him and they knew that they could use him for political reasons as an intermediary with other African leaders.

I remember when we were pushing so hard for reform, the German ambassador and the European Union and the Americans were all on the same script, but we couldn't get the French to buy in. I remember talking to the French ambassador and he said, "Johnny, I can't help you. This man is important to us and we don't want to upset him. I'm sorry I can't join your cause."

*Q: How was he important do you think?*

YOUNG: As I said, as someone they could use as an entrée to get to other African leaders because of the virtue of his position. This was at a time when Mobutu was fading because his health was failing and he was just not as useful. So Eyadema was the number-one man. If you were to look at TV clips of Francophone meetings during that period, you will find Eyadema seated to the right of the French president because that was the number one place of honor. Eyadema lived like a king. He lived very high, no question about it. His office was beautifully done up. I mean you would look at his office building from the outside and say oh, that's not bad, except for some seedy touches here and there. But when you walked inside, it had the finest furniture from France and the finest curtains and on and on. This was equally true for his residences as well; I say residences because he had many. There had been several attempted efforts on his life. They all failed, and as a result the word was that he never slept in the same place two nights in a row and that he always had a different place to sleep. I found that was probably true, because I remember on one occasion I was in a desperate state to contact him at night and I really got a runaround before I finally reached him.

He would have lavish functions where he would host visiting African leaders and would invite the entire diplomatic corps. We would go to these functions and we would begin with the finest caviar. We'd have all of these lovely things to begin the meal and the finest Dom Pérignon champagne and the finest French white and red wines. Then we would have the best filet mignon. You just name it. It was unbelievable. These were not small gatherings for two or three people; these were gatherings for hundreds. He spent a fortune doing these kinds of functions, yet the teachers could not be paid, hospital workers could not be paid, and government workers could not be paid. People were starving. In a country where corruption was already high, people in their desperation resorted to very corrupt measures to get additional cash to take care of themselves and their families. For example, the teachers would only impart let's say sixty percent of what they were supposed to cover.

Togo used to sell some phosphates to the U.S. until we banned it for environmental reasons, but they had other purchasers who were still interested in purchasing it for agricultural purposes.

*Q: It's the sort of thing that passes on tremendous wealth.*

YOUNG: Well, when you can get your cut, it's not bad. For example, if they sell $150 million and receive a nice 10 percent or so, you could live quite nicely off of that I would say. You can rest assured the president always got his cut.

In addition to phosphates, they had cocoa and coffee, which were the principal exports. Some marine items like shrimp and crabs were basically local, with no big production for export.

*Q: Did we have any particular stake in the country?*

YOUNG: Economic stake? None. Basically, our stake was in regional stability and how Togo could contribute to that.

*Q: What was around Togo, which states?*

YOUNG: The states around it were Ghana and Benin and to the north was Burkina Faso. Togo made a lot of money because it had access to the sea. Niger, Burkina Faso, those countries did not have access to the sea, so they could use the port of Lome, Togo, to get their goods, which were then trucked in. This is significant for another reason as well because it was also along this route that AIDS began to develop in Togo. It was through these truck drivers, who would of course do a lot of things that truck drivers do, and the prostitutes would seek them out or they would seek the prostitutes out. Anyhow, that route was a path for the spread of AIDS. We did something original that worked very well. I don't know if it is still working or not, but we were able to win the support of the prostitutes in working with people in the communities and educating them about AIDS. We found that these prostitutes were very happy to receive the heightened status and recognition that they got from being educators and teachers in the community in the fight against AIDS. I thought that was a very effective initiative. The prostitutes helped to distribute condoms and things like that. That worked out very nicely.

*Q: Did you get any trouble from old church groups or members of Congress?*

YOUNG: Not when I was there. Now, it's quite possible that may have happened later on. You have to keep in mind that I was there during the Clinton administration, when that was not an issue. I don't know what has transpired since that time, but this initiative was certainly applauded and recognized for its creativity when I was there.

*Q: Had AIDS made the inroads that it had in some countries, affecting 30 percent of the population?*

YOUNG: No, not to that degree. It had not reached the epidemic proportions that it had in the Ivory Coast, for example. The Ivory Coast was probably the worst area I can recall in West Africa in terms of AIDS. That had not reached Togo, although I had people who worked for me in Togo who contracted AIDS and died. We had one who worked for us right in the residence, and we tried to help him as much as we could. We did not fire him, and we allowed him to continue his work with the residence. When I left and the new ambassador was coming in, we told her about the situation and allowed her to make a decision about what she wanted to do and she decided that she, too, would keep him on. We had a couple of other people that we knew of who worked for the mission and died of AIDS, but at that point it had not reached the numbers that it had in other places in West Africa or in Southern Africa.

I wanted to get back to Eyadema and his style. I mentioned the dinners. Another thing that he liked to do was to go out to the airport and meet all of the VIPs who were passing through Togo, particularly heads of state. If Nelson Mandela was passing through, he would make sure that he stopped in Togo and they met in the airport. He would call out the entire diplomatic corps and we would go out to the airport and wait and wait for the arrival of this person and for the departure of this person. The president would come around with the VIP while we stood in line like God knows what. We shook hands and bowed and that sort of thing. I would go out to these things and would tell my staff, "Okay, I'm going out to sweat for my government," because I was going out to the airport and would have to stand in that sun." Sometimes, of course, you never knew; these things were rarely carried out in any kind of precise time. You would go out and just wait and wait and wait. I remember my French colleague once said, "This is terrible. You know we waste so much time here. We should each be given a Game Boy." I thought that was kind of amusing. There was a practical side to it. At least if you had a Game Boy there, you could sort of fiddle around with your thumbs until the time came to say hello and say goodbye. The president was from one of the minority tribes in Togo, from the north up towards the border with Burkina Faso. He had a home and palace and office up in a place called Kara, which was basically a de facto second capital city. He would sometimes summon us up to meetings there. He would send the jet down. We would get on his 707 and fly up to Kara and have a meeting up there. Again, a very nicely decorated palace with all of the accouterments and furnishings from the best dealers in Europe, and it was really quite up to date in that sense.

Before I went to Togo there were clear signs that there was trouble brewing under the surface. We got there I think in October of '94. I think in that September there had been an attempted coup. There had been the slaughter of a number of opposition people. Other opposition people gathered all of the bodies, put them in a truck, and drove them to the American embassy. They dumped them all in front of the American embassy. I'm told it was a ghastly, gruesome sight, which I'm sure it was, but they were trying to make a point. They were trying to get our attention. They were trying to get us to weigh in to get this man to rein in his boys. When I arrived, there was no question that there were disappearances. People that we knew, particularly newspaper people and opposition people, would disappear. You'd never hear from them again. Later, you would find a picture in the press of their mutilated body. The press began to have some very difficult times with the government and some of those press people began to disappear.

One thing we did that I thought was very successful was to keep the pressure on the government in terms of being accountable for the disappearance of people. We would not let up, the Germans would not let up, and the European Union would not let up. Some of this change came about because of a change in technology as well. Just a few years earlier you could have someone disappear in Togo and it would be written up maybe if some outside source got wind of it, but it would basically be contained internally because the technology wasn't there. The phone system didn't work, cell phones didn't work, the fax system didn't work, and computers were just getting started. But while we were there, these things began to really mushroom and it made a tremendous difference. We would encourage other organizations to send faxes, to keep the pressure on so that when someone went missing suddenly the government was hit from all angles and realized that it couldn't just hush these things up. We had a big hand in making that possible and it was a big success. The people of Togo recognized that the U.S. had a big hand in it and they gave us a lot of credit.

*Q: How did this work? Were the EU or other countries getting together with us and saying okay, so-and-so has gone, let's do something about it?*

YOUNG: Absolutely. I can give you an example about a German diplomat. There would be periods when security in Togo would be heightened because of information the government received that there was going to be some attempt to either invade the country or some attempt on the president's life. Things would tighten up and you could tell when they would tighten up. You would get no notice on the radio or the newspaper or anything like that, but barricades would suddenly mushroom throughout the city. You would get the word that you just had to be extremely careful at night. Well, one night during one of these periods of heightened security one of our German colleagues, I think he was a security officer at the German embassy, was returning home. He was stopped at one of these barricades. They searched his car. I think he became indignant with the fact that he was stopped and searched since he was a diplomat. He got in his car and drove off. As he drove off the police at the barricade opened fire with their machine guns and killed him, thirty-two bullets in the back. It was absolutely horrible.

Well, we went through the government. I asked for a meeting with the government. We got our colleagues together from the diplomatic corps and we marched in to protest this and to demand an accounting. This was one of the occasions, for example, when the French ambassador sat there with his mouth totally shut after this atrocity. He didn't say a thing. Now, here he is, a fellow European, and a German diplomat was gunned down savagely like that and he didn't say one word. I was the one who led the discussion. I told the government how outrageous this was and how they needed to do something about the security situation, where Eyadema had all of these inexperienced people manning these barricades. He did absolutely nothing. The government was very embarrassed by this. It was a horrible thing that happened. As horrible as it was, I think some good came out of it. I think it made the government more sensitive in terms of what was going on, not only with foreigners, but even with its own people. Some transparency began to enter the process and it did make a difference. The government did apologize to the widow of this fellow. They offered her money. I don't know how much, but I think they offered her a pension and all kinds of things like that, which they should have done.

*Q: Did you find that the French were not excluded per se but sort of kept off to one side when the rest of you got together?*

YOUNG: They would always come. Of course they always wanted to know what we were doing so they could report back home about what the American said and what the European Union fellow said and what the group said, but they would never join in. They would never say "Absolutely right, we're going to tell the president such and such." On a couple of occasions we were very unhappy with how the president was treating the opposition, how they were being harassed and not given an opportunity to basically put their message before the public. The government controlled the media, so they didn't have access to television and things like that. We tried to help the opposition to get a fair hearing and they were very grateful for that. They were very pleased with that.

*Q: Were there any forces the equivalent of Charles Taylor or anything like that going on?*

YOUNG: The president had structured the military so that it was totally loyal to him. The top people in the military were all part of his ethnic group; they were not of the majority Ewe ethnic group. All of the top dogs in the military were his people. He had the military right in his pocket and then in addition to that, his son Ernest was a key person in the military although not the top person. That basically assured Eyadema some loyalty at the mid-level through his son, who was quite a rascal in his own right.

*Q: Looking at the dates '94 to '97, were the Russians out of the game completely or were they even there?*

YOUNG: They had left. This was not a country of interest to them any longer, so they had left. They were represented either in Nigeria or through the Ivory Coast, one of those. Prior to 1990 they did have a mission there, but they closed it up. The Chinese were there. You'll find the Chinese just about wherever you find us.

*Q: What were the Chinese doing?*

YOUNG: They were contributing aid to a few building projects and things like that. That's about all, and of course the Togolese buy considerable merchandise from the Chinese. In some African markets such plain simple things as matches are all made in China. Matches and these little coils to keep away the mosquitoes in malarial areas, and what have you, all done by the Chinese. I remember visiting a warehouse with just mosquito coils, which is a very simple thing. I could not believe that they were all from China. It was enough to fill a football stadium. The quantity was so huge

I could not believe it. They buy lots of products; a lot of the toys that are sold in the local markets, all made in China. Soccer balls and so on. The trade is quite significant, but it's basically a one-sided trading arrangement. There's very little that Togo offers to China, maybe some phosphates, because China is not as environmentally rigorous about that kind of thing as we are; and maybe a little coffee and cocoa, but not much. It's more of a one-sided arrangement, with more coming from China than going to.

*Q: Were the South Koreans or North Koreans there?*

YOUNG: No, neither.

*Q: Israel?*

YOUNG: No, none of them were there.

*Q: Did you have any sort of exchange program, or was there much contact with the United States?*

YOUNG: We had a very active public affairs program and we made great strides with the press through this program. We could go out to the provinces and do outreach programs. We could have speakers and all kinds of programs of one kind or another. We had a very active and successful English-teaching program that was self-funded. We had hundreds of students and could have had hundreds more if the State Department had been willing to expand it, but it was not. Again, there was a certain mindset in the State Department at that time. In other words, don't bother me with that country; I have other things to do. Yet this was a key means of influencing young minds, particularly making them favorably disposed towards the United States. These English-teaching programs were among the best things we ever did. So that worked out very nicely. We had one of the best programs I have ever seen anywhere in terms of celebrating Black History Month. We would bring in representatives from schools from all over the country and have them engage in a black history quiz that was broadcast live on radio. We held it in the USIS building and it worked out very well. I would give a speech at the beginning of the thing and then I would award the prizes for the best school. We would have plays and poetry readings. I would go out to the university and do a lecture. It was just a very dynamic, active program in terms of Black History Month.

*Q: How did you and your wife find dealing with the Togolese? Are they open people?*

YOUNG: Lovely people, wonderful. It is a country divided along ethnic lines. We were in Lome, which is in the southern part of the country right on the coast. The predominant tribe in that area is the Ewe tribe, which is made up of an ethnic group that is predominant in Ghana and spilled over into Togo as well. If you recall, at one point Togoland was controlled by Germany as the colonial power. After World War II it was under the UN and eventually in the 1950s people were given an option to either become part of Ghana or become part of Togo. The line was drawn right down the middle. This is again one of those artificial lines in Africa that literally split this ethnic group right down the middle. So you have half of the Ewe people in Ghana, the largest half in Ghana, and then you have the other half in Togo. They are the predominant tribe in the Lome area. You have other tribes as well. I think Togo has some thirty different tribal groups. The president is from one of the minor tribes, the Kabye, from the northern part of the country. Kabye are predominantly Muslim. Ewe are predominantly Christian. You have a big split there, but we got along with all of them very well. They treated us quite nicely and we just felt sorry that such nice people could not have better leadership.

I wanted to cite another example of how Eyadema could be helpful at times. On a couple of occasions we got annoyed with him. We were not fully justified. There were upcoming elections in Benin. President Soglo of Benin was running. The polls were beginning to indicate that as admired and liked as he was, perhaps he wasn't going to win, that perhaps somebody else was going to win. Word got to Washington that the Togolese were meddling in the affairs of Benin. Washington told me to speak to President Eyadema about this and I did as I was instructed. I went to him and said, "Mr. President, we're concerned that there are reports of so and so." He was furious. He said, "That is absolutely not true, I can tell you right now, I am not meddling in the affairs of Benin. However those elections turn out it won't be because of anything that I've done here." He went on, "You have your satellites in the sky, beam them down on me and you can see that there's nothing happening in my country affecting Benin." Frankly, I think he was right. I think we had become so enamored of President Soglo in Benin and we were so anxious to have the Benin story continue along successful lines with President Soglo at the helm that we were prepared to believe anything. I reported that back to Washington in terms of what he said and what he did and that was the end of that. The elections took place and Soglo lost the election to a former head of state named Kerekou, but they were free and fair and democratic and transparent and that was the important thing. It worked out very well.

On another occasion, the situation in the Congo was falling apart. We desperately needed to get Mobutu out of the Congo and get him somewhere, and various places were proposed. Eyadema played a very key role in inviting Mobutu to leave the Congo and to make his way elsewhere via Togo. This occurred after a series of meetings by the Organization of African Unity and the Economic Community of West African States. There were entreaties from us as well for Eyadema to be encouraged in this effort to invite Mobutu to at least spend some time in Togo before moving on. In the end, it worked. Mobutu came and that eased tensions in Zaire for a short period. He spent some time in Lome and then went on to Morocco, where he eventually died, and that was the end of that. Eyadema was very helpful in that regard.

We were concerned about Eyadema's continuance in power and his ascendance to the role of the longest-serving head of state in Africa. I would ask in my meetings with him, what his plans were for running, because elections were going to take place very soon. What was he going to do? He would say, "I've made up my mind. I'm not going to run again. I promise I'm not going to run again. The constitution does not allow it, but I'm not going to do it." Well, I left Togo and the RPT Party, the president's party, controlled the legislature and they amended the constitution to allow him to run an additional year and he subsequently took advantage of that and ran an additional year and just continued on in power. Finally he died on February 5, 2005; I think it was while he was en route to France. He had a heart attack and died. Then power was passed to his son, which was totally out of line with the constitution. Once again his party, the RPT Party, stepped in and amended the constitution, and that allowed the son to become the president. Well, the African Union was outraged: This was a repeat of the kind of thing we had in Africa years ago and we are in a new era now, and we don't do that sort of thing anymore. They put the pressure on and the president resigned and said that he would run in a legitimate election. Of course he ran and everybody knew that he would win. The RPT Party, which the father controlled and the son basically took over, controlled everything. We knew it was going to be less than a fair election. That is where it is.

*Q: I was wondering: did Togo play any part in things like trying to bring about peace in other parts of Africa? I mean, in countries such as Liberia, Sierra Leone, or Rwanda?*

YOUNG: Yes. It played a mediating role. Eyadema hosted a number of conferences and summits that were held in an effort to bring about peace in Liberia. He did play that kind of role, and unfortunately I don't think he was that successful at it. It wasn't because of him; he tried his best. The will was not there on the part of the parties to bring an end to those conflicts; but he definitely played a role there.

I had a very interesting development toward the end of my assignment. I had a young junior officer, Joel Ehrendreich, whom I liked very much. Smart, bright, the future of the Service. I really felt good about him. He did excellent work for us as a consular officer and also reporting on political developments as well until we had a full time political officer, but he was a great consular officer. One day he came to me and said, "I just had a group of people outside there. They wanted visas to go to the States to present some dance." They were people who had been cooks and bottle washers and all of these different jobs of that type. He asked them, "How do I know you can dance?" So, he took them outside in the courtyard of the embassy and said, "Dance for me." So, they danced for him and he was satisfied that they were good dancers. Now, they had come with a note from the government saying that they were going as a troupe basically under government auspices. I said, "Well, that's fine. That's within your prerogative as the visa issuing officer to satisfy yourself that these peoples' bona fides are in order. If you did that fine, no problem." But he did have the presence of mind to come and tell me about it. He said, "Well, you might hear about this from the minister of foreign affairs," who was a moron of the highest order. He was just an impossible, pompous fellow who at every step the president made you could see him dragging behind licking his boot. He was just the sycophantic type. I guess a couple of hours later I got a call from this minister of foreign affairs. He said, "Can you come to the ministry right away?" I said sure. I arrived and he said, "I got a report from our group that we sent over to get the visa that they were asked to dance before they got their visas." I said, "Well, that's within the prerogative of the consular officer and if he felt that that was necessary, so be it." He said, "This is an outrage. We cannot have this. The dignity of the people of Togo has been insulted," and on and on. I said, "Well, I'm sorry about that, but these are our rules. If they want to go this is what's required." That was that.

Later that evening my wife and I went to a fashion show at the French ambassador's residence. It was a lavish event. The runway was strung across the swimming pool and these gorgeous ladies would just come floating across in the evening night with their beautiful billowing gowns. It was just a lovely event and champagne flowed and there were lovely hors d'oeuvres. It was all done in the best French fashion. We had a good time, with good food and good conversation. We were out in the garden, the stars were out and the leaves in the palm trees. I mean it was just wonderful. We got home and said, "Gee, what a lovely evening that was."

Then as I entered the front door, I almost stepped on this huge white envelope with a sign on it, "Urgent." I opened it and there was this elaborate note from the Ministry of Foreign Affairs advising me that the government took exception to the manner in which the dancers were required to perform in the courtyard of the embassy before they were issued their visas. "We find that not proper, beneath the dignity of the people of Togo," and so on. The officer responsible for it, Mr. Ehrendreich, is hereby declared persona non grata and must leave the country within forty-eight hours. Well, I was horrified and so was Mr. Ehrendreich. I called him and told him what had happened. I said, "Don't worry I'm behind you 100 percent. I'm going to do everything I can to keep you here." His tour was going to end in a couple of months in any case. I could have taken the easy way out and said, "Okay Joel, the government has declared you PNG and that's it." I got on the phone immediately. I tried everything.

This is when I basically corroborated the rumor that Eyadema stayed in a different place every night, because I had all these numbers for him and I kept calling all of these different numbers and they said no he's not here, try this number. I tried and tried. Finally I got him and I said, "Monsieur le President, I have to see you tomorrow. Even now if possible." He said, "No, come tomorrow morning at 6:30." I said okay. The next day my DCM and I went to see Eyadema. I told him what I had come for. He knew, but he didn't acknowledge that he knew. This was at 6:30, maybe 7:30 in the morning. Then he offered us lamb brochettes and brought out the Dom Pérignon champagne. There we were, at about 7:00 in the morning in the president's office eating lamb brochettes and drinking Dom Pérignon champagne while the president listened to us and regaled us with stories of his past life. He stood up at one point and said, "Did I ever tell you this story?" I said, "No, Mr. President." He went around to his desk and he walked around and he said, "You know, once I was giving a speech and a man tried to kill me. He shot at me and fired at me. He didn't succeed. You know why?" I said, "No, Mr. President." He reached in his pocket and he pulled out a notebook. The notebook had the passage where the bullet had attempted to penetrate, and he said, "This is what saved me." You could see where it hadn't gone through and it literally did save him. I listened to the story. I looked at the DCM, Terry McCulley, who is presently our ambassador in Mali, and Terry looked at me. We thought, this is weird. Eyadema said, "Thank you very much," and that was the end of the meeting. I said, "But Mr. President, what about the issue I came to see you about." He said, "I'll talk to you later" and we left. As we were leaving, the German ambassador was coming in.

That evening, we were at a function where the German ambassador was present and I said, "How did your meeting with the president go?" He said, "My meeting went well. Did he tell that story about how he was . . . ." I said, "Yes, he did." He asked, "Did he tell you the same story also?" I said, "Yes. I don't understand what that meant." He said, "Oh, there is a method to his madness. He was trying to tell you as God saved him on that occasion he will save you on this occasion as well." That was a little bit too thick for me to comprehend at that point, so I let it go. The next day I called the president and he told me, "Don't worry, it's okay. Mr. Ehrendreich can stay." Joel stayed and completed his assignment and went on. Those were some of our fascinating tales with President Eyadema, who was quite a character.

Whenever I saw him, he said, "When can I get a visit to the United States?" I just ducked the issue each time by saying, "The timing isn't right, Mr. President, we really can't do it." I found one excuse after another, when in my heart, I was saying, "Not on my watch, Buster, no way." I knew I would be laughed out of the Service if I recommended him for a visit to the U.S., particularly with the change in circumstances in terms of our relationship with Africa in the late '90s versus what our relationship had been in the late '80s. In the mid to late '80s, he would have been welcomed once again, but it was a whole new world. We were not in competition with the Communists anymore, so his use to us was not the same. He could not change. He would say, "Well, you invited the president of Ghana, Jerry Rawlings." I said, "Yes, Rawlings came to power the way you did in a bloody coup, but Rawlings reformed and changed and as a result has been recognized and has been given a place of honor in the international community. When you change, the same will happen to you." He couldn't buy that at all. He said, "I was your good friend, I stayed by you through thick and thin," and he did, but the fact was that times had changed. He was not prepared to change with the times, so he paid the price for that.

*Q: Did you feel any of the rumblings of the dispute between the Democratic president and the Republican Congress or the shutting down of the government and shutting down of offices?*

YOUNG: You mean when we closed embassies and that sort of thing? No, we didn't feel that. I felt some of that when I was in Sierra Leone when they attempted to decrease the size of the mission. I said, "Don't do it, this is a terrible mistake," because I realized the great utility of that office, particularly when we had the coup in Sierra Leone. I mean, they provided me with very valuable information.

We had a small staff, but a great staff, and a magnificent public affairs operation. George Newman was the last public affairs officer there, an older gentleman who came into the Service later, basically having two tours that he could do, maybe three, before mandatory retirement. Togo was his second tour and he did quite well. I was very proud of him and we not only became great colleagues, but good friends as well. We're friends to this day.

*Q: All right, then '97 whither?*

YOUNG: I had gotten promoted to my great shock and surprise to career minister. I think this put the Department in a dilemma. In other words, what do they do with me? Here I am, one of the few black career ministers in the Foreign Service and they wanted to give me another assignment. Several proposals had come up and I had spoken to a number of people. I made my case to the Department and I said, "Now, if you're serious about wanting to try and encourage some black officers about advancement in the Foreign Service or even entering the Foreign Service and being able to advance to the top and being able to serve in places other than Africa, I'm your man. You know, you can use me as an experiment to see if this works. I definitely would like an assignment overseas. I'm not interested in anything in Washington whatsoever, But I do not want to go to Africa. I have spent my time in Africa. I've loved every minute of it. I've learned a tremendous amount from it, but enough is enough and it is time to do something else."

At the time, the director general was Tony Quainton and I put my case to him. He said, "You're pretty persuasive. We're going to work with you to see what we can do." I put in various bids of different types. Frankly I didn't think any of them would work. I was not a European hand per se. I was not a Near Eastern hand or a Caribbean hand or an East Asian hand. I wasn't any of those. I said if this is going to work it's going to work because the central system is going to be my advocate in making this work. I will not be the candidate of any of the geographic bureaus for this. I had a series of e-mails going back and forth and back and forth. The woman who was my career counselor at the time, Margaret Dean, was just a wonderful officer. She worked very closely with me and we came down to a couple of possibilities. But they said, "Well, you might be a prospect for Bahrain." I couldn't believe it. The last time I had been in Bahrain or had anything to do with Bahrain was when I was in Qatar from '74 to '77. We used to go over there from time to time because it was like heaven. I said, "I certainly would be interested, but I realize I'm not the bureau's candidate and I know it's going to be very competitive."

Months went by and we kept the correspondence going back and forth between myself, Margaret Dean, the PDAS (principal deputy assistant secretary) in personnel at the time, and Quainton. I remember getting a note that said the D Committee would be meeting on X date and then they would let me know what was what. The date kept being postponed, which is often the case with these committee meetings. Then I got an email saying that the committee had met and that I was going to be the candidate for Manama in Bahrain. Well I was absolutely thrilled. If this all worked out it meant that I was going to be the only black ambassador in the Near Eastern Bureau and one of the few outside of Africa. There were none in Europe at the time and I think there was one in Latin America and the rest were all in Africa. This was going to be a bit of history. I remember announcing to my staff in Togo that this prospect was looking good. Then I left for the States and prepared myself for confirmation. I went on a direct transfer with deferred home leave and stopped in time to prepare myself and to have hearings and meetings and those kinds of things.

# AMBASSADOR TO BAHRAIN

On December 19, 1997 we arrived in Bahrain. Bahrain's national day is on the 15th. The town was festooned with red and white lights, which are the national colors of Bahrain. I remember my wife saying, "Oh, Johnny, look at all of these lights. Isn't it wonderful they have decorated for Christmas?" I had to say, "Honey; this is not for Christmas. These are the national colors of Bahrain." All of the buildings were trimmed with red and white lights and they were decked out in the streets and what have you. Now, that said, there were places that had Christmas lights as well for the expatriate community there.

We arrived, were met by the chief of protocol and then we were whisked to our new residence. We were the first people to occupy this new residence. Before we arrived, we had heard that the former residence was being returned to the owner, who wanted it, and the embassy was looking desperately for a new appropriate residence. Before we left the States we got word from the man who was to be my DCM, George Staples, who said, we think we have found something for you. He made a videotape of the potential new residence and sent it to us. It looked good to us by videotape. We said go for it and that was the house they rented. When we arrived they had transferred the furniture from the former residence, which had been occupied by Ambassador David Ransom, into the new residence. It really did look nice. It was a mini-palace, a lovely place. We could hold a reception for two hundred people in the foyer. The living room was in three sections and seventy-five feet long.

*Q: I'm just thinking, that's not a very big island.*

YOUNG: Oh, but there are some fabulous houses and a lot of wealth on that little island. Six bedrooms, all with en-suite baths, a beautiful family room, and a huge kitchen, plus an outdoor kitchen where you could prepare meals outside without having all the smells come from the kitchen, for big functions. An indoor swimming pool with sauna and steam bath, exercise room; I mean it was just unbelievable. No garden, just a sandpit, so we saw our work cut out for us in terms of trying to make a garden, finishing up the touches in terms of the residence and things like that. The emir of Bahrain agreed to receive my credentials within days of my arrival, so that was very nice. I remember asking if I could take my wife and they said, no, I could not. I understood that these functions are just for the principal and I could not take her. We went to the palace. I had never been in a palace before. I mean I had been in official government offices and other buildings, but these were actually called palaces and were indeed palaces. They were unbelievable and the emir had so many of them it was unbelievable. This was at his palace in downtown Manama.

The deputy chief of mission accompanied me to the palace. Prior to that meeting at the palace, the chief of protocol had instructed me on how I was to proceed in presenting the letters of credence. How I would walk so many steps, stand at a certain line that would be on the floor, then proceed so many steps after that, present the letters, back up, and then stand and wait for the emir to make any comments Then I was to make comments. I had written out some comments and had submitted them to the chief of protocol beforehand. After that I was to go with the emir to a little side area where we would sit and talk. After the whole thing was over, I was to leave. I did all of that. It all worked out very nicely. I was told you could tell when it's over because a server would come with a perfume bottle of rose water. He would sprinkle rose water on your hands and then he would come with burning incense like a chalice. You were supposed to take this incense and bring the fumes of it into your clothing. Then you would take the rose water and rinse your hands. That marked the end of the function.

During our talk we didn't discuss anything of any substance, just little tidbits about our families, where the emir had traveled and how he liked the United States, and how he was so fond of us and we had been so good to the island. I told him they had been good to us, which they were. They were just a fantastic ally. So, the fellow came with the incense and I sort of fanned it into my clothes. We had lived in Qatar and we learned a little something there. He brought the rose water and I rubbed it in my hands and then thanked the emir. Before we left, he said, "You know, I'm impressed. You knew exactly what to do." I said, "Well, thank you, your highness." He said, "You're not like one of the ambassadors we've had here. He took the rose water and he tried to put out the fire in the incense holder." I said, "Oh, no, I wouldn't try that, I learned how to do this in Qatar." He said, "Well, that's very nice." I asked him, "Who was that?" He was reluctant to tell me. He said, "Well, it was one of the former Japanese ambassadors who had tried that." Anyhow we were off to a good start with the emir.

That was quite an assignment for me. Bahrain had never had a black ambassador from the U.S. Frankly, it had never had a black in any senior position in the mission. I learned later they were all curious as to what I was going to be like and how many heads I had and that sort of thing. There was a lot of watching and observing and seeing what I was going to be like, what I was going to say and how supportive I was going to be. They learned very quickly that they had in me a very good friend, impressing on the U.S. what a good friend we had in Bahrain as well. It worked both ways. At the time, we had the Fifth Fleet there, which was managed by Admiral Thomas Fargo, and he was doing a magnificent job. We were very busy enforcing the no-fly zone in Iraq. We were policing the Persian Gulf, interdicting illegal smuggling of petroleum and other products through the Gulf, and also keeping an eye on the Iranians, who were making mischief in the Gulf. We wanted them to know they couldn't do any harm there. The Fifth Fleet was really very important, and key to our interests in the Gulf.

Q: *That was the Fifth Fleet's headquarters then.*

YOUNG: Yes.

Q: *It used to be something called COMIDEASTFOR.*

YOUNG: It was COMIDEASTFOR. They had a big white ship, the *USS La Salle*. At one point we told the Government of Bahrain that we were having a change in policy, that we were closing down that operation, and that this symbolic ship was going to leave. And I think we told them it was going to be decommissioned. Well, as it turned out, the ship was later removed and we changed the name to the Fifth Fleet because the Bahrainis were originally not particularly keen on having the Fifth Fleet. They preferred the COMIDEASTFOR arrangement. In the end it all worked out, but they never forgave us. They always remembered that bit of deception on our part, because the *La Salle* did go to another place. I can't recall where it remained, I think in Italy or a country that was extremely important to our interests.

At the time we didn't have anything comparable to Bahrain. We did have a base in Kuwait following the first Iraq war. The Kuwaitis were very open, but you know, being in Kuwait is not the same as being in Bahrain by any means. We didn't have much in Abu Dhabi, but we did have free access, we could go in and out and the fellows could have some shore leave and that sort of thing. We also had some permanent, but not acknowledged, operations in Saudi Arabia. The Saudis would say, "No, no we don't have anything permanent. We only have temporary duty people here." That was a fiction at the time. We had a little something in Saudi Arabia, and a little bit of something in Oman, and that was it. The commander of the Fifth Fleet in Bahrain controlled all of our operations, big or small, in the Gulf.

Now, my relationship with the commander of the Fifth Fleet was good. I attempted to be as inclusive as I could in terms of including him in any meetings that had anything to do with the military. If I were going to talk about something economic or what have you, there would be no need to include him. That worked out very nicely with Admiral Fargo. With his replacement I think there was some resentment that he couldn't move more freely in terms of his relationship with the host government, but I had to make it very clear that I was the one who spoke for the U.S. government, not the commander of the Fifth Fleet, although the commander of the fleet had all of the assets. That was the way it was. I just tried to be as inclusive as I possibly could. It worked out. We had a good working relationship. We saw, I think, eye to eye on most things until we had the incident of the Cole. That changed how I would look at things or how my mission looked at things versus how they were perceived by the Fifth Fleet.

*Q: Had there been any move towards making Qatar sort of a central command center?*

YOUNG: No, there was talk, but that was it at that point. We had nothing in Qatar at that point. In fact, the Bahrainis and the Qataris were in dispute over territorial issues and had a big case before the International Court in The Hague, a case that had been around for sixty-some years.

Q: *Was that the Hawar Island case?*

YOUNG: On Hawar Island. In fact, it was resolved while I was there. It worked out and was resolved basically in favor of Bahrain.

That was my introduction. I began to make calls, which is standard procedure for an arriving ambassador, on all the different ministers. The foreign minister was an incredible fellow who turned out to be one of my best colleagues, one of the best foreign ministers I think I have ever worked with. He was just a consummate professional, a well-trained Ph.D. from England, a perfect speaker of English, so knowledgeable, and had been foreign minister from the time of independence in 1971. He had already been foreign minister for thirty years or so by the time I got there. He was wonderful. Sheik Mohammad bin Mubarak Al Khalifa. Until recently he was foreign minister and is now the deputy prime minister. The Al Khalifa family is basically a family business. The prime minister was the brother of the fellow who was emir when I first went to Bahrain, Sheik Isa bin Salman Al Khalifa. His brother, Sheik Al Khalifa, was the prime minister and was reportedly the most corrupt of all of the Al Khalifas. He would demand 10 percent of any government project. One major project that was carried out before I arrived was the hydroelectric plant that was valued at $500 million and allegedly his man went from contract to contract to say, okay, now when can we expect your 10 percent. I mean, he was one of the wealthiest men there. It was a fascinating family. Sheik Isa had a brother who was the prime minister and another brother who was just a renegade and a little bit off the deep end, but he was a businessman and the prime minister and his renegade brother even used to have fist fights. It is still a legend in Bahrain that these two had a fist fight at one time and the renegade brother beat up the prime minister. It was over some land dispute or what have you, but this renegade brother refused to put license plates on his many cars and had always traveled with a shotgun displayed in the back window of his car. Nobody would fool with him because they were afraid to. He didn't hurt anyone, though according to legend he did shoot up one fellow or scared him by sort of shooting at him, a top businessman in town. People treated him very delicately. Because he was a member of the royal family I paid a call on him and he took a liking to my wife and me. He invited us to his home and one of the highlights of our stay in Bahrain included some of the tales of visiting with him on his island.

Many interesting things went on when we were in Bahrain. Before I arrived Bahrain was interested in purchasing some additional F-16s, but we had not agreed that they could have them. They wanted to get the F-16s with a certain type of missile. We said, "No, we haven't released this technology to any Arab country." We were thinking, "What would the Israelis think?" We didn't come out and say that, but that was a fact. I remember talking to the DAS (deputy assistant secretary) in PM (Bureau of Political-Military Affairs) at that time, Mike Lennon. Mike would bring me into work in the morning because I was basically on TDY (temporary duty) as I prepared to go to Bahrain. I told him this was one of the things they wanted. He said, "Over my dead body, Johnny. It's just not going to happen. They're not going to get those missiles." I said okay. I wouldn't give up though. I didn't give up on the sale of the F-16s or on the missiles. This country had been our good ally. They said they wanted them so that, if they had a similar situation as in the first Gulf War, they would be prepared so they could be fully integrated and contribute to a joint effort. These missiles weren't going to do any good because they were five minutes by F-16 from Iran. But if they needed them to be a part of a larger effort, then it would help. This was the argument we tried to make, but we weren't getting anywhere. We'd get turned back every time, but we just kept hammering away. As VIP visitors would come over, the secretary of defense and so on, the Bahrainis would make their case over and over. We told them frankly.

The emir was invited for a visit to Washington in May of '98. I accompanied him on that visit. We met with President Clinton. They had a lunch for him. It was very nice, I must say. Before he came, Secretary Albright came and they were all very grateful for the role that Bahrain was playing in the no-fly zone and also in hosting the UN team searching in Iraq for weapons of mass destruction. They were all supported out of Bahrain. Logistically this was where they would fly in and fly out. When they came out, I would meet with the head of the team to debrief. He would meet with me, and with the Brits, the French, and the Russians. We would debrief, then of course we would fire that right back to our governments and discuss whether they needed any special help on some things. I mean there were certain things that we would do that we didn't tell the Russians about or we didn't tell the French about and that sort of thing, because this was such an important mission. That was when I met the Swede who was the head of the UN inspection team at the time, Hans Blix.

We were very appreciative of the role that Bahrain was playing in support of this activity. Whenever our VIPs came out, they would give them a big pat on the back for the role they were playing. They would play up how important it was, because we would also launch some of our retaliatory attacks on Iraq from Bahrain.

Now, I'm going back to the time prior to the emir's visit because of something that happened that I want to get on the record. In March of 1998, Madeleine Albright was coming out to visit. She was basically visiting the region and also wanted a blank check in terms of the launch of attacks on Iraq from Bahrain. Before she arrived I got a call from the royal chief of protocol and he said, "Johnny, I want to talk to you." I said, "Okay." I went over to his office. He said, "Johnny, I called you in because I don't want a repeat of what happened the last time Madeleine Albright visited Bahrain." I said, "What happened?" He said, "She arrived and the minister of the interior was the acting minister of foreign affairs. He met her and he got ready to get in the car with her and was pushed aside and told, "You can't ride with her." He was outraged that this had happened and he said, "Okay, if you don't want me to ride with her, I won't ride with her." Now, this man was representing the emir of Bahrain as the acting minister of foreign affairs because the minister of foreign affairs was out of the country at the time. It was not appreciated at all. He said, "I don't want a repeat of that. I don't want it." I said, "Okay, I'll make sure that this is made clear to the secretary and her party." The advance person for her visit was David Hale. I explained what the situation was and I said, "Would you please send a cable to her party advising what we should do, that the foreign minister plans to meet her plane side and expects to ride with her. If that is not possible we need to tell them up front. The royal chief of protocol wants to know." He said, "Okay." He sent a message and I was amazed that we had quite a bit of going back and forth including messages from Tom Pickering on this issue of the minister of foreign affairs riding from the airport to the initial meeting with the emir and the prime minister. We finally got an okay, after much going back and forth.

Now, mind you, this is a government of Bahrain that agreed to give us something like fifty hotel rooms and thirty Mercedes, all for free. I remember specifically asking Dick Shinnick, whom I know, if we could accept this and he agreed that we could, that the government had given us this to carry out our mission. Here, we got all of this free and we're quibbling over the foreign minister riding for just a few minutes literally to a meeting with the prime minister and the emir. I would then ride with the secretary from that meeting to the embassy, where she was going to meet with the embassy staff and take a few photos. Well, in the end it worked out very well. The secretary arrived and the foreign minister rode with her and then I rode with her to the embassy and that all turned out very well. It was a one-day visit and they all spent the night in the hotel and the next morning when it was time to leave we were supposed to reverse the procedure. The foreign minister was to meet her at the hotel. He would wait downstairs for her. When she was ready she would come downstairs and join him. They would get in the car together and go to the airport, which was all of fifteen minutes away.

Well, that morning, I was sitting in the little room with the foreign minister when the phone rang and I was told, "Oh, it's for you Mr. Young." It was the secretary's chief of staff. I've forgotten the name of this woman, but she was a horrible woman and she said, "The foreign minister can't ride with the secretary." I said, "You must be kidding. I'm sitting right there." He wasn't right next to me, but I said, "The foreign minister is in the room here downstairs waiting. I cannot go over to him now and tell him, Mr. Minister, you cannot ride with the secretary to the airport, which is fifteen minutes away. If you want to turn what has been a very successful visit into a disaster, then I'll go over and tell him." They thought about that for a while and then she got off the phone and then she put David Hale on the phone. He said, "Johnny, this is terrible. We can't have this. We never have people ride with the secretary. Now the foreign minister rode with her once. He shouldn't be expected to ride with her a second time. This is going to look bad on your record." I said, "I really don't care. I've had a wonderful career and I have to watch this relationship, that's what's important to me. If you want to ruin this relationship or really put a blemish on it at this point, you proceed with what you've just told me." I was just livid. I could not believe the insensitivity of people who were working so closely with the secretary that they would do something like this. I said, "This is just awful." After some hemming and hawing and some threats to me and what have you, they said, "Okay, he can do it this time, but if we come here again, this can't happen." I didn't have to go and carry out that dreadful message to the foreign minister. The plans proceeded as they were laid out. The secretary came out downstairs. The foreign minister met her. They got in the car together and less than fifteen minutes later they were at the airport.

I asked someone, "Why is this?" They said, "Well, you know, she likes to sleep in the car. She likes to doze in the car." I said, "She's going from here to Egypt, that's about four hours on the plane, she can certainly sleep plenty on the plane to Egypt." Anyhow, I got in the car with Martin Indyk, who was the assistant secretary for Near Eastern affairs at the time. I said, "Martin, this is just what unfolded while I was waiting there at the hotel. They threatened me that this is not going to look good on my record and on and on. Martin, I don't give a damn. I don't care. I've had a wonderful career. I could care less. My job is to protect this relationship. It is of maximum benefit to the U.S. government." He said, "I understand, Johnny. Don't worry about it." Well, I accepted his word for it. Would you believe, two months later I got a call from the deputy assistant secretary of state for Near Eastern Affairs, Ron Neumann, who eventually replaced me in Bahrain. He said, "Oh, Johnny, I'm just checking in to see how things are going." He tried to do it in a very casual kind of way. He said, "Well, I just want you to know that if the secretary comes out there again we can't have a repeat of what we had with the foreign minister riding in the car with her." I said, "That's not a problem, but we've got to let them know ahead of time that this is her preference. Otherwise they'll make other arrangements and they won't have the foreign minister there. They'll have some clerk meet her."

Q: *Politically they were people of such little consequence after she departed the scene they were never heard again.*

YOUNG: Well, I'm not so sure.

Q: *Secretary Baker had a court and they're still around because they were good.*

YOUNG: Yes, well, I'm not so sure about them not being heard from again. I think the woman I was speaking of was named Elaine Schouse. As I said, David Hale was a Foreign Service officer just trying to please the secretary of state and he was basically taking orders from Elaine and others around her. For example, when I rode in the car with the secretary from the prime minister's office to the embassy, where she was going to take pictures with children, I asked her about that and she said "Oh, I love to do that sort of thing." Her staff had told me just the reverse. They told me, "Oh, she really doesn't like that and she doesn't want to be bothered with it." But she said, "I love that sort of thing." I think that, in that particular case, they did her a disservice. But, that said, I saw another side of her. For example, on the day that we had the official state visit of the emir in May of 1998, I was invited to her office to brief her before the emir paid her a visit. I walked in her office and there she was with a few other people and she said in a nasty arrogant tone, "The *last* thing I want to hear about today is Bahrain," Now, here I am, the American representative there. I went to her office to brief her on what the issues he would likely raise and that was the greeting that I got as I walked into her office. I was not impressed.

I would add that for a woman of her standing and stature, I expected a little bit more in terms of how she made her presentations. I will never forget that meeting with the emir when she sat there with her legs crossed wearing a relatively short skirt, shall we say, which was not appropriate for that kind of setting in the Arab world. I mean, she was dressed very nicely, but that kind of position was just not the right one for that kind of setting. She had these five-by-eight cards and she would basically read her presentation from the cards. On that visit, Tom Pickering was with her and a few other big shots. Pickering had visited Bahrain before and they just adored him. On another occasion, when Pickering was coming out on a possible visit by himself, I remember the prime minister saying to me, "Oh, I love that man so much. He's so bright. He doesn't use those cards." That told the story right there: "He doesn't use those cards." Well, that's how she made her presentations. That's how she made them to the emir, to the prime minister, and to the foreign minister. You know, thanking them for their help and support and blah, blah, and asking for basically a blanket approval to launch attacks from Bahrain on Iraq. And the emir would not agree. He said, "Launch them from one of your ships at sea." He said, "We're going to have to live with this guy after you've gone." The other thing he said was, "We don't think you're serious. You talk about getting rid of Saddam, but what you're doing is strengthening him. You hit him a little bit here and you hit him a little bit there. It doesn't get rid of him. It weakens him a little bit, but then he gets stronger. He wins sympathy from others in the Arab world. If you're serious, we're with you. But otherwise we have to think more in terms of living with this guy." That was the emir's take on it.

Now, unlike Madeleine Albright, who came out there just once, the other top visitors were the secretary of defense, William Cohen, who came nine times during my assignment there, and the head of the Central Command, General Zinni, who also came many, many times. The Central Command really had control over the Fifth Fleet and the entire region. It was all that theater. These guys were great visitors. They knew the importance of how you massage a relationship in the Arab world and how you keep that friendship going just on a friendly level, so that when you need them one day you can go in and say, hey, can you help me out here, and they'll come through. They always did come through for us.

Well, anyhow, when the emir came to the States, he put his case before President Clinton and before the secretary of defense and in the end we were successful in getting them the planes. They bought a dozen F-16s and they got the missiles they wanted to go with the F-16s as well. That was a major achievement. I was very pleased with that.

Things continued to go along very nicely. We continued the policing. We continued these periodic attacks on Iraq, as we say, to demean and diminish his various sites and equipment. In the end, it sort of broke down things a little bit but really did not make a significant difference. Then Secretary Cohen came out for a visit in March of 1999. Cohen, other members of the team, and I met with the emir. The emir was not his usual lively self. We met for forty-five minutes. We had a couple of moments when we had pregnant pauses where we had to sort of pull things out of him and he did acknowledge that he did not feel particularly well that morning. We left his office. It was a good, cordial, friendly meeting. The emir said, "Well, if I hadn't agreed to meet with you I probably wouldn't have come in today, but I agreed." He kept his word. That was the kind of man that he was. The prime minister and the foreign minister were in the meeting as well. The minister of defense was there. I was sitting next to Cohen. We had a couple of other people from the embassy, the note-takers and so on. The plan was that we would then proceed from the palace to the ministry of defense, where we would have a lunch and from that lunch Cohen would fly out directly.

It was March 6. Following the meeting with the emir, we went to the lunch. I was at the head table with the secretary of defense, together with the minister of defense and the chief of staff of the Bahraini armed forces. I was sitting next to the chief of staff and the secretary was seated next to the minister of defense.

Everything was going along nicely, but we were there for a very short time when the minister of defense got up and left the room. He came back and then he got up again and he left and he came back and then he got up a third time and he didn't come back. Very shortly after that, the chief of staff leaned over to me and said, "Sheik Isa is dead." I said, "I don't believe it." He said, "No, he just died." Well, we were all speechless. We passed the news immediately to others in the room and the secretary learned of it because he was at the head table with the rest of us. We were absolutely stunned. We just could not believe it because we had left him literally no more than fifteen to twenty minutes earlier and we learned later that he died of a massive heart attack. Well, our secretary of defense was going to proceed with his plans, but I told him, "You can't proceed with your plans. We have to stay. You have to stay and pay your condolences to the family. You have to go to the new emir who assumed power immediately upon the death of Sheik Isa." His son Sheik Hamad became the new emir. So, Cohen discussed it with his party and agreed that that would happen.

Of course as you can imagine, the telegrams were immediately flying back and forth to Washington over this. After a while we returned to Sheik Isa's palace, where his son greeted us. The secretary extended condolences on behalf of the U.S. government and on behalf of himself personally. I did the same and when we left, the new emir grabbed us both and hugged us. It was an incredible moment. I cannot remember, and I would guess that former Secretary Cohen probably cannot recall, a meeting where a head of state embraced him so emotionally as happened on that occasion. It was such a touching moment. Well, those of us in the embassy were deeply saddened by this death. Sheik Isa was a remarkable man, a man of enormous generosity, kindness, and great understanding, loved by his people. The Shi'a community represented about 65 percent of the population, but the country was run by the Sunni Al Khalifa family. Despite internal turmoil and setting off bombs all over town and things like that by those who wanted to get the attention of the government to implement the changes in the way things were done in Bahrain, Sheik Isa never allowed security to be put in place in his biweekly meetings with the population. At the time we were in Bahrain, the local tradition of the population coming once or twice a week to pay deference to the head of state was still the practice.

*Q: It wasn't just deference. It was sort of a majlis.*

YOUNG: It was a majlis.

*Q: They would come and present petitions.*

YOUNG: Oh definitely, come and present petitions. If anything, it was their form of democracy in a sense. It was their way of staying in touch with the people and listening to the will of the people at least in terms of what the people wanted in a material sense. That worked out very nicely, because he would meet literally thousands in the course of a week and they would come and say well, I need this and that and can you help me with this and that and he would say, well, see Mr. so-and-so on my staff, or here's some money for this, here's some money for that. I mean he was literally the father figure dispensing kindness and largesse to his people, and they loved him. They respected him enormously. I think it's a very revealing fact that despite this turmoil that had really been in effect for a couple of years, at no time did he allow his people to put in security where he would screen and frisk people and tighten up measures. People came in freely. They left freely. They embraced him. They shook his hand. It was truly remarkable and it went on until the time of his death. That to me was indicative of the kind of respect that the people had for him; no one harmed him or wanted to harm him. In keeping with Muslim tradition, the emir was buried immediately in a traditional Muslim ceremony, cleansed, washed, wrapped in very simple cotton or muslin material and placed in a very simple grave outside of Bahrain. Later on, we went to the gravesite and it was as simple as you would expect. There is a more prominent marker there than the others, but nothing terribly elaborate, nothing in the grand style that you would find in so many cemeteries.

March 11, 1999 marked the day of a major change in governance in Bahrain as well. The new emir certainly was aware that one day he would assume power, but he didn't know when that would be. It was totally unexpected, but he was prepared for it. I thought it was interesting that prior to his father's death he had said certain things to us that we found quite interesting and quite surprising. For example, he had indicated that if he were in power he was prepared to open up the system to a much greater degree than his father. Now, he did that very carefully. He didn't do it in any open way to criticize his father while his father was living. In our meetings with him immediately following his father's death he was considerably expansive in that regard, saying that he wanted to open the system up, that he wanted to give people an opportunity to participate in the government more and to take the country in a new direction. He began to do that. In the meantime we continued our pressure on Iraq. It was clear to us that we would continue to get good support from the new emir, that he was as cooperative as his father, perhaps a little bit more deliberative than his father. We could go to his father and say "Oh, Sheik Isa, can we do so and so," and he'd say, "Sure go ahead and do it," and that would be that. With this new fellow, it would be "sounds like a good idea, sounds reasonable, let me think about that. I'll get back to you." It was a different way of doing business.

*Q: It sounds like somebody who hasn't been on the job that long, you know.*

YOUNG: He wasn't, but of course he was in close contact with his father and in the decisions taken by his father, and he had been the minister of defense.

He was the crown prince and the commander in chief of the armed forces and he took great pride in his military training. He had been trained as a military man. He had spent time in Brussels, at Sandhurst in England, and he had spent a year at the Army Staff College at Fort Leavenworth in the United States. In fact, both Emir Sheik Hamad and his wife Sheika Sabika have said separately that their year in the United States was one of the best times in their lives. I remember the Sheik Hamad saying that when he left people cried. That was not true when he left England and it wasn't true when he left Belgium, but when he left the United States the outpouring of affection and the friendships that he had established were unprecedented. He had not had that kind of experience anywhere else. I remember Sheika Sabika saying to my wife that her time in the United States was so wonderful and so liberating. She gave the example of being in a room where these ladies were working on a project or something like that and suddenly this lady from the other end of the room said, "Hey, Sabika, can you come over here and help me with so-and-so?" She said she was absolutely startled when she heard that, because she had always heard, your highness this, your highness that, but she was treated as just a regular person and she loved it. She really, really liked that. Again, she spoke of the friendships and the emotional attachments of that period in the United States with great fondness. That had a great impact on them and, as a result, it helped to make them even better friends of the United States.

We wanted to move as quickly as we could to bring the new emir to the United States to meet with the president. We wanted to seize the opportunity to put a stamp on them, so to speak, to encourage them to move ahead with the reforms that he had in mind. We began to push for an official visit and eventually got one. Once again, in May of 2000, I had the privilege of accompanying the emir back on a visit to the United States. He met with President Clinton. It was an opportunity to reaffirm the relationship. It was also an opportunity to put in his plug for some military equipment and missiles that they wanted. It was also an opportunity to ask for something that he wanted restored, which was to have the military dependents return to Bahrain. Following the incident of the USS Cole and some other security threats that were occurring in the region, the commander of the Fifth Fleet had decided to send the dependents home. A good number of the dependents returned to the U.S. and no new ones could come out. This of course created quite a problem for the school, which was a DOD (Department of Defense) school. It was one of the most unusual schools in the entire DOD system. Although it was set up primarily to provide for the education of military dependents, it had a very large community of Bahrainis and international students. It was more of an international school than a DOD school, with an international baccalaureate program and advanced placement programs, many of which were not usually found in DOD schools. The new crown prince, the son of the new emir, had his two children in the school and he himself was a graduate of the school. That was also a factor in the support that the school received from DOD. Those were the key things that the new emir took up in his visits with the president, the secretary of state, and the secretary of defense. Those were the three key individual meetings that he had and it was great.

I remember certain things about that visit. For example, we knew that the emir had agreed to stay at the Four Seasons Hotel, a very fine hotel. The hotel staff certainly made it clear that they would accommodate in whatever way they could. I was part of the receiving party at the airport when his plane arrived at Andrews Air Force Base. We met him and we took the long route back, sort of a little tour, and then we arrived at the Four Seasons Hotel. Mind you, I was back on TDY (temporary duty) to stay for the duration of his visit, but of course I could not stay at the Four Seasons Hotel; there was no way that per diem would cover me for that. So I stayed at a hotel two blocks away. Anyhow, the emir said, "Well, why don't you stay here with me? Don't worry about it, I'll take care of it." I thanked him very much, but said, no, I could not and I stayed at my hotel. He said, "Please come on up to my room, my suite." I went up there and the other person who met him and accompanied him on this trip was the former Saudi ambassador to Washington, Sheikh Bandar, who had also been the dean of the diplomatic corps at that time. We went up to the suite and I could not believe my eyes. I looked around and I could have been in one of the emir's palaces back in Bahrain. The hotel had literally pulled out all the stops imaginable and had made his suite look exactly like one of his palaces in Bahrain. It was a remarkable job. God knows what it cost them, but of course money was not a factor. It was one of those little things that I'll remember.

It was a good visit and lasted a couple of days. The emir met all of the people he wanted to see. In the end, he achieved what he wanted in terms of getting the military equipment, or at least a commitment in principle. He also got an agreement to have the dependents return, which worked out very well. I mean, this was important in terms of the image of Bahrain, a country that prided itself on being such a good friend of the United States and a rock of stability in the Gulf. They were very concerned about that.

*Q: Could you talk a little bit about your impression of the meeting with President Clinton and how he engaged in this?*

YOUNG: Yes. President Clinton is a master at these kinds of things. He has the ability to make the person he is receiving the center of everything that is going on around him; and that was the way he was in this meeting. I mean he was truly remarkable. He had a way of taking that person aside and, as he walked with them through the White House, pointing out different little historical things here and there: "Here, let me tell you a little something about this picture," and so on. He did the same with the emir's father, Sheik Isa, as well. That was quite a picture, as you could imagine. I mean, Sheik Isa was about five feet tall and Clinton was about six-two, so it was a wonderful picture of this little emir from the Gulf with all of his regalia and President Clinton looking as smooth and as easy as possible with this fellow. He was just remarkable and also very supportive in terms of how he addressed issues without making any commitments that would not be cleared by his staff, and that sort of thing. He knew how to do it in such a way that the person putting the petition to him leaves feeling that he's been heard and that there's hope, and he did it beautifully. He's a master, just one of the best there is. Of course he's so articulate and what more can I say on that score? He made us all very proud.

I'd like to go back to February of 1999, when I decided to visit a cardiologist in Bahrain because I was having some chest pains. I had spoken to Sheik Isa and he had said to me, "I want you to go to the military hospital. It has the best cardiologist in the country and they'll take care of you. If you need to be flown out I will fly you out. I will take care of everything," and so on. I went to this cardiologist, who examined me and said I had a blockage in one of my arteries. I had an angioplasty there in Bahrain at their army hospital, which was as good as you'll find anywhere. The State Department was quite alarmed that I had agreed to do it there. While I was in the hospital the regional medical doctor flew in from Saudi Arabia to check things and see what was going on. He satisfied himself that it was as good as you were going to get. They even made a DVD, a CD-ROM, of everything they did to me. It was incredible. Later on, I took this CD back to the States for an evaluation of what they had done. They looked at it and said, "Wow, this is as good as it gets."

Sheik Isa was just incredibly supportive during that time. When I was in the hospital there was an outpouring of affection for me, or for the position, I don't know if it was for me or for the position, but it was unbelievable. I received 125 bouquets of flowers, there were so many they couldn't keep them in the hospital anymore; they had to take them out because they said this may cause allergic reactions among other patients in the hospital. I felt like I was either dead or something. I had never seen so many flowers before, and these flowers were arranged in the most elaborate fashion you can imagine. I mean, very little is done simply in that part of the world, but with great elaboration. Anyhow it was wonderful. The emir could not have been better. I will never forget that after I went home, he called me one day. I answered the phone and said "Hello, who is this?" He said, "Hello, this is Isa." That was all, not this is Sheik so-and-so. "This is Isa. How are you doing? How are you feeling? Are you getting better? Do you need anything;

do you want anything?" I mean, he was that kind of guy. Then he came out to the house to sit with me and to see how I was doing. It was just another example of what an extraordinary person he was.

In 2000 his son, Sheik Hamad, visited the States. As I said, that was a very successful visit. We returned and continued our work with the Bahrainis in terms of their support for what we were doing in Iraq in policing the no-fly zone and occasionally having these hits on Saddam's facilities, either his radar facilities or some bunker or something like that, none of which really did him any great harm. From the new emir we continued to hear what we had heard from the former emir, which was that if we were serious in our efforts to take down Saddam, they would be with us. The emir said, "Until you do that, what you're doing is not helping the case, but its enhancing Saddam's standing in the region. We've got to live with this guy. If he survives he's going to be the tough guy in the neighborhood and we've got to be able to deal with him." That was how they felt about that at that time.

During this period, differences began to develop between the embassy and the Fifth Fleet in terms of how we saw the security situation there. It was serious. The situation of Palestinians had a very serious impact on sentiments in Bahrain and in other countries in the Gulf. That said, I still saw us as being in a relatively good, secure situation. The commander of the Fifth Fleet was considerably more cautious. I think that what was in his mind was that, "Look, this *USS Cole* incident occurred on my watch. I can't have anything else happen on my watch." That is an understandable view. If I had been in his shoes I would probably have thought with the same amount of caution and carefulness and would have made my decisions accordingly. He was truly frightened and would not take any chances at all, which was why the dependents were sent home and why they weren't letting replacements with dependents come in. That situation continued for quite some time.

July 4, 2001 was an example of how this came to a head. It was a glaring example of the difference that the two of us saw. Leading up to July 4 we were seeing a lot of chatter in intelligence channels about the possibility of something happening in the region. No one knew what it was going to be: when, where, how and what have you. This made us all very nervous and if it made us nervous at the embassy you can only imagine that it made the commander of the Fifth Fleet even more nervous. We always had a very elaborate and remarkable July 4 party. We held it in one of the top hotels in Bahrain and thousands attended. About 2,500 people attended, perhaps more like 5,000, huge, elaborately decorated, the best food you could think of. Each year we had a theme. One year it was Main Street, USA and another year, the last year I was there, in 2001, it centered on our diversity. We had foods to fit the different ethnic groups that you would find around the United States. We held it at the Gulf Hotel, which had the largest conference center in Bahrain. The money for this didn't come from the State Department.

This event ran like $40,000 to $50,000 and it all came from contributions from American companies there, primarily IBM and Microsoft and particularly the American banks, Citibank and banks of that type. It was just unbelievable. We had agreed with the hotel. We had worked out the menu. I was working on my speech or rather people were working on my speech. We had everything set up. We had an agreement with the daughter of a fellow who was an officer with the Fifth Fleet for her to sing the National Anthem. We were going to then have a Bahraini fellow sing the Bahraini National Anthem. We had the band from the Bahrain Police, a top-notch band. So everything was arranged. Then, as I said, this intelligence chatter picked up in pitch and it looked like something may go down or was going to go down in Bahrain. I'll never forget that July 4. It was one of the most troublesome days of my life, because at the very last minute we had a piece of very credible intelligence that indicated that there could be something. Of course we shared this; we shared everything with the military. I had gone to the minister of the interior and to the emir. I told him, "We're down to the wire now. Either I cancel this whole thing or we proceed and we have to have every security measure in place." I conferred with my country team, with the security officer, and I got support from all of them. There was only one member of the country team who was not sure of going ahead with this thing or not. It came down to a decision that I had to make myself. I thought about it hard. I thought about the assurances I had from the government. I thought about the material we had looked at, the intelligence we had looked at. I thought about the physical arrangements we had made and I decided I would proceed with the event.

At about the same time the admiral of the Fifth Fleet issued an immediate order to his people prohibiting them from attending the Fourth of July function at the Gulf Hotel. We had invited hundreds of his people and we were particularly counting on this young girl who was a dependent of one of his officers to sing the National Anthem. At the last minute, the DCM asked Joe Mussomeli to ask his daughter, Alexis, to sing the National Anthem. First of all I didn't know that Alexis could sing and I'd never heard her sing. To my knowledge, she had certainly never performed in front of any large groups. She had no time to rehearse because this was all decided on the day of the function itself. She didn't have time to practice with the band that was going to be there and that sort of thing.

Anyhow, we proceeded with the function. Thousands came. We got to the point in the program where the national anthems were played. The Bahraini sung his and then Alexis got up and she sang and she did a magnificent job. I mean, it was like listening to an angel. We were moved to tears: my wife, Joe Mussomeli, his wife. We just couldn't believe it. Here this young girl, she was no more than about fourteen or fifteen at the time, just did a truly magnificent job. I mean talk about stepping up to the plate and taking on this kind of challenge. She did it and hit a home run. It was something I will never, ever forget. The function was a great success. We didn't have any security problems at all and I was very relieved that it turned out so well in the end.

*Q: I take it the admiral did not show up.*

YOUNG: Oh, no, not at all. Normally he would have been in the receiving line with me because he was a key official.

*Q: How did this go with the Bahraini authorities?*

YOUNG: They were disappointed that he was not in the line, because they'd been coming to these things for years and expected to see him there. But they also understood his sensitivity to the security situation in Bahrain at the time. Our work proceeded as usual. We continued to receive all kinds of VIPs. I think I mentioned earlier that Secretary Cohen came out nine times during my visit there. I thought he was absolutely wonderful in how he would try to keep this relationship well oiled, shall we say. He would come out sometimes with no particular request, just because he was in the region. He wanted to say hello to our good friends. This kind of expression of friendship is deeply appreciated in the Arab world. They don't like it when you come just when you want something. They like it when you come and chitchat and say "Hello, how's the family?" in their tradition. It is part of the thing that you do when you're in the desert. I may be exaggerating here, but it is related to that tradition that was developed in the desert as people would pass through and sit in tents and visit. This way they knew that when they needed help they could get it. Secretary Cohen was just a wonderful guy, and of course we had visitors from the Central Command and many others, all kinds of VIPs. It was just an endless number.

One day in 2000 I got a call from the director general of the Foreign Service, because I was supposed to leave Bahrain in 2000 and my mind was made up that I was going to retire. I thought my days in the Service were finished and I was going to leave. If all went well I would leave in December of 2000, after three years. Anyhow, I got a call from the director general, Skip Gnehm, and he said, "Johnny, this is Skip. I'm calling to ask a favor." I said, "Now, what have I done wrong this time?" Because the only time they would call me is if I'd done something wrong. They never called to say, "Hey, you're doing a great job." I asked, "What have I done wrong?" He answered, "Nothing. I want to call to ask you something." I said, "What is that?" He said, "Would you mind staying another year?" I thought about it literally in a second because although my mind was made up that I was going to complete my three years and leave, I said, "I don't mind. What's the problem?" He said, "Well, your replacement," and Ron Neumann had been named my replacement, "his nomination is in trouble and there's no way he's going to get confirmed by the Senate this time around. So, would you stay the extra year?" I said, "I don't mind." That was what extended me from 2000 to 2001.

*Q: I was wondering could you just give us a little bit of the workings. Do you know what the problem was?*

YOUNG: It was a security problem, I learned later on. Skip did not go into the details at that time; he just said it was a security problem. If you recall during Madeleine Albright's tenure as secretary of state, there was a security problem with computers.

*Q: Yes, a couple of laptop computers disappeared.*

YOUNG: Right. Well, Ron's computer didn't disappear, but I guess one that he had on some of his trips with Martin Indyk was checked and found that it hadn't been secured at all times as it should have been. So that was the problem. I mean, the secretary had made this bold move that no one would be spared if they were caught violating the rules on security and that sort of thing. That made it impossible for his nomination to then be advanced to the Senate. Ron Neumann didn't make it on that round, but there were elections in 2000. A new regime came in. His name was forwarded again, and he made it through, was confirmed, and replaced me in 2001.

I left at the end of September 2001. I would like to mention two things about the time prior to my departure. The first and most important of course was September 11. I will never forget, I was in my office and someone called and said, "Turn on the TV. It seems like a plane has crashed into the World Trade Center, one of the buildings in New York." I turned on the TV right away. Several people had come to my office. There was an immediate replay of what had happened with the first plane and we looked at it and all of us said immediately, "Well, maybe it was an accident." Then we began to talk about it and we said, "Maybe, but how could that be? A plane that size wouldn't make that kind of error." While we were watching the screen, plane number two hit the second tower. We knew immediately then that this had to have been a terrorist act, no question about it. We were all in a state of shock over this. We got immediate expressions of sympathy and concern from the government of Bahrain. The calls began to come to the embassy and we began the procedure of setting up a condolence book and things like that and we began to work immediately on a memorial service, which we held in one of the local hotels. In fact, we held it in the same hotel where we had the Fourth of July reception.

It was a beautiful service, a very respectful and dignified service. It was an interfaith service, where we had Muslim and Catholic prayers. I don't think we had any Jewish prayers, because there wasn't any kind of rabbi available, and then the different chaplains. It was nice. We had these huge candles and we had a candle for the fifty states and a candle for each nationality that we knew of. As we called the names of each state, we would light a candle. Then we called the different countries, United Kingdom, France, Germany, and a candle was lit until the entire stage in this huge hall was lit with candles. Somber, respectful, beautifully done. The hall was packed with people. It was really a very sad time.

Well, as you can imagine, I continued my arrangements to leave. I continued my round of farewell calls. Then some days before I was to leave, maybe a week or so, we got a message that we were positioning our assets to go into Afghanistan. I got a request to ask the government of Bahrain for permission to base refueling tankers in Bahrain. At that point the little island was already packed with planes from the Fifth Fleet because of what we were doing in Iraq, and there just was not much room. Nevertheless, I went to the emir and I relayed the urgency and the importance of the request. I was given forty-eight hours to get back to the military on this. Prior to this, messages were going back and forth to the mission asking: what is your assessment of this, what is your assessment of that? Messages were also going directly to the defense attaché without my inclusion. It was clear that DOD was doing one thing and the State Department was doing something else. I was getting calls at all hours of the morning and night telling me to do this or that. I'll never forget a screaming match with Jim Larocco, who was managing all of this at the time, screaming at me like a mad man.

Q: *Where was he located?*

YOUNG: Jim Larocco was back in Washington. He was the principal DAS (deputy assistant secretary) in the Bureau of Near Eastern Affairs. I forget that particular request, but I knew what I had to do. I did not have to have him scream at me. Anyhow, he was screaming about this particular request that had to be done in forty-eight hours. I went to the government and the emir said, "Yes in principle, but we need time to work this out with our people before we give you the final okay." That was within hours of my receiving the request because I met with him literally right away. That was not good enough and I would get calls. "Have you got it yet? Have you got it yet?" I said, "In your message you said forty-eight hours. It isn't even twenty-four hours yet or thirty hours or anything like that." The pressure was on me. I could not sleep. I was irritable. It was quite a time. Of course the military was just pushing, pushing to move ahead on this. I'd get calls from them as well on this. "Have you got the okay yet Johnny?"

About thirty hours had gone by and that morning I got a call from Washington saying the planes were on the way. I had not gotten the okay from the government yet, so I scrambled like a mad man to get the emir and everyone I possibly could. It had to come from the emir, because no one else could issue that authority. I had visions of these tankers arriving and having them turned away. Anyhow, I chased the emir down. I literally tracked him down and said, "You know, you've got to help us on this one. This is when we really need you," and I added, "The planes are on the way." He said, "Don't bring them here." I said, "There's no alternative, they're on the way." He thought about it and he called me back later on and said it was okay and then I conveyed that and the planes came in.

Then it was a question of getting the fuel to fuel them. That became a logistical issue, but now that they were in place we could work out the rest. We had special tankers to travel many miles over the desert to fuel these things, and in the end it did work out. That was the last big crisis before I left, and I left a matter of days after that. The last day of my time in Bahrain the former commander of the Fifth Fleet, Admiral Fargo, had come into town and asked for a courtesy call on the crown prince, which we agreed to. We had that meeting with the crown prince, which was basically to say that Admiral Fargo was going out to Diego Garcia to take charge of operations in preparation for what was going to go down in Afghanistan. So that all turned out very nicely. It gave me an opportunity to once again say hello and farewell to Admiral Fargo. I returned home to finish my packing, and when I was in the midst of packing one of the suitcases, the doorbell rang. The staff went to the door and they said, "Oh, here's something from the crown prince." It was a tube about twelve feet long, and about twelve inches in diameter. My wife and I opened it up and it was the most magnificent carpet that you could imagine. My guess is that that carpet must have been worth about $25,000 or $30,000. It was just magnificent. I sent a note of thanks and I called the DCM and said, "I'm leaving it for the embassy. I can't take it and you know that, but I want that documented that I left it here with you." We left it and later on that evening we went out to the airport, took the plane and said our farewell to Bahrain. It was on the 30th of September, 2001.

*Q: When the attack of 9/11 happened, you were all Middle East hands. Did the finger point almost immediately in your mind to Bin Laden or was that the consensus?*

YOUNG: Clearly, there was no question as to who might have done it. It looked like it was his footprint or handprint or whatever you call it. That was clear. There was no question, because we had sufficient evidence of the kind of activities that were going on in Afghanistan. In fact, we were one of the posts that was able to intercept two trainees who had been in camps in Afghanistan and had questioned them and then we turned them over to the Saudis. They were Saudi citizens, but we were able to get our hooks into them before they were turned over to the Saudis.

*Q: As vice consul in the late '50s, when Bahrain was part of my consular district, we were worried about the Shi'as, particularly of Iranian influence. While you were there, how did we see the bombs going off and security things? Were the Iranians behind what was going on?*

YOUNG: I think that is a lingering concern among the Sunnis in Bahrain that Iran has a hand in these evil acts that people would perpetrate against the government. There was no trust of the Iranians. There was an Iranian ambassador there, but after one attempted coup some years earlier, Bahrain had put a curb on Iranian activities. They closed the school down; they closed their club down and things like that and would not allow them to reopen. When the Ayatollah came to power in 1979, this emboldened the Shi'a in Bahrain quite a bit. They felt that their day had come. They thought this was their time to ascend to power in Bahrain and that Iran would back them up, and therefore they began to agitate for change. The Bahrainis cracked down and they remained very suspicious.

I want to discuss the political reforms that occurred in Bahrain during my time there. The emir indicated that he was willing to open up the system, and he had two key elements of change in mind. One was to basically have what he called a national charter, a new type of constitution. One of the criticisms of the government up to that point was that his father had suspended the constitution and that was what ended the parliament, which was never allowed to restart. The new emir, Sheik Hamad, realized that there were flaws in the old constitution and that if it had operated as it had been written it would have ended the power of the Al Khalifas in Bahrain. He initiated and actively supported the idea of a new national charter. This charter would be drafted by a wide range of business and civic leaders and scholars and what have you, and it would then be put to a vote. The people would agree with this and the charter would then lead to the creation of two legislative bodies. One already existed, the Shura council, which was a consultative body. It had no real power to enact legislation. With this new arrangement there would be a two-house chamber. One would be consultative, similar to the Shura council, and the other would be legislative. Legislation would require passage in both chambers before the emir could sign it into law, but veto power rested with the emir. He could veto any bill that was passed by these two chambers. After much discussion and all kinds of TV programs and involvement in the press and what have you, this charter was put to a vote. I think on Valentine's Day, February 14, 2001, this national charter was passed. It was very well received and passed with a huge margin. We sent out people to monitor things to see how the elections were going. They were free, fair, and transparent, I mean it was very nicely done. We have to keep in mind that Bahrain did have some tradition of voting prior to the suspension of the parliament back in the 1970s.

This was the beginning of major changes in Bahrain. Those changes have not been without problems. The country continues to this day to have these eruptions, primarily from the Shi'a community. Although I'm not there now I do follow events and I must say that, like it or not, what has occurred in Iraq has emboldened the Shi'a in Bahrain. Keep in mind that there are three countries in the Gulf with majority Shi'a populations: Iran, Iraq, and Bahrain. In Iraq, the Sunnis were the key leaders and in Bahrain, the Sunnis are the key leaders, but the situation has changed in Iraq. It is now the Shi'a who have come into power and this has given encouragement to the Shi'a in Bahrain. So they continue to press for more and more change. This is something that I think we will have to watch very carefully. We press for change in the Middle East, we congratulate Bahrain on the changes it has made, but let's face it, if we pressed all the way and true democratic change came to Bahrain in terms of one person one vote, that would be the end of the Sunni regime. There is no question it would bring into power the Shi'a who would be aligned 100 percent with Iran. It would be a whole new ball game in that little country and I think we would have to look at sort of packing up our bags and moving on.

Now, the Saudis don't want to see this. Let's be honest; we don't want to see it either. We want a country that is stable and that is still friendly to us, so it is in our interest. It is in the interest of the Al Khalifas also to try to find some accommodation that pleases the Shi'a community.

*Q: I realize you left shortly after 9/11. But by the time you left, were you and your staff and others around you, maybe our military, thinking about Iraq's involvement in this?*

YOUNG: Absolutely not.

*Q: Were we looking at Afghanistan?*

YOUNG: We were looking at Afghanistan. We were dealing with Iraq as a separate issue altogether. Iraq was not the center of terrorism. We were dealing with Iraq in terms of weapons of mass destruction and a rotten leader there, but not in terms of having been the place that harbored the people who did us harm on September 11. That was the formulation that came about later.

*Q: Then you left and retired?*

YOUNG: Oh, no. During the time that I was asked to stay and given that extra year, I then began to let it be known that I was available. I had been promoted to career minister and had not really been assigned as a career minister to a new assignment. I made a case once again to the central personnel system that there were not that many blacks at my level in the Service. In fact there was only one other at that point, and that was George Moose. George was already assigned and I said I was interested and I think the Department wanted to do something with me. They did not want to throw me to the wolves at that point. Frankly, I was a symbol that they could use. I was prepared to be used as a symbol. I had no problems with that at all, but I did have my limitations. I said I did not want to serve in Africa, that I had done my time in Africa, and that I thought it was time once again for the Service to demonstrate that it could assign minority ambassadors to regions other than the traditional places in Africa. I had put in my wish list, which consisted of ten different countries, and I remember the order of them very well. Number one on the list was the Netherlands. Number two was Sweden. Number three was Jordan and number four was Slovenia, and then I had a whole lot of other ones down the line. I knew that the Netherlands would go political. I knew that Sweden would go political. I thought Jordan could be a possibility and Slovenia I frankly thought, well, you never know. It was in Europe, a lovely country, a country doing a lot of things right. A beautiful, nicely situated place, so I thought, why not. That's a possibility. The other thing I figured was that I could be used not just in terms of my color, but as a career administrative officer who could possibly hold this assignment of career minister, that I could be used in that kind of argument as well. I think my color even added to it. The first two that I mentioned didn't work out. The third one, Jordan, may have been a possibility, but at the last minute they had to find a place for Skip Gnehm. All of the other places that might have worked out for him were all gone.

*Q: He was a Middle East hand.*

YOUNG: Right, and they gave him Jordan. He went to Jordan and I got a call that the D Committee had selected me for Slovenia and I was very pleased about that. Now this was in the summer of 2000 when the committee made its selection. Well, that didn't go anywhere because all of those selections made by the committee died because of the elections, and then they resurfaced again. Some of them had changes in them when they resurfaced and I was lucky that my name was selected when it was resubmitted the second time under the Bush administration. That's how I got to Slovenia.

# FOURTH AMBASSADORSHIP: SLOVENIA

*Q: You were in Slovenia from when to when?*

YOUNG: I arrived in the fall of 2001. Prior to my arrival in Slovenia, I came back to the United States for my hearings. I was preparing myself all along in terms of the issues that we had with Slovenia. I had my hearing and there was a moment in it that I thought was quite memorable. I was up with Dan Coats, who was going to Germany. The fellow who was going to the Czech Republic was the cousin of the president. Ambassador Lynch was going to Ireland. It was quite a nice hearing. We were all treated very nicely. No great controversy. For Dan Coats it was like a love fest, since he was a former senator. Senator Sarbanes introduced me. My daughter and son were seated behind me and I had the pleasure of introducing them to the members of the committee. Senator Sarbanes was chairing the committee at that time, but at one point Senator Helms came in and he was allowed to speak. I'll try to imitate his voice. I'm not sure I'm that good at it, but he said, "Ambassador-designate Lynch, you're going to Ireland. There's something I want you to do for me when you get to Ireland." Ambassador Lynch answered, "Yes, Senator Helms, I'd be glad to. What is it?" He said, "I want you to meet somebody who is going to be in Ireland and I want you to take good care of him. He's a good man and he does good work and I want you to treat him fine." Ambassador designate Lynch said, "Why, by all means I'll be happy to have him. Yes, I'll be glad to take care of him." Helms chimed in again, "I can assure you this is a very good man and I want you to take good care of him and I appreciate your pledge that you're going to take good care of him. His name is Bono." Well, my daughter kicked my seat behind me and later told me, "Dad, I thought I was going to lose it at that point. When Helms told the ambassador-designate to

Ireland to take good care of Bono, I couldn't believe that that would come up at a hearing." And I couldn't either, nor could anyone else.

*Q: You might explain who Bono is.*

YOUNG: Well, Bono is the lead singer in the U2 rock group and he does incredible humanitarian work, particularly in Africa.

*Q: He made Man of the Year.*

YOUNG: He's been knighted by the Queen of England. That aside, you would not think of Senator Helms, this right of right fellow lining up with this knee-jerk liberal doing humanitarian work, but they became great friends. I thought it was interesting. We were asked a few questions and it all turned out very well. I had a statement prepared and I remember at one point Senator Helms saying, "Well, this looks like a really nice group of nominees here. I think they're all fine. We're going to break because we have to take a vote. I think we ought to wish the best to this group and thank them for coming here." We just put our statements in the box at the end of the table. Such is the prerogative of the Senate. They can do whatever they want in terms of how they interpret their role to advise and consent. You can prepare and prepare, but in the end if they tell you to just drop your statement in the box at the end of the table, that's what you do. I mean, we did have a small amount of time to make our individual statements, which we did. We were asked a couple of questions, but Sarbanes brought it all to an end and that was that.

I decided after I was confirmed that I would do something completely different for my swearing in. I had had three previous ceremonies in the Benjamin Franklin Room, where hundreds of persons were invited. I was told that the secretary of state would swear me in if I decided to hold it in the Department, but this time my decision was to have the swearing in outside of the Department, and take it to my high school in Philadelphia. I attended a vocational, technical high school there. It was a school that catered to underprivileged kids in the inner city and I wanted to do it there as a symbol of what is possible for kids coming from that kind of school, not that they could all aspire to be ambassador or what have you, but to offer them a symbol and some encouragement.

I had my swearing in at the Edward Bok Vocational Technical High School in Philadelphia. I asked my mentor, Assistant Secretary Mary Ryan, to officiate and she agreed. We arranged for a federal judge, the wife of then mayor of Philadelphia Ed Rendell (he is now governor of Pennsylvania), to swear me in. It was in September and it all turned out very well. Following the swearing in, which was something that these kids had frankly never seen before, we had a little reception in the library, which had been named for me, the Johnny Young Library, which I thought was very nice. The local TV station covered it and it was written up in the newspaper. "Philly Boy makes good," that sort of thing. There was one thing that made me feel particularly good about the whole thing. I was talking to a young girl who was graduating from this high school and she said, "I wasn't sure that I wanted to go to college until today. Now I know I want to go." If she is the only one that I touched on that occasion, it was worth it.

*Q: Absolutely. What was the situation in Slovenia?*

YOUNG: In my statement before the Senate Foreign Relations Committee, I had mentioned several items that I knew were controversial and would kind of get things stirred up, but I wanted them to get things stirred up. I used that as a deliberate mechanism to engage the Slovenes in dialogue on these issues. One was the return of property confiscated during the time of the Tito regime, property that had not been returned to American citizens. Mind you, the property had been confiscated before these persons had become U.S. citizens. Nevertheless, they were making claims now on their property. Upon its independence, Slovenia was one of the countries that said that it would return property. This was something that they decided to do on their own, and that was a good thing. It was something that was looked upon very favorably by the trans-Atlantic institutions they wanted to join, such as NATO, the European Union, and the like. That was one issue.

The other issue was intellectual property. Slovenia had the reputation of its pharmaceutical companies taking the data developed by American drug companies and using those data to manufacture generics. This had the pharmaceutical industry up in arms. That was an issue I wanted to flag. Another was Slovenia's candidacy for NATO. The U.S. had not yet committed to supporting Slovenia's candidacy and I wanted to keep the dialogue open on that. I also wanted to make sure that we could get as much leverage out of this as possible before we committed to supporting Slovenia's candidacy. Another was, of course, to try to help the country in whatever way we could with its transition from a centrally directed economy and state to one that was more open, with open markets, and that was democratic and things like that, to support their civic institutions.

I arrived in Slovenia. The press had interpreted my remarks about the return of property as meaning that we would not support Slovenia's candidacy for NATO if these changes in terms of intellectual property rights did not occur in a positive way. Immediately, I had to try to correct that misunderstanding, because it was clear that it was going to follow me everywhere. That was one thing that I found right away. The Slovenes were very thin-skinned; they didn't like criticism at all. They were worried about me. I began to see right away racial comments about me in the press. I was portrayed in local cartoons in an unflattering way in terms of my race and what have you. I said right away, "Look, if I am going to have any relationship with the people of Slovenia and with this government, then we've got to take race off the table. There's no way that this is going to fly." I said, "You can challenge me, you can challenge my government on anything that you want, except it cannot be based on race. Let's put that aside, and if we put that aside we can be friends and we can discuss business and we can work together. If that's going to be on the table, I can't deal with you." That cleared the air. I did it on television and in editorials to the press. I made it very clear that this was a topic that I would not accept as a responsible basis for any kind of dialogue. The government never engaged in this sort of thing, but it certainly could affect my relationship with the government. We got that cleared up right away and we could then move on to do business.

After being in the country a very short time, it was clear to me that Slovenia was indeed a very good candidate for NATO. I favored strongly supporting their candidacy although we had not committed yet. I continued to press them on reforming the law on intellectual property. What happened was, in preparation for their European Union candidacy, Slovenia had passed a law that made it illegal for companies to use the intellectual property of someone else to support generics. That was good, but they did that well in advance of their candidacy for European entry. Their own pharmaceutical companies were furious and they realized what this meant to them. They pressured the government, which immediately passed a law that rescinded the law that it had passed. Pharmaceutical companies reverted back to using these data developed by other drug companies.

*Q: When you're talking about pharmaceutical companies, you're talking about the indigenous pharmaceutical companies.*

YOUNG: Yes.

*Q: Because in no way could a country join the European Union if it is engaging in stealing intellectual property.*

YOUNG: That's correct. That was why they passed this law, but they passed it almost two years before they had to meet this requirement. For the pharmaceutical companies, that was two years during which they could continue stealing. So they rescinded the law. Of course, the American companies were furious. I continued to pressure. They thought, "Oh God, if we don't do this we won't get the U.S. support for our candidacy for NATO" and they knew that if we didn't support them for NATO they would never get in. They had an opportunity to join NATO in 1999. It was a foregone conclusion at the time that of any of the countries to be considered, Slovenia was going to be number one, not the Czech Republic, not Hungary, not Slovakia. But in the end Slovenia was cast aside and I think it was Hungary, Poland, and the Czechs that were brought in. The Slovenes were devastated.

*Q: What was behind it?*

YOUNG: Well, no one has heard the definitive answer why. Some say it was the French who screwed them at the last minute and did them in because they wanted these others in. Some said, no, it was the U.S. who did it. I don't know what the pressures were, but we never got to the bottom of it frankly. Anyhow, they were devastated that they didn't get in. They wanted this more than anything else. To them, this was a badge of respectability and of status and, you know, it really made sense. Also it meant that they could reduce the amount of money they were spending to defend their small territory and basically count on the umbrella that would be provided by NATO and channel their funds in a more efficient way. It really made good sense.

We made the case to our government that we should support Slovenia, but we were not getting full support. There was a great deal of opposition by one element in the Department of Defense to this. I don't know how it started, but there was the feeling out there at the time that Slovenia was somehow arrogant about its candidacy, that it was too sure of itself, that it was too cocky. If you looked at it in terms of GDP (gross domestic product), in terms of democracy, economic reform, in terms of the kind of disciplined military they had, all of these kinds of issues, they were at the top of the list. But the feeling developed that, because they were number one in all of these categories, they were arrogant. They were not taking it seriously enough. They needed to do more to demonstrate that they really wanted this in the worst way. Well, the Slovenes' response was, "We do want it in the worst way, but don't you remember what happened to us in '99 when you screwed us?" They said, "We're like a rejected suitor. We tried the first time and we were turned away. We're trying again, but we are afraid we may be turned away again. So we are reserving a little bit of enthusiasm and are being a bit guarded just in case this doesn't work out. We will not be as devastated and disappointed as we were the last time." This didn't fly. Nobody bought this in Washington and, as I said, the biggest obstacle to more immediate support from the U.S. side came from the Department of Defense.

*Q: Any particular branch?*

YOUNG: Yes, specifically the office run by Ian Brzezinski. I don't remember the specific office. He was determined to make Slovenia a case to demonstrate the seriousness with which we were taking this whole business of the expansion of NATO, that we weren't going to just take a country because they were good in every respect, but we were going to really be tough and hard on them.

*Q: It sounds like, let me put it in diplomatic terms, somebody in a bureau or a place in the government showing they had balls. At the same time picking on the small country when they knew they couldn't get away with it elsewhere, say with Poland or someplace.*

YOUNG: That's the bottom line.

*Q: "I can prove to my guys at the golf club that I'm really tough." Did you get that feeling?*

YOUNG: Oh, no question about it. Here we had this little country that was doing things its way and we feel that little countries frankly should dance to our tune. When we want them to do something they should do it and that should be that. Slovenia was a very successful country, one that succeeded because it did things its way. For example, the World Bank and the IMF had counseled Slovenia to take a certain approach in its economy following its independence in 1991. Slovenia didn't listen to that advice at all and did it its way and was able to demonstrate in black and white that if it had taken the approach suggested and recommended by the IMF and World Bank, it would have been in a terrible state compared to where it was. So it made it very difficult for subsequent IMF and World Bank teams to come out and tell them to do something a certain way, because they had done it themselves. That was in their nature; it's part of their nature. They're very stubborn people and I always said that was part of the reason why they existed for 800 years under Austrian rule, because of a certain stubbornness and a certain cautiousness and carefulness as well.

Anyhow, we had this resistance on the part of DOD, whereas we had said we were going to do this. In terms of a few other countries, we'd said it informally; we hadn't come out and said so publicly. There was good support in Congress for Slovenia's inclusion. There was support in other quarters as well. All of the European countries, all of the European members of NATO were fully committed to Slovenia, but we had not committed yet. Anyhow, in May of 2002 we succeeded in getting a visit to the United States by then Prime Minister of Slovenia Janez Drnovsek. He was able to make his case with President Bush, who had visited the country in June of 2001, when he met Putin for the first time. They had their meeting in Slovenia. When I had my photo-op with President Bush in August of 2001, he greeted me and said, "You're going to Slovenia?" I answered, "Yes." He said, "You're going to love it. It's a wonderful country. I loved it. Laura and I had no idea that it was so beautiful and that the people were so nice" and so on. He said, "You're going to enjoy this."

When I met him again in May of 2002 for the pre-brief prior to the meeting in the Oval Office with Prime Minister Drnovsek, the first thing he said to me was "How do you like Slovenia?" I said, "It was just as you said, Mr. President. It is absolutely wonderful." He said, "See, I told you so." Then we got down to discussing the issues and he said, "Well, what are the problems?" I said, "The problem is Slovenia wants to join NATO and it would like our support. I think it should be a member of the alliance. They continue to make the reforms necessary to complete their application for NATO membership and they're doing a good job in reforming their economy. It's a solid democracy," and so on. He listened and then we had the meeting. The photographers came in and they were snapping away and then the word was "get them out." Like rats leaving the ship, they all left and we were left there to have our discussion with the Slovenes. President Bush, Secretary of State Powell, and Scooter Libby were in on that meeting. Condoleezza Rice left to attend another meeting. I'll never forget that because I have a photograph of it.

*Q: Libby being the principal aide to the vice president.*

YOUNG: I don't know what role he was in at that point, but he was in the meeting and Dan Freed, who was the head of the European office in the White House, was in on the meeting as well. There were a couple of amusing incidents during this meeting. Of course the Slovene expressed his friendship and solidarity with the U.S. in terms of September 11. They were with us and they wanted to help us, and what a good relationship we had, and what an important role we had played in terms of Bosnia, and how important a role Slovenia played in that as well. When we were getting ready to do the bombing, we had asked for over-flight clearance from Austria, which Austria denied, and then we asked Slovenia and Slovenia agreed. So, the planes came over Slovenia and then into Bosnia.

The president was at one point reared back in his chair, with just his shoulders resting on the back of the chair and his legs way out. His heels basically on the bottom of the floor and he was sort of swinging a little bit. The prime minister said, "Oh, we'd love you to come back to Slovenia," and the president said, "Well, I don't travel. My secretary of state doesn't like me to travel. He's afraid I'm going to make a faux pas." We all had a good laugh and Powell didn't say anything, he just looked on. The president asked good questions. He was briefed and knew exactly what to ask. He asked how the reforms were coming along and how the country was doing, and so on. Then President Bush said, "I don't know why, but there's this reputation that Slovenia has taken for granted that it's going to get into

NATO. There's this feeling that Slovenia is arrogant about this whole process. Mr. Prime Minister, do you have any idea why that happened or why this has gotten out and is circulating?"

Prime Minister Drnovsek is a very sour-looking fellow with sort of a pear-shaped face; he looks almost like something out of Munch's painting, *The Scream*. He literally has that kind of head and that kind of tight mouth. A very serious intellectual, he was a brilliant man. He said in his perfect English, "Mr. President, I have no idea where these things circulate. I, too, have heard rumors of that type. But, I want to tell you there's no basis to them whatsoever. We work very hard to try to meet all of the requirements of our NATO membership application. We will be a good and responsible member of the alliance if we are selected. I don't know how these things get started. Maybe some low-level person on your staff has put this in a report and it's gotten its way up to you." At that point, the president turned to Dan Freed and said, "Dan, did you put this in my report?" Well, I thought I would fall out of the chair. Dan said no or didn't respond, I'm not sure which it was. It was really quite something that he would do that, because at that point Dan wasn't fully committed either, I must say. But I give Dan full credit for the reporting cable; he reported that incident in the telegram, which I thought meant a lot. That showed a great deal of integrity on his part. He was at least faithful to what transpired, although it was sort of in a light moment. It was a good meeting. In the end the president kind of let slip when he said to the prime minister, "I'll see you in November at the summit," which was the big meeting that would decide who would be invited into NATO and who would not. That was a slip, but it was a positive one because the president did not commit in that meeting. He was as supportive as he could be, but he did not commit our support. It was a good meeting. The prime minister left happy. I left happy and all turned out well. That was May of 2002.

The big NATO summit was scheduled for Prague in November of 2002 and it would be at that meeting that the decision would be made. Now, prior to that we had many meetings in the United States, trying to firm up our position. Prior to the Prague summit we received a cable in which I was instructed to go to the government and tell them that the U.S. would support Slovenia's candidacy for NATO. That was one of the most wonderful moments that I can remember.

*Q: Did you feel that the prime minister's visit had sort of trumped the opposition from the Department of Defense? I mean, I'm sure the prime minister knew exactly where the problem lay.*

YOUNG: Yes, I think that it was certainly beneficial. I think that there were two meetings that were crucial and helped. The prime minister also had a separate meeting with Donald Rumsfeld, the secretary of defense. Now, Rumsfeld had been an ambassador to NATO, so he understood, I think, to a much greater degree what was involved, versus members of his staff, including Brzezinski with all of his brilliance.

*Q: This is Zbigniew's son?*

YOUNG: Yes. So those two meetings were key, plus of course the meeting he had with the secretary, where the secretary was very favorable and very positive. I think it was basically those three meetings that helped to bring it all together and we had piled on the reporting. We had put it on every way you could possibly think of in terms of our analysis of the economy, of the political situation, of the reforms of the military; all of the data were there and clearly positive in terms of what should happen. As I said, that glorious moment did come when I could go to the government and say, "We will do it." The cables went out to all of the posts at the same time. I think it was either in Estonia or Latvia that the ambassador went in and told the prime minister or president of the U.S. support. The official said, "Read it to me one more time. I want to hear it again." It was truly a glorious moment.

Then in November there was the summit where it was all formalized. The day following the summit, Rumsfeld visited Slovenia to reaffirm what had occurred. He said, "Now that this has happened, we want you to follow through on these reforms." Brzezinski was there and was just chomping at the bit to say, "You got in, but let me tell you, let me just slap you around a little bit." But he was kept in check. I remember later on in a private meeting Rumsfeld saying to Brzezinski, "I knew you wanted to say something, but I'm proud of you that you kept quiet." It was really a good meeting. It was with the prime minister, the president, and the foreign minister and all. That was my first time meeting Rumsfeld, the most charming guy you'd want to meet. Smart as a whip. It showed Slovenia at its most glorious, so it was really wonderful. That was in November of 2002.

*Q: Do you want to discuss intellectual rights and explain what the problem was?*

YOUNG: At my confirmation hearing I had put down a marker in terms of intellectual property rights being one of the issues that I would take on. I knew that this would get people stirred up in Slovenia, but I wanted them to really engage with us in dialogue on this particular issue. I arrived and the press was waiting for me to just shock me to pieces. The pharmaceutical companies in Slovenia had put pressure on the politicians in the country and on the press to go after me. The issue was a very simple one. American pharmaceutical companies had spent considerable money in developing their brand name products. Slovenia has a very extensive and successful generics industry and they would take the data developed to support the American brand name products to produce generics and then sell these generics throughout Europe, Africa, India, you name it, making lots of money.

*Q: With no money going to the drug companies?*

YOUNG: Oh, absolutely none, no money going to the American drug company for the use of their data. The drug companies were very upset. All of them, Pfizer and Wyeth and all of them were there and they were quite upset. They appreciated that I had taken this on as an issue. They wanted me to move ahead on it and I did in press conferences, in TV interviews, and in special press conferences that I would call to speak on this issue. I was just relentless in raising this and in making it known that this was something that had to be dealt with.

*Q: Would you call it stealing?*

YOUNG: Well, that's what it is. We just said it was wrong and Slovenia knew that it was wrong. In preparation for its candidacy to enter the European Union, it had passed a law that prohibited the illegal use data and intellectual property. That was fine. It had passed this law well in advance of the time that it was required to pass it. As I noted earlier, the pharmaceutical industry in Slovenia then pressured the politicians to repeal the law that they had passed. They basically said, "We've got a good thing here. We don't need to have this law in place for another year and a half to two years. So why do we do it now? Let's repeal it and enjoy for the next two years the benefits of being able to use the intellectual property and data from these American companies." The other Europeans didn't concern themselves with this. It was only the Americans who were carrying the ball on this.

*Q: Were the pharmaceutical companies doing this in Slovenia homegrown or were they sort of offshoots of other outfits in other parts of Europe?*

YOUNG: These were locally developed companies. These two companies were Slovene inventions and were part of the Slovene success story. Together they had sales of $1 billion, which is quite substantial for a small country of two million people. They were just quite a force to be reckoned with. During my time there, one of them was bought out by Novartis and is a part of Novartis at the moment. I had all kinds of meetings with the parliamentarians and I told them, this is not going to look good. If you want to be a real member of the alliance you've got to demonstrate that you carry yourself in a way that is consistent with the standards expected of the members of the alliance. I used that as part of my argument as well.

*Q: Was there any illicit threat on our part?*

YOUNG: No, our only threat was how they would be viewed in the alliance and the kind of support we would give them. We were giving them military support as well in order to prepare them for their membership in the alliance. No out and out threats. This was through jawboning and moral persuasion that we finally succeeded and we got the law repealed and the American pharmaceutical companies were very happy. The Slovene pharmaceutical companies were not, though it was amazing how they bounced back after that. For example, shortly after one of the companies became part of Novartis, they began bidding on American contracts for generics. They still had some requirements to fulfill before they could really succeed in that way and they finally did and then began selling generics to the United States. It was a win-win all the way around. Now, that didn't end all of the problems in terms of pharmaceuticals. Let's face it; I don't think American pharmaceutical companies are 100 percent happy in any country that they are in. They are constant moaners and groaners and that's just the way it is and it's our job to try and help them in whatever way we can.

Their next complaint was that the government had concocted a scheme to bring down medical costs which is something that I think governments around the world are faced with and it's no different in this country as well. The government's program was very similar to one in Italy and similar to one in practice in one or two Scandinavian countries. It was basically to limit the amount of reimbursement patients could receive for their medications with the highest reimbursement going to those patients who use generics versus those who use name brand products. Those who used name brand products got a very small reimbursement. This had an impact on those American pharmaceutical products because all of the American products were name brand and some of them of course were able to stand on their own and really didn't have generics to equal them. This was another complaint. They wanted my support in trying to get the government to implement a scheme that would be more generous to brand name products. I did my best on that, but really there was little defense that I could offer for that. This was a problem that is being dealt with internationally.

I just wanted to add one thing on the success of our program in Slovenia. It was cited in telegrams that went out worldwide as an example of how this can be done. I remember Tony Wayne, the assistant secretary for economic affairs, sending out a telegram and we took great pride in that I must say.

*Q: What was the reaction among the Slovenian contacts, the ones who were not specifically connected to the pharmaceutical thing? I mean, did they understand what they should?*

YOUNG: They did. Many Slovenes who were anti-the-regime-in-power gave me a pat on the back. You're showing them. This government needs to be shown that it can't get away with anything and it needs to do the right thing. They were pleased with the moral implication of pushing the government to do the right thing. That is not inconsistent with Slovene morals. They are very strict, moralistic people. They don't look for sideways to do things. They're very straight.

*Q: How did you find the reaction in the government officials you would meet? Were they just sort of uncomfortable?*

YOUNG: They knew that it had to be done. They knew that it was something they had to do. It was a requirement to join the European Union.

They just wanted to postpone it for as long as possible. I got cooperation from the folks in the government and they knew that it was political, that it was the money and the influence of the pharmaceutical firms that brought about this problem.

*Q: How did you find the response from the media?*

YOUNG: The media was after me. They were after me because of what I had mentioned earlier in terms of Slovenia's entry into NATO. They thought that I was going to sabotage Slovenia's entry into NATO by working to deny them support from the U.S. government for their candidacy. They learned very shortly that they had one of the best allies they could find in me and applauded my efforts.

*Q: Were there any other intellectual property problems, like books?*

YOUNG: No, you didn't find counterfeit books or counterfeit CDs and tapes and that sort of thing. They had a good record in that regard, but that was petty business. It's not a country that specializes or has much of that kind of gray market trade.

*Q: Sometimes border countries are basically smuggling countries. It's what they do for a living.*

YOUNG: Yes, but this is not a smuggling country. Slovenia is a very successful country with a developed economy and a sound political system so they don't have those kinds of problems. It was just in pharmaceuticals because it was such a big business. The two pharmaceutical companies there were national treasures and they were regarded as part of the patrimony. These companies were incredible. In many ways they were exactly like Hershey, it's not just the product that they produce, but it's their impact on the total community where that product is produced. That was true in the case of these two pharmaceutical companies. They run schools and clinics, they have basketball teams, soccer teams. I mean they have all of these different institutions that you find in the community and very often maybe just supported in a small way. I mean, they literally run them and it's so funny to see the basketball team. They brought in a couple of black players from the United States and those few black players and myself were the only blacks in the entire country. Of course they stood out even more than I did because they were so tall.

*Q: What were some of the other issues you were dealing with?*

YOUNG: We tried to contribute to the development of civil society. We tried to help with funding small groups that had begun to support and encourage democratic governance in various areas at the community level. We attempted to help groups that would try and help with wayward youth and with the elderly. We tried to work with the judiciary in areas of judicial reform, particularly in the implementation of the alternative dispute procedures. That was very important particularly with the judiciary. Slovenia had a wickedly backlogged judicial system. Our goal was to try to break that up so that justice could be administered in a more efficient and faster manner. We brought over judges and we sent judges from Slovenia to the United States to meet with judges to show them our court system in all of its different levels and had terrific dialogue on that particular issue.

One big problem was in trafficking of persons. Slovenia was not a destination point, it was a transit point for people coming out of the Dalmatian coast, Albania, Macedonia and Serbia through Slovenia and into Italy and then into Europe. There were some who remained there. The majority of the people trafficked were women. There were really no organizations set up to deal with that problem. One group began during our time there and we helped to fund them to get them started. They opened up a shelter for women who were trafficked and we worked with the government in providing them some money so that they could continue this work and expand it. We had some leverage there because Slovenia was a category two country. We classified countries in their trafficking as category one, two or three. Category one is basically the top of the line, no problems of any significance and category two countries have some problems and government needs to do more. Category three countries are where you have major problems. Slovenia, as a new member of the alliance and as an aspirant to the European Union, wanted to be in the same company as European Union countries, which is category one. The leverage was in persuading the government that it had to do more to get into category one. At the time of my departure we were lucky in maintaining them in category two because there was a push to move them into category three.

*Q: What was the problem? I mean, I think of Slovenia as being so small and you have this all going through and as long as they don't stay.*

YOUNG: The government had no laws on the books to protect people who were the victims of trafficking. The problem was to persuade the government, the parliament to do something, to put some laws on the books, to protect those who were trafficked. What you raise is a very good point. You would go next door to Italy and trafficking was as obvious and as flagrantly practiced as you would find anywhere. In the middle of the day in Rome, you could pass little alleys and see women waiting there, African women and Asian women, waiting to be solicited. We raised this with the folks in Washington. Why was Italy with this kind of open practice in category one, and yet a country like Slovenia where you didn't have that kind of behavior at all was a category two? They said, as bad as it is in Italy, Italy has laws on the books. So people who are trafficked can actually go to the courts and say under law number twenty-three or so-and-so my rights have been violated. There was nothing like that in Slovenia.

*Q: I'm thinking since Slovenia was not the ultimate destination, there would be no particular problem for them to pass a law.*

YOUNG: Well, they finally did, but it took a lot of pressure to get them to do so.

*Q: They didn't see a need or were they forced to say don't do this because we're making money?*

YOUNG: Slovenes are inclined to let things alone if they do not see it as a problem. I don't think that was unusual. I don't think they're unique in that regard. They feel that if it is not a problem, there is no need to bother with it. They didn't see it as a problem. It took a lot of sensitizing to get them to see it differently and they also view sex completely differently than we do. We think it is immoral and wrong to have people trafficked and engaged in prostitution and that sort of thing. Their attitude is different. I forgot the number, but there were some sixty private clubs in Slovenia where prostitution was practiced and the government knew that it was practiced and it was legal. It's a completely different attitude.

Q: *What about relations with Italy? For years, particularly around the area of Istria, there were Slovenians trying to have Slovenian taught in the public schools, the Italians were vehement about this and all. How did that work?*

YOUNG: I think overall I would say relations with Italy were good, but there would be flare-ups from time to time. As you probably know, there is an Italian minority in Slovenia and there is a Slovene minority in Italy around the border areas where the border had shifted back and forth before the lines were finally drawn. Anyhow, the Italians do have a member in the Slovene parliament, but I don't think there is a Slovene in the Italian parliament. I could be wrong, but I know there is an Italian in the Slovene parliament. Relations were good. Problems occurred when Slovenia was moving towards its entry into the European Union. One of the minority parties in Italy rose up and said it was going to block Slovenia's entry because Slovenia had not settled debts from World War II with the Italians who had lost property and business interests in Slovenia at that time. That was not true. There had been a settlement on those issues. In fact the U.S. government was party to it, but despite having signed the agreement at the time the Italians had not moved to collect the money that had been put in the accounts to settle those disputes. That would flare up from time to time. Slovenia was a little bit uncertain about Italian support for its entry to NATO. I mean, it finally did get it and for its entry to the European Union.

As far as Croatia is concerned, there were border dispute problems. There were some other problems that had been around since the time of independence in 1991. Those issues were believed to be resolved in an agreement that was initiated by the prime ministers of both Croatia and Slovenia in 2001. Everyone breathed a sigh of relief that this agreement was resolved. The borders were established, property claims were settled on both sides and a number of other issues as well. Number one was the border and the demarcation of the territorial waters. That was a major issue as to where the Croatian line was and where the Slovene line was in the Adriatic. This affected fishing and lobstering and that sort of thing. This was a very nice agreement. Prime Minister Drnovsek was very pleased with it and the Croatian government seemed pleased but little by little it began to fall apart. The Croats said we're not going to adhere to it, this is no good; the party that raised this was a party that was campaigning to be elected in place of the party that had signed this agreement with Drnovsek. The Slovenes just stood their ground. They said we signed the agreement.

We're not going to budge. That's it. It's up to you to honor it. This went back and forth. When I left in 2004 it still had not been resolved, but the Slovenes had not backed up at all. Special envoys were appointed to go negotiate between the two countries, but when I left in 2004, nothing had been resolved. It was basically the status quo.

There were flare-ups during my time there when Slovene fishing vessels were seized and then Croat crabbing vessels or lobstering vessels were seized. They had these little spats going back and forth. Then you'd have Slovenes who would say, well, I went down to Croatia for my vacation. I was treated like a dog. They were disrespectful and it was nothing but contempt and they looked down on me. Mind you, they'd go by the tens of thousands to their vacations in Dubrovnik and Cortula and all of these lovely places along the Dalmatian coast. Some of this resentment goes back decades because when they were all together in the Republic of Yugoslavia, Slovenia was the most envied of all of them. The other members of the republic thought the Slovenes were haughty and arrogant and disdainful of them and the Slovenes thought the others were a bunch of slackers because the Slovenes work hard. They had the most successful economy in the republic. They made up about a thirteenth of the population, but produced a quarter of the GDP. They were very proud of this and they are very proud in any case. Then there was also the feeling that when Slovenia broke away in 1991, they left the others holding the bag. Some of them said, well, yes, those Slovenes broke away and they had a war that lasted ten days, but the rest fell on us. That's not quite the case either. There are a number of reasons for that kind of resentment, but nevertheless things were good. As I said, relations stayed fairly even. You'd have these flare-ups over fishing, you'd have flare-ups at the border and the Croats would decide all of a sudden that they were going to slow things down and the cars couldn't get through and they'd be at the border backed up for tens of miles and that sort of thing. Overall, pretty good.

Slovenia knows that the best place for Croatia would be in the alliance and in the European Union.

*Q: The alliance, you mean?*

YOUNG: NATO. That these are key anchors for stability in the region. The only one who has that at the moment is Slovenia, but Slovenia would like to see the other members of the former Republic of Yugoslavia become members of these institutions as well. Relations with Austria were good except for some of the same reasons that I mentioned earlier in terms of Italy; you have a Slovene minority in Austria. You don't have it the other way around. You have some of it, but not too much. You have more the other way around, with a small Slovene minority in Austria. Unfortunately, it was in the region of Styria which is the area headed by Haider.

*Q: I was going to say Haider, we've talked about him.*

YOUNG: Yes, well, he's quite a guy to say the least, a real troublemaker. Austria had laws that said there would be bilingual education in the schools where the Slovene communities were located. By law and by affirmation by the courts of Austria, there would also be bilingual signs and things like that. Haider said, I don't care what the courts say, we are not having bilingual education any longer and we're going to take down the signs and they're going to be in German and that's that. Of course this got everyone riled up and by the time I left, things were still pretty much the same. There would be these flare-ups in the region of Styria where Haider was.

*Q: Haider had been prime minister for a little while, wasn't he?*

YOUNG: Oh, yes, he was impossible.

*Q: He was essentially seen as a neo-Nazi.*

YOUNG: Well, he is.

*Q: Certainly an extreme nationalist.*

YOUNG: An extreme nationalist is a gentler word.

*Q: He had a following in Styria?*

YOUNG: Yes, Styria. You know the Slovenes were ruled by the Austrians for eight hundred years and that has put a certain stamp on the Slovenes. I think their sense of orderliness and their drive to work hard, I think there's a streak in them that you find in Austria as well.

*Q: Sort of Germanic.*

YOUNG: Yes, Calvinistic I would say. They work very hard, do not take too much outwardly, and do not make very outward shows of emotion and pleasure. I went to a dinner hosted by the U.S. government for the graduates of a program we had in the region to send college graduates to the States for graduate education and master's degrees. It was for the Balkans and for Central Europe. I remember the speaker giving awards at this function. He said, "Now we have an award for Mr. So-and-So of Romania." There would be some applause. Then he said, "We now have such and such an award for Mr. So-and-So of let's say, Hungary," followed by applause. This went on and on. Then he said, "We have an award for Mr. So-and-So of Slovenia," with very quiet applause. Then he said we have an award for Mr. So-and-So of Serbia. Well, the room went crazy, with all kinds of yelling. The Slovene fellow next to me gave me a nudge and said, "Serbs." In other words, they're full of emotion and you don't get this outward show of emotion on the part of Slovenes. They certainly have fun and they make jokes and what have you, but they are completely different in terms being more Germanic and more Austrian in that sense of the word. The Slovenes have this great admiration for Austria and they take pride in it, they're also neat and clean and as I said orderly. That is why if you travel from Slovenia into Austria it's a seamless transition. You travel from Italy to Slovenia or from Slovenia to Italy and you can see the difference. You travel from Slovenia to Croatia you see the difference. You travel from Slovenia to Hungary, you see the difference, but into Austria it's a seamless transition. It's amazing.

Relations with Hungary were very good. No major problems there. The Slovenes looked at Hungary as a model of what they could do in terms of being a member of NATO. Hungary had not yet entered the European Union. They were in the same line of candidates as the Slovenes. There is a Hungarian minority in Slovenia and there is a Hungarian who is a member of the Slovene parliament, but not the opposite way around. Overall, very good solid relationships there

*Q: From 2001 to 2004 how did the Balkan troubles play in, particularly Bosnia and Kosovo? I mean, were you seeing new repercussions or was Slovenia somewhat removed?*

YOUNG: They were removed, concerned, and received many thousands of refugees as a result of this. As removed as they were, they were affected. They played a key role for us in the bombing of Serbia because when we were ready for the air strikes, we asked the Austrians because that was the shortest distance to fly, and the Austrians declined. They would not allow us to overfly their country. Then we asked the Slovenes and the Slovenes said yes. We did it and the Slovenes felt it was the right thing to do. They knew that this problem had to be put to an end.

Q: *It was a tremendous crisis.*

YOUNG: They got all of these refugees in, mostly Serbs. They got some others as well, but the majority were Serbs and that created some problems for them. They had to find a place for them, and then at some point they gave them the opportunity to become permanent residents there and they handled it fairly well. In 2001, however, this issue of refugees who had come in became a political issue. One party said that the people who had come in had been given permanent resident status and was then stripped of that status and were not allowed to vote and things like that. This particular candidate wanted that whole issue reexamined and it became a huge issue in the campaign for prime minister in 2001. It was a significant issue and the guy who raised it became prime minister. He ousted the regime that had been in power since the time of independence.

Q: *Was this a major factor?*

YOUNG: It was a factor, definitely. But I think the main reason why the opposition was elected was because people had grown tired of the regime that had been in power since independence in 1991 and wanted to try something different. The feeling was that in some ways this was basically like the old Communist days with the old regime. Everybody knew everyone and everything got done through these connections and they felt that the time for that was over.

Q: *Were there any other developments of this political nature? Did we get involved in the refugee matter at all?*

YOUNG: No, we didn't. We got involved to the extent that we kept emphasizing human rights, the need for the rule of law, the need for fair play, and those kinds of things. These human rights cases were amazing; some of them were just unbelievable. There's a small Muslim community in Slovenia. The Muslim community had been campaigning for years to build a mosque, and the government finally gave them land or agreed that they could buy land in this particular area for this mosque. Then this became a huge issue, whether they were going to get this mosque or not. They got the land and then questions were raised as to putting this issue to a referendum or just allowing it to go forward on its own. We knew that if it had gone to a referendum it would have been defeated. Then it would have gotten into another area in terms of a religion not being able to practice freely. To the government we kept emphasizing the importance of demonstrating that there was religious freedom in Slovenia and that this mosque would move forward. In the end it got into the courts and everyone got involved. I mean, these things that seemed so small became an emotional issue. This was a serious issue though. In the end they agreed. I think it was a result of a court decision that basically said that even if they had a referendum they could not abridge the right to religion or freedom of religion. That was a basic right that everyone enjoyed.

*Q: What was the role of the Catholic Church?*

YOUNG: Good question. If you ask a Slovene what religion he or she is, they will say Roman Catholic. About 85 percent are Roman Catholic by profession, not by practice. You could go into a Catholic church on Sunday and count the number of people in the church.

*Q: Particularly all women.*

YOUNG: The majority, you're right there, but that's not unusual anywhere.

*Q: It was like that when I was in Italy.*

YOUNG: Yes, that's very true, but you ask men and they will tell you they're Catholic. My wife and I are Roman Catholics and we would go to mass there on Sundays. We would make these observations like you have: look, it's all women. The Catholic Church had considerable influence and had owned extensive properties at one point. Following independence, the Slovenes said they would return property to former owners and one of the former owners was the Roman Catholic Church, which owned forests and basically state parks, I mean what came to be a state park that encompassed hundreds of thousands of acres, way up in the mountains. They had these schools, monasteries, and chapels all over. The Church played quite a significant role in the evolution of the country going back to the time of the attempts by the Turks to conquer that area. For example, there is a church on every hill, placed there for strategic reasons. They would serve as lookouts and there was always a wall around the church. The person who was the lookout would keep an eye out for the Turks. If he saw Turks coming he would give the signal, the villagers would come into the yard of the church, and they would fight the Turks from the wall of the church. The role of the Church in being able to defend the country from subjugation by the Turks is just one example of their influence in Slovenia.

They also ran all of the schools at one time. They ran the universities. They have had a tremendous impact in the evolution of the country, but under Communist rule, the Church was cut out. Basically the Church was brought back into society at the time of independence. People were allowed to exercise their right to practice their religion, so the Church was basically reborn at the time of independence. But it was not happy with just being able to practice as it wanted to, it wanted the government to give it more money. The Church wanted the government to insist on religious education in the schools and things like that, but that just would not be acceptable to Slovenes. So you had this tension between the Church and the government. While I was there an agreement was hammered out between the Vatican and the government that allowed the Church to operate freely, to have Catholic education in its own schools but not have it in the public schools and not get huge amounts of money from the government. The archbishop was a very controversial fellow named Rodey who has subsequently moved on to be one of the key figures working with the present pope in the Vatican. He was very outspoken and on occasion would inflame the situation in Slovenia, particularly among the Muslim community. In one public statement he equated them to all being terrorists, and the government had to be careful to be sure that it was not encouraging them in their terrorist activities and that sort of thing. Well, everyone went ballistic when they heard. He would do things like that.

The archbishop was very influential, for example, in terms of persuading Slovenes to vote for NATO and also persuading Slovenes to vote for entry into the European Union. Slovenia was the only country of the candidates invited to join NATO that had a referendum on it. The referendum succeeded. I wanted to go back to that a little bit because it leads to what was happening in terms of the war in Iraq. In 2003, at the beginning of the year, the talk of a possible war was getting louder and louder and as it got louder the opposition to it in Slovenia grew in intensity. It was very clear the Slovenes wanted absolutely nothing to do with the war in Iraq. The referendum on NATO and the European Union was scheduled for March 21, I think, in 2003. Little did we know the war would begin literally within days in March 2003. We had no doubts about the Slovenes agreeing to enter the European Union, but the polls indicated that it was very uncertain about the Slovenes voting for entry to NATO. We were afraid that with the war on the horizon the Slovenes would vote against it. In the end, two-thirds of them voted for entry to NATO and 90 percent voted for entry to the European Union. That was a big success.

*Q: Were certain assurances given at that time, saying the war in Iraq is not a NATO matter?*

YOUNG: Despite those assurance and what have you, NATO was looked at unfortunately through the prism of the U.S., that this is a U.S.-run institution and if we vote for this we are voting basically for the U.S. and we're agreeing to war with Iraq. A very important thing did occur just before the war started. We knew we were going to go into Iraq. I got a message from Washington instructing me to go to the government to get permission for our planes to overfly Slovenia to get to Iraq. I put the request in and the government was very quick to get back to me. They said no thank you. I communicated that back to Washington. They were very unhappy, as you can imagine. We literally had hours to move, because the instructions were given that we were going to go that night. The planes were going to come out of Aviano in Italy and over Slovenia and then on down. But we couldn't do it, so they went over Macedonia.

*Q: Did they have to go over Albania?*

YOUNG: They did that as well, and so those two countries became our best friends, among our dearest friends, as a result of that. Slovenia ended up in the doghouse. That was a major item. The war started. The opposition just grew and grew in intensity. We had all kinds of demonstrations outside the embassy. My car was attacked one day while I was leaving for home.

The editorials in the papers were all anti-U.S. and it was all directed at President Bush. It was all seen as a result of this man. It was Bush, Bush, Bush. Nothing we could do would deter them from this. I continued to give access to the press any time they wanted it. They were relentless in asking me about the war and what the U.S. was doing and how wrong it was. I would give the spiel about what we were trying to do there and how we were going to build democracy and how this was necessary and we got rid of a wicked dictator and that sort of thing.

I don't know if I mentioned what had happened with Slovenia's signing on to the Vishegrad Statement. This was when Powell went to the United Nations. Well, that was a big issue. We were looking for support in terms of proof that Iraq had weapons of mass destruction and that the United Nations should support the secretary in what he was proposing to the United Nations. We went to the ten countries that were proposed for membership in NATO and/or the European Union. They were called the Vishegrad 10 and all of them except Slovenia had signed this letter. I remember calling Foreign Minster Dimitrij Rupel and saying, "This is going to look really bad. You want to look good. You want to be counted among those who have signed this letter. We've got the proof," holding up like Powell did later on, "we've got the proof." He said, "Well, I've got to run this by a couple of people here and I will get back to you," and I think I gave him fifteen minutes and I called him again and said, "We're waiting in Washington, you know. They're waiting for you. You're the only holdout on this. We need this. This is so important. This is critical; we've got to have it." He said, "Well, I've got to run it by more people."

I learned later that one fellow who was sort of a real anti-American member of the ruling government was pressing the foreign minister on how to tweak the statement and Rupel did make a few little tweaks, but nothing significant in terms of the substance of it. This letter basically said, based on the evidence that Secretary of State Powell has represented to the United States, we believe that the United Nations blah, blah, that this is what they should do. That was pretty powerful stuff. Anyhow, I kept after the foreign minister. I was relentless in my pressure on him and in the end he signed. We were able to communicate that back to Washington, and that was one of the statements that Powell used in his discussion with the United Nations. The Slovenes regretted that later on and Powell did too as a matter of fact, but anyhow that was what happened in that particular case.

*Q: Being number one, the most powerful country in the world, obviously brings resentment. You can't help it, This just comes with the territory. And the fact that Bush seemed to give no attention or care to European sensitivities allowed all this anti-American resentment to well up and concentrate even before the Iraq war. Did you feel this?*

YOUNG: Yes, at the time.

*Q: There was the idea that a little could have been done to assuage the sensibilities of the Europeans, which other presidents, like Bush's father, had done, but he didn't. Did you have a feeling that this was kind of built into it?*

YOUNG: There's no question that that was the case. When Bush was initially elected there was not euphoria at his election, but there was certainly a willingness to stand back and give him a chance, to see what he was going to do. Then he took these unilateral moves, abrogating agreements that we had signed and what have you.

*Q: Anti-ballistic.*

YOUNG: Yes, an alarm went out, not only an alarm, but also opposition and criticism and it just never stopped. They felt that, well, if we are members of an alliance, if we have this relationship, that's very special, and not just the Slovenes, but Europe in general, then we should be consulted. I remember having a discussion with Secretary Powell and I said, "You know we don't do a good job in communicating with our friends in telling them privately, not going public but handling it in a private way, that this is how we feel about a particular issue, that we know they don't feel that way about it, but we want them to know this is how we're thinking, this is how things are shaping up in the U.S., this is how it's likely to come up." I think that would have had a different result than just barreling ahead without any kind of consultations at all. That's just not the way you deal with a friend.

*Q: How did Powell respond?*

YOUNG: Well, he listened. I think he was just in a listening mode at that point. I think Powell was a believer in this. He was a believer in consulting and conferring with friends, but this was a little bit beyond him.

*Q: I have to state my prejudice. I feel this has probably been the darkest period of American foreign policy since World War II, I mean as far as our ability to exert our influence through diplomatic means is concerned. Did you find yourself, and also your officers, having trouble dealing with this major reverse in American foreign policy?*

YOUNG: We did, but we kept that to ourselves. We realized that we had a responsibility to represent the president and to do that in a professional and resolute way, and if the situation got so bad that we couldn't do that anymore, then it was really time to leave. For myself, I knew that upon completion of my assignment I was going to leave and that I would be a free man in a relatively short time. So that sort of helped me to stay the course. The others would voice their views privately. They would not even voice them at all to non-Americans, but amongst ourselves there was great disappointment with the direction we were going. I think it may have changed a little, but I think the secretary has done some positive things to try to change it.

*Q: I've talked to someone who was serving as the DCM at a European post. He had a lot of trouble, because people would come up and say, "All right, you've talked about this and you've presented it, but what do you really think?"*

YOUNG: Oh, we get that, yes. If you're dealing with the press, you have to be extremely careful or else it will get out: "Although Ambassador Young said so and so and so, he privately believed so and so." I never let my private thoughts out in public.

*Q: Did you have much consultation with your fellow ambassadors around the area?*

YOUNG: They were very nice, very gracious. You mean the fellow American ambassadors?

*Q: Fellow American ambassadors.*

YOUNG: We'd have a conference in Washington once a year, which was always interesting, because we'd have fifty-four ambassadors there. I was the only black in the entire room and I would say that I was president of the Association of Black Ambassadors in Europe. Later on we got one more, the guy who was in Iceland, and so I told him, "Now you're the vice president. I'm the president." These conferences provided an opportunity for informal discussions. The career people did their job in terms of defending the president and speaking out and not trying to hide and duck from the issues. I think some of the political people took a very low profile and wouldn't speak out and wouldn't have the same kind of relationship with the press that they would normally have. So, we would meet there. NATO would have an annual regional conference and we'd meet at that conference as well, but that was about it.

*Q: How did your public affairs officer deal with this matter? This was a very difficult time?*

YOUNG: An extremely difficult time. I was very fortunate in having one of the best public affairs officers I have ever worked with, a woman named Laurie Weitzenkorn, who worked with me in seizing every opportunity imaginable to do exactly what I wanted to do, which was to show the U.S. government in a very positive way. For example, if we were doing something with the judiciary and an alternative dispute resolution conference or something like that, she would arrange for me to have press conferences. She would arrange for me to give the keynote address and of course this would be carried in the papers. Then she would arrange for me to be on a panel or something like that with other ambassadors or jurists. Again, all of this would be picked up in the press, and it was neutral; it wasn't political at all. That worked out very nicely. We had a good-sized Fulbright program and she would arrange to do something with the Fulbrighters, such as programs with scholars and speakers on different issues. She programmed me to the hilt, but always with one goal in mind. She didn't skirt those occasions when it was clear that the reporter or the press or the television wanted something said politically; that was what they were after. She did her best to prep me and to get me ready for this, and it all ended up very nicely. She was just an extraordinary public affairs officer. She was engaged, creative, full of energy, and very well connected in the community, particularly among people in the press and academia, just what you would want.

*Q: How did you find life in Slovenia?*

YOUNG: I always tell people that I certainly enjoyed the issues and enjoyed my time there. I could not have asked for a nicer post to conclude a career and to do so in a country that was democratic, that had open markets, that respected the rule of law, that believed in integrity, that didn't have problems of corruption, that was moving ahead, and that believed in reforms. Slovenia was doing all of those things that we had attempted to do in one way or another in so many countries that we had been in over the years. To be able to do that in a country that was so spectacularly beautiful was an extra treat. Also, to do it in a country that took such pride in culture and art and music was also an extra treat. I went to more concerts in Slovenia than I have gone to in total in the United States and other countries combined. There were all kinds of world-class performers. They had a world-class orchestra of their own. The little country had three symphony orchestras. Just unbelievable. We just soaked it all up, traveled all over the country, and just loved it.

I attended the ski-flying competition in Planica. I had never been to a ski resort, let alone to a ski—flying competition. We were at the foot of the mountain, where the skiers land, to see them come off of this run. Slovenia has the longest run in the world for this kind of jump. I think its 250 meters, which is just unbelievable. To see these people go up in the air and then come down, they literally were like birds, and it's just absolutely spectacular. I have never seen anything like it. It was one of the most breathtaking and thrilling things I have ever seen. I went every year I was there except the year that the war started, but I had wanted to go. I had been talking about it for a long time, but my country team advised me not to go. They said, "You're going to be very visible, there's no question about that. Although you'll have 40,000 people there, you're going to be a very visible person in that 40,000 crowd." That was the only year I didn't go, but I did go the next year and loved every minute of it. It was wonderful. Slovenia is a gorgeous country. Ljubljana is just a delightful town, a small city of 325,000 people. One person described the country to me I think in a very apropos way. She said that if Disney created an Alpine village it would look like Slovenia. I think there's some truth in that. It's just gorgeous.

*Q: Do you think there is anything more we should discuss about Slovenia?*

YOUNG: No, I think we've covered the major issues. The intellectual property and the Iraq war continue to be big thorns in our side. After the war started, Slovenia was asked if it wanted to be a member of the coalition of the willing, even a silent member of the coalition of the willing, and they said no thank you, we don't want to be a part of the coalition of the willing.

We have to also keep in mind that at the time, Slovenia had a new prime minister. He was afraid of taking any stance that was inconsistent with public sentiments for fear of not being reelected, which he was not, but he was not about to stick out his neck at all. He would say the right things when we met privately and he talked a good game, but he was not prepared to back us. We were pressing him to send some forces to Iraq, to send some forces to Afghanistan, but they were not prepared to do any of that unless it was under the cover of NATO. Slovenia was not about to break ranks on its own with its European Union allies in order to demonstrate support for the United States. If it demonstrated any support for the United States it would only do that under the umbrella of NATO or the European Union. Now, for example, they are about to send I think a few people to Iraq, but this would be under the NATO training program that is being worked out. They do have people in Afghanistan. That started while I was in Slovenia, but again this is not a unilateral thing; it is part of NATO. They are part of the NATO alliance and they're demonstrating that they're good members. They don't have huge numbers out there. I forgot the number, but its small, ten, twelve, fourteen or something like that. As we know, it's the symbolism that's important in this. We talk about the coalition of the willing, but if you look at the real numbers, it was still the U.S. that was doing this. It was just symbolic.

# SELECTION AS CAREER AMBASSADOR AND LIFE AFTER THE FOREIGN SERVICE

*Q: Well, you retired in 2004?*

YOUNG: I left Slovenia in September of 2004. I put in my papers to retire and then I got word that I had been selected to career ambassador. Now, this created a problem for me because I had no idea when that position would be confirmed by the Senate and I had signed up for the retirement seminar. If I had taken the retirement seminar, particularly the job search portion of the retirement seminar, when you conclude the job search portion of it, you must leave the Service or you have to pay back all of your salary that you've been paid for the past two months. I spoke to a number of people in the Department including Ruth Whiteside in the Office of Human Resources and a couple of other people. They said, well, that is a problem, but we'll help you sort it out. Then I spoke to someone in the Board of Examiners and asked if I could spend some time over there until this whole matter of Senate confirmation of this nomination to career ambassador was sorted out. They agreed to allow me to come over there. I canceled my registration for the retirement seminar and instead went into the Board of Examiners. That worked out very nicely and then the Senate did confirm the nomination. I think confirmation was in November and the minute they confirmed, I put in my papers to retire. I had a very nice ceremony with Colin Powell. He called us all up to his office together with Deputy Secretary of State Richard Armitage. The nominees were Marc Grossman, Beth Jones, Ryan Crocker, Larson from economics, and myself. It was very nice and quite dignified. We had a nice exchange with the secretary and with Armitage and a little champagne after, and that was that. I put my papers in and left.

*Q: What have you been doing since?*

YOUNG: Well, I had made arrangements to work for the Office of the Inspector General as an inspector. One of the first things I did with them in January of 2005 was a study of how we staff the mission in Iraq. We looked at how we got the people to go out in that first round, how we were getting them to that second round and what would likely happen in that third round. What we found was really a great demonstration of patriotism, volunteerism, and professionalism in that first round. People went out and they did a great job. We found some of that in that second round of staffing as well, but we could see problems in the third attempt to staff, because the pool of people had already been tapped. There weren't that many more out there. We offered some ideas on additional incentives that perhaps the Department could offer in enticing people to go out.

That study was done in two parts. My team did the domestic overview and then Ambassador John Monjo went out to the field and looked at it in terms of what was the right level of staffing. That gets to be such a subjective matter in terms of what is the right size for a mission. That was what I did for a couple of months. Then I joined a team that went on an inspection of Santo Domingo in the Dominican Republic in May and June. We were also supposed to do Haiti, but Haiti was not doable, because the security situation there was deteriorating so rapidly. We were monitoring it daily and it was getting worse and worse. We finally called and said, "Look, you're evacuating the post, how could we possibly go in when you're evacuating and do an inspection? The last thing you need is to have us around." We never got to Haiti. At some point it will have to be inspected. It's a mess. The people there were doing a great job. Based on our preliminary work we saw a really dedicated, hardworking staff doing tough work under extremely difficult situations. Since I had postponed my entry to the retirement program, in August and September I joined the retirement program.

*Q: Which would be 2005?*

YOUNG: 2005. I did that for a couple of months and since October, I've been kind of looking around to see what might be out there that I might be able to do. I've been letting friends and colleagues know that I've been looking for something. What I would like to do, I think, falls into three areas. One would be to sit on a corporate board for pay, which is not easy to do though. You really need friends, relatives, and well-placed colleagues. So that has not worked out, at least not for pay. I'm on enough committees gratis. Then, I think I could run an association of some kind. I think that's a possibility. We're looking into that. The other would be to engage in the international operations of a private firm, of a profit-making firm, I should say. So, that's what I'm looking at. In the meantime, I'm also active in my Rotary Club. I'm active in the Washington Institute of Foreign Affairs. I'm on the membership committee there. I do the program committee for the Rotary Club. I'm in the American Academy of Diplomacy, but I haven't done a thing for it. This exercise, the oral history, here at the Association for Diplomatic Studies and Training, we've been doing this for a bit, and I'm involved in other organizations as well. We have the retirees of Maryland, the Foreign Affairs Retirees of Maryland, and different groups like that. So, I've been busy.

I wasn't sure that I had covered an event that occurred in Bahrain. If I didn't, I'd like to add it now so that it is included, because it was an important event that happened in the mission and demonstrates what can happen.

We had a regional personnel office at the embassy in Bahrain and a regional diplomatic courier office. Those two were attached to the mission. We had three couriers, they would go out and deliver their stuff and then come back. On the 23$^{rd}$ of August, 2000, my wife and I were getting ready to host a dinner party. We were waiting for the guests to arrive and the phone rang. It was the security officer. He said, we think we have a problem here. A plane has crashed in Bahrain and we believe that our diplomatic courier, Seth Foti, is on that plane. So, I said, call the country team, meet at the embassy, I'm on my way.

I went in. The country team was there. We decided that we would assign certain responsibilities. First of all, we needed to establish if Seth was on that plane. We needed to establish if there were other Americans on that plane. We needed to get certain things going right away, notifying the Department.

*Q: Also, the classified material.*

YOUNG: Oh, yes, that was important as well. We were concerned with the person first. The DCM handled the group that we established. I immediately got on the phone to the minister of transportation and to a couple others to try and assess what was going on. A key thing that we wanted to get our hands on was the manifest from the plane. I called the minister of transportation, who was in Paris. I called him in Paris and he agreed to release a copy of the document to us and we got it and we went through it. We were also in touch with our embassy in Cairo to establish that Seth had gotten on that plane and when we got the manifest, we were then convinced that he was on the plane. The next thing then was to find his body and find survivors. The U.S. Navy had already gone out on a search-and-rescue operation where the plane had come down. They were able to mobilize their resources faster than the government of Bahrain. They took the lead in the search-and-rescue. A fellow from the courier office and one of the national employees went with them. They did find the different bodies.

I left the DCM in charge of operations in the embassy, and my wife and I went to the home of this fellow to be with his wife. They had been married on the 3rd of June; they were just the happiest, loveliest couple. He was a young, handsome, smart fellow and I remember that when he first came to the embassy I sat him down for my usual talk with people and because of his education and his background I teased him; I said, "You know, I think you're a closet political officer." He says, "Oh, no, no." I said, "Given your college education, you speak Russian fluently and all of these things, you've traveled. If you are, that's okay. We just want you to do a good job in this job and then take that and move on to something else." I was convinced that the guy had the potential to do really wonderful things in the Service.

My wife and I rang the bell. She came to the door. She looked at us. She didn't know what to expect and I told her that it looks like we had a very bad situation here. A plane had crashed. We're trying to determine if Seth was on that plane and as soon as we got any news we would let her know. We wanted to stay with her until we got the news. We waited and waited and then I got a call that confirmed they had found Seth's body and that he was dead, and how he died was not very pleasant. I had to tell her that her husband was dead. That was the most difficult thing I've ever done in the Foreign Service, to tell this young bride that her husband of just a couple of months had been killed in that plane crash. He was the kind of fellow that everyone loved. We all took a liking to him. Everybody loved him. He was very pleasant and smart and didn't have a bad word to say about anyone. He was always dressed in a suit and a tie and I mean he really looked more than the part. The mission was just devastated, both Americans and the national employees in the mission.

We then began to make arrangements to take his body back to the States. I agreed that I would accompany his wife back to the States with his body. Before that happened, we had a little memorial service in the embassy. We then began the trip back home. Marc Grossman, the director general at the time, met us when we got to Washington. The assistant secretary for diplomatic security was also there, because the couriers came under that bureau, along with the top people in the courier service. The body then went from the airport directly to his home in a place called Browntown, Virginia, a little tiny town. A day or two later they had a lovely ceremony in the garden of his home and the sad thing was that the ceremony was in the garden that his parents had built for the wedding of this fellow and his new bride. So, his urn sat right under the canopy that had built for him and his new bride. It was a lovely, very touching ceremony, well attended. People came from all over and it was very nice.

Then I had a battle with AFSA. I returned to post and asked AFSA when his name would appear on the wall.

*Q: The plaque.*

YOUNG: Right, for those who have died in service. AFSA said his name would not appear. I was stunned, absolutely stunned. I could not believe it. They said, "Well, we don't think the circumstance is warranted." I said, "You must be kidding. The man died in the line of duty carrying a diplomatic pouch in his hand and guarding others in the hold of the plane." They would not agree. So, I sent a telegram in which I said if AFSA didn't reconsider that I would withdraw my membership and that other members of the mission would withdraw their membership as well. I sent the telegram to all consular and diplomatic posts all over the world. Replies started to come in, cables from so-and-so stating, "We're going to withdraw our membership" and so on. It was really snowballing fast. As a result of that, AFSA changed the rules and allowed Seth's name to be placed on the wall. When they changed the rules, they sent out a telegram asking if people knew anything about the deaths of several other people that they had in this questionable category.

One of the persons in that suspense category was a woman by the name of Marie Burke, who was murdered in London in 1989. She was a consular officer who was found killed in her apartment. I was able to give them some information in terms of her having died while on duty as well. There was another fellow who had died in a plane crash in Togo. Anyhow, this was a revolutionary change for AFSA and I was so happy that I was instrumental in bringing about that change. I wanted to make sure that I mentioned that particular incident.

*Q: Well, I'm very glad you did. As sort of an up-to-date note, just last week they had a very solid free election in Palestine, which the fundamentalist Hamas won. And you said earlier that you thought the fundamentalists could well win if there were a full democracy in Bahrain.*

YOUNG: I think that would be the case if it were a one-man, one-vote system, because it's clear that with three quarters of the population being Shi'a, and the Shi'a being very sympathetic to Iran and to other Islamists, and sympathetic to the Shi'a in Iraq, that would probably be the outcome. And I don't think that would be in our interests, frankly.

*Q: We're pushing democracy, but at the same time it's a complicated world out there.*

YOUNG: It is a very complicated world. I don't know what will finally prevail in Bahrain, but they do have a charter that was voted in democratically and that charter does provide for some participation by the citizens through those who represent them in the legislature. As I mentioned, final veto rests with the king and the king wants to maintain his power. In fact when the former emir ran into difficulty with the legislators—that is, Sheik Isa—he disbanded it. He disbanded the parliament because it was clear that if the parliament continued to exercise the power that it did, he and his entire family would have been out on the street. He disbanded them and they had no legislature until his successor, his son, made this new arrangement as a result of the national charter that was voted in.

Made in the USA
San Bernardino, CA
13 January 2014